ROUND ABOUT
THE UPPER THAMES

BY

ALFRED WILLIAMS

AUTHOR OF "A WILTSHIRE VILLAGE"
"VILLAGES OF THE WHITE HORSE"
"SONGS IN WILTSHIRE" "POEMS IN WILTSHIRE"
ETC. ETC.

WITH FOUR PHOTOGRAPHS AND A MAP

Copyright © 2013 Read Books Ltd.
This book is copyright and may not be
reproduced or copied in any way without
the express permission of the publisher in writing

British Library Cataloguing-in-Publication Data
A catalogue record for this book is available from the
British Library

A Short Introduction to the History of the River Thames

The River Thames takes its name from the Middle English *Temese*, which is derived from the Celtic name for river. Originating at the Thames Head in Gloucestershire, it is the longest river in England, flowing a total length of 236 miles, out through the Thames Estuary and in to the North Sea. On its journey to open water it passes through the country's capital, London, where it is deep enough to be navigable for ships, thus allowing the city to become a major international trade port.

The earliest evidence of human habitation on the river is a Neolithic bowl (3300-2700 BC), found in the river at Buckinghamshire. Other Pre-Roman sites have also revealed watermills, navigations, burial mounds, and settlements along its banks. As with many geographical features of Europe, it was the Roman Empire that realised its strategic and economic importance. In the first century BC, under Emperor Claudius, they built many fortifications along the Thames Valley. They also established a trading centre at the river's lowest point on two hills, now known as Cornhill and Ludgate Hill. They built a bridge there and named the settlement Londinium, a settlement that would eventually become the City of London.

During the Middle Ages the river attracted great prosperity, being a hive of activity in the fishing, milling, and pottery industries. However, the success brought with it unwanted attention, and in 870 AD the Vikings swept up on the tide creating havoc and destroying buildings such as Chertsey Abbey. When William the Conqueror arrived in

1066 AD he was rightly concerned with protecting the Thames Valley. He built many castles along its banks, such as those at Windsor, Rochester, and the magnificent Tower of London. This cemented his strategic position and gave him a base from which to control the rest of the country. He was also responsible for giving us the Domesday Book (1086), a hugely detailed survey, which gives us great insight into the activities on the Thames in the Middle Ages.

In the 16th and 17th centuries the river became a hugely important tool for transporting goods such as timber, livestock, and foodstuffs, from Oxford to the capital. It helped the City of London grow with the expansion of world trade and the wharves became packed with shipping vessels. It was also during this period that the country endured a series of cold winters that froze the Thames. So solid was the sheet of ice that 1607 saw the first Frost Fair, where tents were set up on the river offering various amusements such as ice bowling. By the 18th century, London was the centre of the mercantile British Empire and the river became one of the busiest waterways in the world. Docks were expanded and locks were built, allowing for easier navigation and even greater method of trade.

Among the many uses of the Thames, unfortunately one of them was as a dumping site for the city's waste products. This had been the case since the Middle Ages, but the more populous the banks of the river became, the more it became an environmental hazard. This problem reached its zenith with the 'Great Stink' of 1858, when the stench from the raw sewage in the river caused the abandonment of a sitting at the House of Commons. A concerted effort was then made to clean up the river and the construction of massive sanitary sewers was undertaken. This was part of a great engineering drive in the wake of the Industrial Revolution that saw pollution decline, water sources become cleaner, and railway bridges reducing the congestion on the river.

Although the Port of London remains one of the UK's main ports, the growth of road transport has largely superseded the Thames as a medium of transport. There are also far fewer heavy industries utilising the river, and as a resulted it is cleaner than it has been in hundreds of years. The Thames has played a key role in the development of a nation. Its story, both geographically and with its human uses, is a long and fascinating one. As John Burns, MP for Battersea, said in 1929 'The Thames is Liquid History'.

[W. Dennis Moss, Cirencester.]
The Round House, and Junction of the Coln with the upper Thames, near Lechlade.

[Frontispiece]

TO
REUBEN AND LOU
IN MEMORY OF
MANY PLEASANT EVENINGS
SPENT TOGETHER IN THE VILLAGE
WITH THE FLOWERS AND BIRDS
AND THE OLD FOLKS

OFT, as we waited for the nightingale,
We passed the peaceful hours with jocund tale,
Till all Heaven's starry eyes beamed in the blue,
And the young rose drank deep the fragrant dew;
Then through the scented dusk you stole away
Like Youth, light-hearted on a holiday.

PREFACE

THE following chapters were written in the early part of 1914, and were serialised in the *Wilts and Gloucestershire Standard* in 1915. Since then many changes have taken place, which must have a permanent effect upon the life of the countryside. At the same time, such changes are not entirely radical. Work and wages are the principal things affected; the fundamental spirit remains much the same as formerly.

There had already been a decay of village folklore and tradition. The discontinuance of farm festivals and fairs had much to do with this. They had provided the people with convenient means of association. The ballad-singers with their bundles of broadsides, travelling players, in fact any who could tell a good story and provide entertainment at the inns never failed to attend, and were listened to by an appreciative audience. By the process of natural development, or evolution, that condition of things came to an end, and none now wish to see it restored. It had its evils; I nevertheless imagine that rural characteristics were stronger and sturdier, and the village provided better physical material than it does to-day. When the smallholder tilled his land with the breast-plough, and the hook and the scythe did the work of the mowing and reaping machines, and the threshing was done with flails, the exertions conduced to make men tough and muscular. This accounted for the astonishing number of healthy, aged men throughout the Thames villages, some of whom followed their occupations and did useful work to the age of ninety, and even ninety-six years.

Village people are healthy now, but the farm labourer lacks the power of endurance possessed by his forerunners of two generations ago. Who now would have the strength—to say nothing of the courage—of " Old Jonathan " of Highworth, who laboured with the bricklayers at London and walked home, a distance of nearly 80 miles, and returned every week-end ? Or who could compare with Giles Draper, of Hannington, who mowed two acres of grass a day, and kept up the effort for a week; with Tom Fowler, another local champion, who, at the end of a day's mowing, could lift a heavy farm waggon unaided ; or Gabriel Zillard, who, at the singing contests held at the inn, could sing continuously for eighteen hours ?

The ground covered by the chapters is, roughly speaking, that lying between the Thames Head and Radcot Bridge, *i.e.* the first twenty-five miles of the river's course, and it embraces portions of three counties—Wiltshire, Berkshire, and Gloucestershire. This represents a distinct locality, with a common speech and folklore. The river Thames brought about this, for it had through the ages a unifying effect on those dwelling within the sphere of its influence. As the rainfall between the Cotswolds and the Wilts and Berks uplands is gathered into the channel of the Thames, so the principal life and commerce of both sides of the valley flowed down to the river's banks, and people differing in several respects came to be blended and united in their characteristics by the processes of intercommunion and close association.

The scope of the book is principally nature and life, speech, story, tradition, and humorous incident. Whatever of this is contained in the chapters was gleaned on the ground, and is, I believe, for the most part original. In traversing the circle of villages in the area I have attempted to avoid historical references, which are often tedious, though it was obviously impossible to eliminate them altogether. The question always is whether a particular locality is in itself sufficiently interesting to merit attention. This I leave for the reader to decide; his judgment and not mine must determine the issue.

Since my object was to portray as much life as possible—not its sufferings and tragedy—I have made free use of persons, and these not fictitious, but real, who inhabited the villages within the memory of those yet living, believing that such records can never become stale or valueless, and that here, as elsewhere, a little fact is more convincing than a goodly array of fiction. It was in support of this that I have retained the account of Squire Archer, of Castle Eaton, and have given the extraordinary list of worthies of the villages of Blunsdon and Hannington, with the prevalent beliefs in sorcery and witchcraft.

I suppose that one locality is not much superior to another in the interest of its life and traditions, since that district which is most thoroughly explored usually exhibits the richest treasures, both as regards the human element and wild nature also. At the same time, no one can pretend to be the discoverer of life, but only its interpreter ; and however great may be the amount which he has succeeded in setting forth in any given locality it could be no more than an infinitesimal fraction of the whole comprised therein.

My thanks are due to Mr. W. Scotford Harmer, editor of the *Wilts and Gloucestershire Standard*, for his ready assistance at all times ; and to Mr. Dennis Moss, of Cirencester, who kindly provided me with the photographs for use in the book.

A. W.

CONTENTS

CHAPTER I
PAGE

The Haymakers—The Thames Valley—The River Coln—Scenery of the Thames—Sketch of the Ground—Local Opinions—"John and Sally" 17

CHAPTER II

Highworth—The Town and Church—Mixed Features—Harvest Chant—"Tib Day"—The Eccentric Squire—John Drew and "Peggy" Tawnley . . . 32

CHAPTER III

The Avenue—Shrivenham Village—"Admiral of the White"—Court Leet—Beckett House—Weather Signs—Local Tales—Lord Craven and the Farm Boy . . . 45

CHAPTER IV

Watchfield—The Stolen Church—Blackbirds—Tales and Gossip—Coleshill—The Luck of the House—The Lord Radnor—Anecdotes—"Mose" and the Farmer—"Old Polebrook" 62

CONTENTS

CHAPTER V

Crossing the Ford—Discoveries in the Field—The Hawk and the Blackbird—Inglesham Church and Village—The Round House—The "Grand Old Man of Inglesham"—Steam Ploughing—A Storm in the Vale . . 79

CHAPTER VI

The "Ha'penny Bridge"—Buscot—Squire Campbell's Works—The "Water Gardens"—Herons—Visitors to the Lake—The Woodman Naturalist—Eaton Weir—Floods at Kelmscott 95

CHAPTER VII

The Journey up the River—The Rat and Kingfisher—St. John's Bridge and Priory—Lechlade "Flea Fair"—Holders of the Manor—Curious Items of Church Expenditure—Local Witchcraft Tales . . . 111

CHAPTER VIII

The Cotswolds near Northleach—Carl the Carter—Valley of the Coln—The Mill Pool—Fairford Church and Windows—Hard Fare—Gipsies—Harvest Home Healths—Sheep Stealing—"Cotswold Ale"—"Tig" . . . 129

CHAPTER IX

A Cotswold Ploughing Match—Old Acquaintances—The Carter's Criticism—Progress of the Ploughing—The Prize-Winner 148

CONTENTS

CHAPTER X

A Cotswold Carter's Cottage—"Chasing the Cock"—Native Wit and Humour—On the Coln—Whelford—The Smithy—The Mill—Old Elijah's Tale 165

CHAPTER XI

The Fatal Jackdaw Nesting—Hannington Wick—Kempsford—"The Lady of the Mist"—The Boatman—A Trip by Water—The Home-made Loaves—Rustic Medicines—Rhyme of the Shorthorn—Tales at the Inn . . 182

CHAPTER XII

Squire Archer, of Lushill—The Vanishing Stag—Castle Eaton—Tragedy of the Roach, Heron, and Fox—"Darby and Joan"—Queen Victoria's Coronation Dialogue—The Trout Stream—The Landlord and the Farm Boy . 200

CHAPTER XIII

Source of the Thames—Water Shortage—"Wassail" Song—Thames Head Villages—Cricklade—Election Scenes—"Open House" Expenses—A Local Execution—"Bark Harvest"—"Looking through the Rafters" . . 218

CHAPTER XIV

The Upper Thames Valley in the Making—The Youth and the Traveller—The British Camp—"Slan" Feast—"Rat-Catcher Joe"—Jack and the Squire—"Joe the Marine"—Moll Wilkins and Tom Hancock—Bet Hyde, the Witch of Cold Harbour 234

CONTENTS

CHAPTER XV

PAGE

Roman Remains at Bury Town—Stanton—Fulk Fitz-Warrene—Burial of the Dead—The Lake and Woods—"Moll Taw's Corner"—"Man-Traps"—The Wood Sale—Tom Fowler's Feat—Tricks and Conundrums . . . 254

CHAPTER XVI

Bide Mill Brook and Wood—Wych-Elms—Hannington Village—Giles Draper and the Cobbler Clerk—Farmer Baden's Courtship—Whistling Joe, the Blacksmith—Lye-Droppers, Potato Starch, and Rush-Lights—"Bang-Belly" and "Frog-Water"—Wooding Rhyme—A "Journeyman Farmer"—Riddles—Rustic Lore—"Oby" and "Scamp" 273

CHAPTER XVII

A Retrospect—The Thames in Flood—Gramp's Cottage—"Farmer Bernard and Yellow-Breeches the Lawyer"—Healths and Toasts—"Parson Jingle-Jaw's Adventure"—"Sweet Peggy, O"—Skit on the Fast ordered by Parliament at the Time of the Cotton Famine—The Mumming Play of Robin Hood and Little John . . 292

INDEX 317

ILLUSTRATIONS

The Round House, and Junction of the Coln with the
Upper Thames, near Lechlade . . . *Frontispiece*

                                                                      FACING PAGE

Inglesham Church : date, Twelfth Century . . . 86

Kempsford Church and Porch 186

Saint Sampson's Church and Cross, Cricklade . . 226

Map . . . . . . page 315

ROUND ABOUT THE UPPER THAMES

CHAPTER I

The Haymakers—The Thames Valley—The River Coln—Scenery of the Thames—Sketch of the Ground—Local Opinions—"John and Sally."

"THER', ther', ther'. Pat it down. Pat it down. A little bit more on the fer far corner. Put on a thunderin' good load but don' strain the 'osses. We be in for a wet un to-morra, as sure as thy name's Jack Robbut."

"Aa, zur. The owl' zun bin a-zuckin' an't up all th' aat'noon awver Castle Yetton yander."

"An' the cows be moonin' about, an' the martins be clawss to the ground, an' tha's a sure zign o' casulty weather, as my owl' faather used to zaay."

"Aa, an' the dew's a-vaallin', an' this aay 'll soon be as wet as muck, an' the rick's a-yettin now, an' us shan't a done bi doomsday if ya don' look sprack. Go farrud, bwoy, an' pull towwerd a bit. Coom e! Gip now!"

"Lar! dwunt chaestise the poor craturs, maester. The little mer's a-tired. A bin in the shafes all day, ver' nigh."

"Hello! Jin. Hast thee found thy tongue? Wher's thy man got to to-day?"

"A yent very well, zur."

"Aw! Wha's the matter wi' he, then?"

"Got a naesty cowld on 'in."

"'Ev a bin to the chimist?"

"Ae! A went to Hyvuth tha smarnin', awhever. Tha telled un a'd got the—— I caen't tell 'e what tha zed."

"What is it?"

"I caen't tell 'e. You'd oni laaf at ma if e was to't."

"Come on. Out wi't."

"I caen't zaay't."

"Yes, tha cast."

"Tha telled un a'd got the infli—zummat."

"The what?"

"The infliwinzy cowld. Yellacks! I zed you'd oni laugh at ma."

"What! 'Ev a bin sleepin' out under the aaycocks agyen? Thee must kip un a-twhum o' nights, Jin."

"Lar! Chent no use to tell 'e nothin'. A takes no moore notice o' I than a crow do o' Zunday."

"Tell tha what, Jin. Go down to the kitchen, an' missis ull gi' tha a bif bwun. Bile 'e up wi' some suety dumplins. That'll cure 'is cowld, as sure as God made little apples!"

"Sartintly, zur, an' thenk 'e. Tha's what I'll do, when us a done."

"An' 'ow's that you byent 'elpin' yer father wi' tha ship to-night, artful? Ood you sooner be along wi' tha 'osses? What be us to make on in, Dannul?"

"'E don' keer for tha 'osses. It striks I 'e's a-veerd an 'em. 'E can get an wi' tha ship tha yezziest."

"Aa. 'E's like I. 'E can 'andle the ship better

THE HAYFIELD

when tha bin under the pot-lid. Never mind, sonny. Tha't be a man now afore thi mother!"

Enter, by the gate, a rustic, with a note in his hand.

" Be you the maester ? "

" I be zummat, awhever."

" Was to gi' ya this, then."

" Wher' d'ye come from ? "

" Hyvuth."

" Wha's yer name ? "

" Mister Ferris."

" An' wha's yer maaster's name ? "

" John Whitful."

" Well! You can tell Maaster Whitful I'll meet 'e at 'Anninton, bi the Jolly Tar, at two o'clock to-morra."

There were six toilers engaged with the waggon gathering up the hay. First were the two pitchers —always considered the principal men of the field; next was the loader; then the two rakers, Jin, the fogger's wife, and Aaron, the odd man, and, last, the youngster to lead the horses, and feed them with handfuls of sweet hay from the wake. A small green elm bough, cut from the tree, was hung over the mare's forehead, half veiling her eyes, to protect her from the troublesome insects. In the middle of the field, beside a haycock, was a large wooden bottle containing the ale, with a tin cup turned upside down over the handle of a spare fork thrust into the earth to render its whereabouts visible.

The hayfield was situated about half-way between Lushill and Castle Eaton, in the valley of the Upper Thames, near to where the four counties of Wiltshire, Berkshire, Gloucestershire, and Oxfordshire come into conjunction. A hard road ran through the field, bordered by a high hedge on one side. Here the beautiful wild rose, shell-pink and creamy-white, with sweet crimson-pointed buds and wax-like petals, infolded, or curved outwards underneath, expanded like a saucer, or depressed like an umbrella, hung in luxuriant trusses and clusters from the top of the hedge down to the ground, shedding a soft radiance, and emitting a faint tea perfume. Between the rose boughs, along the shallow ditch, crept the dewberry with occasional blossoms and exquisite bluish fruit; here a teasel, light green in foliage, with prickly buds and thin rings of purple flowers growing from tiny cells like honeycomb, stood boldly up alongside a stately thistle, to the large head of which a drowsy humble-bee was clinging, though all her companions had long ago departed homewards to their nest in the mossy bank.

Running along at the bottom of the field was a deep ditch, like a brook, one of those made to conduct the water readily into the Thames, and relieve the river in flood-time. Here, bordering the tall flags, and shaded with boughs of guelder rose laden with milk-white flowers, were banks of forget-me-not and brooklime; the snow-white watercress leapt out of the ditch upon the bank, while here and there shone a yellow iris, or a tall spike of pink valerian showed above the reeds and added to the beauty of the border. In the bed of the ditch, if you could have peered through the dense flags, plants, and grasses, you would have seen the moorhen with her brood of tiny young wading and swimming in the shallow water. As it was, they were out of sight, and their presence would have been unsuspected if the mother bird had not indiscreetly uttered a loud " cirr-rr-rr," thereby discovering their whereabouts. In the oak-

THE THAMES VALLEY

tree, standing down the hedgerow, a trim-looking magpie hopped deftly in and out among the branches. On one side the tall taper top of the rick, nearly completed, was visible in the farmyard; on the other the stately tower of Kempsford church rose above the elm-trees and peered majestically over all the valley round about.

Now a large dark cloud, like a bat, with head distinct and wings outstretched, rose slowly out of the west, covering the sky, and causing the interiors of the elms to show blue-black. The moist night wind, laden with the warm scents of the hay and the stronger smell of the ricks heating in the farm-yard, came puffing up from the river, and the hay-makers hung their rakes on the hedge and left the field, the rumbling of the heavy waggon echoing loudly down the road in the twilight.

The Upper Thames Valley, roughly speaking, comprehends the whole of the ground between the base of the Cotswolds and the northern extremities of the Wiltshire and Berkshire Downs, running from Swindon to Wantage. This tract of country is more commonly known as the Vale of White Horse, since it is dominated by the huge chalk hill upon which the ancient figure of the White Horse is graven at Uffington. But the actual bed of the Upper Thames, or Isis, is really much smaller in extent, and covers no more than half that ground. This begins near Cirencester and continues eastward towards Oxford, bounded on the north, past Burford and Witney, by the Cotswolds, and, on the south, by a low ridge of stone hills running in an almost direct line from Purton, past Highworth and Faringdon, to Cumnor and Hinksey.

The part of the valley in which our scene chiefly

lies is that between Cricklade and Lechlade, and the small conical-shaped Lushill occupies the centre of the field. There are five conspicuous landmarks in the locality. First is the splendid tower of Saint Sampson's at Cricklade; next is that of Kempsford church, on the Gloucestershire side of the river; then Highworth tower, perched high upon the hill, and visible for many miles distant. After this comes Lechlade steeple, rising like a needle from the river's side, and, last of all, and higher than any, though not as permanent as the rest, is Faringdon Folly, a lofty clump of trees upon a high mound outside the Berkshire town, where, as tradition says, King Alfred laid down the crushing burden of life eleven centuries ago.

The waters of the Thames, in the neighbourhood of Inglesham and Lechlade, are augmented with the addition of several tributary streams that flow down from the north and south, draining the localities through which they pass. The principal of these are the Coln, the Cole, and the Leach. The Coln is a swift-flowing trout stream rising in the Cotswolds and joining the Thames at the Round House, near Inglesham church. The Cole has its origin at the foot of the Wiltshire Downs, and flows by way of Sevenhampton and Coleshill; and the small river Leach, also a trout stream, bubbles out of the rock near Northleach, twelve miles distant to the north-west.

Of these tributaries the Coln is the most beautiful. It is like a lovely laughing bride, crowned with flowers on her marriage morning, fresh, sweet, and pure, radiant with happiness, whose face, kissed with the morning sunshine, sends a gleam through the world and rejuvenates everything, shedding a new

glory—" the light that never was "—on all around
her, and adding an unspeakable gift—a moment of
immortality. And how lightly and gaily she trips
along, with feet that seem not to tread the ground,
moving half on earth and half in the air, with a graceful, jaunty, bird-like motion that only blithe-hearted
youth could execute, bewitching in her exquisite
ease and simple natural loveliness ! Even so beautiful
is the Coln, swimming along over her stony bed
through the fields, laughing aloud in the sunlight,
flowing, flowing, ever flowing, clear and pure as
though composed of nothing but freshest dew-drops,
each one resplendent with the morning, twinkling
in the glorious light of the unutterable dawn hours.
The smile on her face, the musical ripple of her voice,
the sweet pouting of her lips where the stones oppose
her passage, the shadow no sooner received than
dispelled, the snow-white foam flakes borne like
bunches of lilies on her breast, her long flowing hair
streaming in the crystal, the graceful and voluptuous
sweep of her skirts at yonder curve, the silver sandals
of her restless gliding feet, her gauze-like garments
of the summer fields, green and gold, white, opal,
and purple, the flash of multicoloured light reflected
from the plumage of her attendant kingfishers, her
joy and bloom and perfect beauty are all-powerful
and irresistible. Heaven is in her eyes ; Laughter
is in her soul ; the spirit of eternal Youth is about
her and within her, and she has no secrets. She is a
symbol of Life at its earliest and holiest hours, when
the earth is newly awake and full of sunshine and
song, and all things are freely and easily fathomable,
before Sorrow's fruit hangs on the bough, the heavens
are overcast, and we draw near to the depths that
conceal who knows how many pains and afflictions,

filled as they are with the doom of ourselves and all other earthly things.

The origin of the Thames is said locally to be in the neighbourhood of Cricklade, which error may easily have arisen since the river is not usually identified until it reaches the vicinity of that small town. This view of the inhabitants is quaintly and tersely expressed by the old man who keeps the tiny shop at the top of Blunsdon Hill, overlooking the valley, and to whom I applied for a glass of refreshing drink after climbing up the steep slope one broiling day in midsummer.

" This hill is very steep, and the sun scalds like a furnace to-day," said I.

" Yes," he replied slowly, and then galloped away with : " This is Broad Blunsdon 'Ill, Noth Wilts. You be close to Gloucestershire here. All this below is the Thames Valley, and you be jest come through Cricklet. The Thames rises in the meadas close to Cricklet, an' runs away, an' gets bigger an' bigger, an' jines the sea at Greenwich, an' don' mix wi' the salt water for miles out, an' the skipper ull tell 'e when you gets into salt water."

Everything about the valley—pasture, tillage and crops, vegetation, birds, and animals, the keeping of flocks and herds, work, business, pleasure, recreation, the whole life, in fact, is governed by the river, that operates in a hundred ways, openly and secretly, determining all things, and whose decrees are absolute and irrevocable. The invisible processes of draining, flushing, and exhalation go on year after year, producing a luxuriant growth of plants and foliage, unequalled on the hills and plains, or thirsty downlands stretching away to the south. On the hottest day of summer, when the down air is exceedingly dry, the whole valley will be full of vapours exhaled by the river. They float like a sea over the warm fields, enveloping everything—a spiritual food for leaf and flower, an invisible heavenly dew for the nourishment of Nature's garden; and at night the thick mist rises and condenses on the leaves of the trees and hedgerows, and makes the meadows " sopping " wet, and so waters and feeds every form of vegetation. The existence of vapours may have something to do with the prevalence of thunderstorms in the vale, that develop along the course of the river in the summer months. The hills on the one side and the river-bed on the other attract the greater part of the summer rains, leaving the intermediate region comparatively bare and dry.

How old is the river, and what first determined its zig-zag course through the level bed of the valley, so slowly and dreamily it wanders on, turning this way and that, doubling and redoubling, traversing the same ground over and over, lengthening out its sinuous coil for very fantasy, mocking at the mad haste and impetuosity of man, yet, by that very deliberateness of motion, figuring out lines of rarest and gentlest beauty? Perhaps the hills could answer the first question, for they were the earlier born. The second is more difficult to decide, since the composition of the river-bed is fairly uniform, and there was not likely to be serious opposition to the passage of the waters in any one direction. But Nature sees not with the eyes of man; she dreams out her plans and designs with more than mortal wisdom. Little by little, as the mighty stream that once filled the valley subsided, the remaining waters resolved on their course and slowly sank into their channel, determined to loiter, having no object but to prolong their stay in the heart of the island and lengthen out their journey to the inevitable sea.

There is a delightful irregularity in the course the Thames takes, and a sweet confusion and uncertainty in the signs by which one is wont to trace and locate the stream from a distance. The round clumps of hawthorn standing down the fields and along the banks of the river are strikingly beautiful, and especially if you chance to view them in the spring, in their first greenness, after a shower, when the sun peers from behind great masses of woolly clouds and sheds a soft light upon them, causing them to stand out in gentle relief against the more sober background of the shade-wrapt trees and woods. But the lines of willows and poplars, which the stranger immediately concludes to mark the course of the river, are often some distance from it, standing along the margin of a small brook, or back-water. Even the hawthorn clumps are not infallible evidence of the river's nearness, but may be ranged along some half-dry course in the field. Very often, in one's first pilgrimage in the vale, one happens suddenly upon the river, when one felt certain it was a mile or two away in another direction.

Two series of small towns, villages, and hamlets are scattered throughout the Upper Thames Valley. Of these some follow the course of the river; others are perched upon the stone hills running parallel with the stream at a distance of four miles to the south. Beginning with the river, a few miles from its source, are Ashton Keynes, Cricklade, Castle Eaton, Kempsford, Whelford, Fairford, Inglesham, Lechlade, Buscot, Eaton Hastings, and Kelmscott; along the ridge, and winding to the south-east towards the Berkshire Downs, are Blunsdon, Stanton Fitzwarren, Hannington, Highworth, Coleshill, and Shrivenham.

PREHISTORIC RESIDENTS

Of these the hill villages are the more ancient, having been occupied long before those were built by the river and in the level bed of the valley, while, in fact, all the country below was dense forest and swamp, swarming with big game and wild-fowl. At Blunsdon, besides its Roman ruins, the remains of an ancient camp or prehistoric village exist, high above the valley; Roman and British occupation is evidenced at Watchfield, Coleshill, Stanton Fitzwarren, and Highworth.

The *Belgæ*, who settled in Britain several centuries before Cæsar came to the island, are said to have held the land south of the Thames. They were noted for their skill in building and in agriculture. They were also more highly civilised than were the majority of the Gallic tribes, and it is not to be doubted but that they taught the natives useful arts, as how to till the land well and make butter and cheese, for which the locality was famed down to a few years ago.

In times still more remote, before the knowledge of agriculture, the inhabitants of the valley subsisted on raw fish from the river, and tender roots obtained from the swamps—of bulrush, reeds, and flags. They also ate the wild carrot and parsnip, young twigs and buds of trees, wild apples, beech-nuts, walnuts, and acorns. The eating of the last-named, in later historical times, may have been responsible for the custom of making an acorn pie every year at a village feast celebrated on the downs to the south of Highworth.

The hunters of the valley, who belonged to an age more recent than that of the root-eaters, slept sometimes in the trees, and sometimes in houses made of fir-boughs interlaced, similar to those fashioned by the woodmen in the coverts and plantations. They used the goat's horn, heavy clubs, spears of wood sharply pointed and with tips hardened in the fire, sharp stones and darts for weapons, hiding in the boughs and leaping out upon the beasts as they came to drink at the pools. They saved the skins of the animals taken and used them for clothing and bedding; and when they had been unfortunate in their hunting and were hard pressed for a meal, they well washed the newest of the skins, burnt off the hair, roasted them over the fire, and shared them out among the hungry multitude. The young male children were trained to the hunt and taught to hit the mark exactly, and if they missed they were punished with the loss of their dinner or supper, and were packed off to bed in the trees at an early hour.

Old Aaron and Daniel, the haymakers of Lushill, are sceptical when mention is made of prehistoric times. For the physical features of the earth and the fossil remains discovered in the quarries, and ofttimes built into the walls of their houses, they hold Noah's Flood responsible. They believe that stones and minerals grow, and affirm that the sarsens in the meadow get visibly bigger year by year: some of them, they say, are as large again as when they were boys. They are, moreover, positive that bones grow when they are buried in the earth, and that the skeleton of a man or animal will ultimately be enlarged to very much more than its original size. They consider that the prehistoric camp at Blunsdon was made by Oliver Cromwell. The first hunters, according to their idea, were Robin Hood and his merry men. The earliest battles fought were those between King Alfred and the Danes; and they believe that man sprang direct from the Biblical Adam—there can be no doubt whatever about all these things.

But neither Daniel nor Aaron is given to deep and speculative thinking. They love, most of all, during haymaking, and at dinner-time, sitting beneath the thick hedge, fragrant with blossom, or around the trunk of the shady elm or willow beside the sunny river, to talk about past toils and conquests in the field, or divers experiences here and there. Daniel's chief diversion is to tell of the suspicious old farmer who always took a loaded gun to bed with him; the Inglesham Ghost, that appeared in the shape of a black dog, or old Bet Hyde, the witch of Cold Harbour; while Aaron's forte is the unromantic tale of John and Sally, first told by the local roadmender.

John worked on the road for many years, and Sally was his wife. By and by John got old and tired of his work. John said to Sally:

"Zally, I thinks I shall gie mi job up."

"Well, if 'e caan't get on wi't, a know, John, gie 't out," Sally said.

John said: "I'll gie mi nowtice in to-marra."

"Aa, zo do," said Sally.

In the morning John went to master. "I must jack it up, maester. I caan't manage it no longer."

"Well, if you caan't manage it, John, you must gie 't out," said master.

John went home to Sally. "I chocked it up, you!" exclaimed he.

"Aw right, Jacky. We shall get on zum'ow, mun."

The next day John walked about and seemed very miserable.

Sally says to John: " Whyever dossent make thizelf contented ? "

" I caan't, you! I must get another job."

" What should 'e like to do, then, John ? "

" Thinks 'e should like to go to school agyen."

Sally says: " I'll go an' zee schoolmaester about it."

This she did, and said to him: " My owl' chap wants to come to school agyen, you ! "

" All right," said the schoolmaster. " Tell John he can come; we'll see what we can do for him."

Accordingly John went to school. When he came home at night Sally said: " ' 'Ow dist get on at school ? "

" Didn't get on at all, you."

" 'Ow's that, then ? "

" All the bwoys pinted at ma, an' called ma girt 'ed, an' thick 'ed. Byen a gwain ther' na moore."

The next day John was as miserable as before. " Zally," says he, " I ull go an' ax gaffer to let ma go back to mi job agyen."

" Well, zo do, if tha cassent make thizelf contented," replies Sally.

Then John went to master and told him about it.

" Yes, John," said he, " you can go to your work again."

John went back with the shovel. Passing along he saw something lying on the road. When he came to it he found it was a small leather bag. John said to himself: " This'll do aw right vor Zally," and took the bag home.

" Now, Zally, I got zummat var tha. This'll do djawwsid [deucid] well to kip thi candles in. Durzay thee cast awpen in, Zally, but I caan't."

After dinner Sally opened the bag, but did not

tell John what it contained. It was full of money and notes.

The next day John was out on the road again when a traveller came by. "Old man, how long have you worked on the road?" said he.

"Aw, zum time, you," John replied.

"Did you find a bag?"

"Aa-a!"

"Where is it?"

"Too-am. I gied un to Zally to kip 'er candles in."

"Could I go home and have a look at it?"

"Aa-a! smine t'oot."

They went home together.

"Zally, this vella wants to zee the bag what I vound."

Sally produced the bag.

"Looks very much like my bag. How long have you worked on the road, old man?"

"Aw, gwain in vifty year an' more."

"And when did you find the bag?"

"The vust day I started to work on the rawd."

"Well, that can't be mine, then," said the traveller, and took his departure.

"Aa! but 'twas the zecond time as I worked on the rawd, Zally, ye zee," John said afterwards.

CHAPTER II

Highworth — The Town and Church — Mixed Features — Harvest Chant — "Tib Day" — The Eccentric Squire — John Drew and "Peggy" Tawnley.

THE town of Highworth is perched upon an eminence, half-way between the Cotswolds and the Wiltshire Downs. The hill commands a series of pleasing views, not all of equal extensiveness, but of such a variety as to fit in with the several moods of the inhabitants, being changed and modified according to the light and atmosphere—strong and clear, soft and tender, pale blue, greenish blue, or indigo, magnificently distant, or charmingly near, full of detail, or indistinct and mystical, calling into play the spirits of fancy and imagination. To the south, ten miles distant, are the exquisitely graven downs, with ever-varying hues, from the gleaming chalk fallow-land to the tender green of the corn springing, the bright yellow charlock, or vivid red of the poppies, purple sainfoin, or autumnal gold of the wheat crops. Eastward, opening out from behind high avenues of elms, is the charming valley of the Cole; to the west, through a gap in the stone hills, is a view of the Cotswolds beyond Cirencester; while, stretching from west to east, by the north, in an unbroken panorama, is the Thames Valley and hills beyond, extending to Cheltenham, past Witney, and into Worcestershire.

Four main roads lead from the hill town, in as

many directions, and connecting it with other towns situated to the right and left, at various distances. Each road, where it climbs the slope, bears the name of a particular hill, as though there were many of them, while, as a matter of fact, there is only one. But accurate localisation is a characteristic of rural people: every slope, angle of the road, field, dell, uncommon tree, or other outstanding feature is given a name, to ensure its immediate identification, and also to provide some small pleasure for the nominators and inhabitants at large.

There is a double advantage in dwelling upon a hill, especially such a one as this, where the mound is isolated and in an independent position. There is a greater share in the scenery of the earth and of the heavens. Here one may view both sunrise and sunset; catch the first red gleam of morning and the last gold of evening, and follow the course of the sun from east to west without a moment's interruption. And at night, when the stars come out, he may watch them rise over the low downs, or see the pale moon steal up the sky and sink again to her bed of silver saffron in the early morning hours. Or, if the night be dark and stormy, and the wind rushes madly up the steeps and howls along the roofs and among the chimney-tops, one may yet be interested in counting the number of towns indicated by the ruddy glow of their street-lights reflected on the skyline. In addition to this, the day itself is longer and the night shorter on the hill; there is more light, air, freedom, vigour, and power, and consequently more life than about the valley and lowlands.

In prehistoric times the site of the town was occupied by a British village. When the Romans came, they used the hill as an outpost for the observation and defence of their territory along the Thames; then it fell into the hands of the Saxons, who built a high wall around it and called it the " High warded enclosure," from which the name of Highworth is derived. The Danes seized upon it for strategical reasons; later it was a Royal Manor, and when the town grew and became commercially important it was presented with a Charter and styled the Borough of St. John. The Danish occupation is certified in the names Eastrop and Westrop—" trop " from " thorpe," Danish for village—and, if this is inconclusive, there is the evidence of the danewort, or dwarf elder, which grows in profusion in the locality, and which is said to have been introduced by the Danes and never to be met with but in the regions they occupied.

The church is of Norman foundation. The building bears witness to several architectural periods, but is chiefly Perpendicular in style. In the stonework of the tower is a round hole, caused by a shot from the cannon of Oliver Cromwell, when he besieged the church after the battle of Naseby. Here he was defied by a garrison of troops, under one Major Hen, for three hours, at the expiration of which time the gallant defender " took down his bloody colours," and surrendered, handing over prisoners and arms. The missile that struck the tower is preserved, hanging in chains within the church. The common report is that the shot was fired from Blunsdon Hill, three miles off, but Cromwell's cannon were not sufficiently powerful to inflict damage at such a distance.

There is a charming confusion in the arrangement of houses and shops in the principal street and about the market square, which is in pleasing contrast to the formal and monotonous regularity observed in more modern towns. The roofs are an extraordinary medley. Some are very high and others low, with gable end towards the street, or sloping sideways, or having an end wall covered with stone tiles overlapping like a "tortoise"—a military formation of shields used by the Romans in an attack upon an entrenched position. These are narrow and pointed, those are broad and square, with an indescribable outline, and nearly all have tiny gables and windows inset, quaint and picturesque. The chimneys are tall and rakish, with parts superadded at different times, and they possess a certain gracefulness of outline. The grey colours of the stone walls and the darker brown of the tiles on the roofs match well together. The green and blue of the distant vale, visible through the gap at the end of the street, harmonises with the town itself and reminds one of its position and surroundings.

How knowingly and wisely the old tower, black with age, peers down from above the roofs and chimney-tops, looking at you with a kind of arch countenance, as though half amused at your insignificance, pitying your condition and the limitation of your knowledge, as though it should say: "I know something," and "I could tell you if I would," and "I have seen that which would surprise you." Standing in its shadow, with gaze averted, you have that indubitable feeling of being watched by someone, and you instinctively look up at the tower and seem to catch an upward motion of the stonework, as though you had really felt a person's gaze upon you, and, glancing up quickly, were in time to see the other's eyes suddenly raised, and catch the look of stolid indifference and unconcern immediately affected.

But though the old tower seems always *about* to tell you something, and whisper some secrets of its mysterious past and the scenes enacted in the hoary church and round about the shadow of its high walls, it comes to no more than *nearly*, and always disappoints one of the utterance.

Yet stirring times have certainly been around the pile, of high days, festivals, and civic functions: when the town was in its prime; when the mayor and aldermen, clad in their robes and followed by an enthusiastic multitude, attended in state; when the bells rang out and the people were on holiday to celebrate the termination of a mighty war and the blessings of peace; or at election times, when contending factions surged to and fro and came into collision, and made a dash for the belfry to get possession of the ropes and clash out a derisive peal, provoking to fury the hearts of their opponents.

There were two high wooden galleries in the church. In one of these, opposite the parson, sat the musicians, like " Timotheus up on high," and provided harmony for the worshippers. Their instruments were—the violin, the key bugle, clarionette, baritone, bass viol, the " horse's leg," and the big wavy trumpet, commonly called " the Serpent," from its resemblance to that beast. A difficulty was often experienced in getting away with a hymn, as the two clerks were at loggerheads, and could not suppress their rivalry, even within the sacred building itself and during the service. " Peggy " Tawnley, the weird little woman, accounted a witch, started the singing; there was no surpliced choir, trained with hymn-book and psalter. " Peggy " also made pilgrimages to the village churches, and led the singing; that duty devolved upon one of the congregation. The churchwarden's aged aunt undertook the pulling of the "ting-tang" before the services; the paupers from the local workhouse stood or sat upon the floor, up the middle of the nave. The tunes were arranged to suit the instruments, and the Serpent had pieces specially composed for itself, and called "Trumpet Notes," the style of which is indicated in the following refrain:

> "Soon shall the trumpet sound:
> Soon shall the trumpet sound:
> And we shall rise, shall rise to immortality;
> Shall rise to immortality."

At Harvest Festival the people of Highworth observed a partial fast, and ate nothing more sumptuous than a rice pudding. The special harvest chant used at the church was as follows:

HARVEST THANKSGIVING CHANT

O bless the God of Harvest, praise Him through the land.
Thank Him for His precious gifts, His help and liberal love:
Praise Him for the fields, that have rendered up their riches,
And, drest in sunny stubbles, take their sabbath after toil:
Praise Him for the close-shorne plains and uplands lying bare,
And meadows where the sweet-breathed hay was stacked in early summer:
Praise Him for the wheat sheaves, gathered safely into barn,
And scattering now their golden drops beneath the sounding flail:
For mercies on the home, and for comforts on the hearth,
O happy heart of this broad land, praise the God of Harvest.

The vicar—a plain, outspoken man, and a friend of the people—attended the domestic feasts—weddings and baptisms—and frequently entertained members of the congregation at his house. There the tables were laden with homely fare and an abundance of the nut-brown liquor. "Now, gentlemen, we've nothing to drink but beer! Pass round your jorams," the parson would cry, and the company responded with alacrity.

Markets and fairs were held periodically. There were no steam roundabouts or electric switchbacks then, but there was a large assemblage of shows and booths, with boxing and wrestling, comic acting and plays, such as *The Tragedy of Maria Martin*, a ghost piece on the subject of *Hamlet*, and another play called *The Flying Virgin*. In the booths was step-dancing to the tunes of "Charlie over the Water," "The White Cock Hen," "Triumph," and "The Old Woman tossed in the Blanket," with entertainments by the strolling Ballad Singers. A tribe of gipsies, thieves, and fortune-tellers attended the fair, and were soberly engaged making money in one way or another. On the morrow—called Tib Day—they got drunk and disgraced themselves, and were promptly hurried off into the gaol hard by and confined there. The town possessed its market-house, and it also retained its "Jury" and public Ale-taster down to the year 1850, or thereabout.

For a long time the old Bull Inn was remarkable for a large human skull that had been dug up with skeletons near by, and which was preserved upon the shelf among the mugs and bowls as a curio. But giants did not only exist in olden times, for it is said of a local corn merchant, one John Hall, who lived in the town fifty years ago, that he was as big as four ordinary men; that in conversation his voice could be heard half a mile away, and that his grave

A TYPE OF LABOURER

was wide enough to hold a fat ox. Over the breasts of some of the skeletons large flat stones were laid, which caused the local wits to suggest that they had been placed there in order to prevent the corpses from walking in their last sleep.

"Ther's nar a road neether comin' in, ner it gwain out o' Hywuth, but what carpses laays at," says "Old Jonathan." He dwells in the most ancient cottage in the town, and is tended by a middle-aged deaf-and-dumb daughter, who is unable to communicate with her father except by the primitive methods of nodding and pointing. He is aged ninety-two, is minus an eye, and very grey, but he is of robust health and indomitable spirit. As a young man he worked with the masons at London, and walked to and fro at week-ends, covering the distance—seventy-eight miles—in about twenty-two hours. He had many experiences on the road, and was often robbed of his earnings and forced to beg his food on the way home. The roads were very rough at that time. The railways were not made, and the stage-coaches and waggons passed him regularly on the way. He often stepped aside to view executions at different places. At one time the death sentence was for farm firing, and at another for "sheen-breakin'"; the hanging took place in the open, before a crowd of spectators. He reckoned to walk nine hundred miles with one pair of boots.

The industries of the town were important. The principal were—bell-casting, soap and candle making, saddlery, coach and waggon building, rope-making, and straw-plaiting. The town was also noted for the excellence of its wooden ploughs. Of the industries nothing now remains but the rope-making and coach-building, but there is a modern cocoa-nut fibre mat factory, which employs over a hundred hands.

The coach-building yards have long been famed for the excellence of the work made, and especially for the high quality of the wheels. It is astonishing to learn the great age of some of the vehicles in for repairs. Here is a waggon nearly a hundred years old, with wheels still more ancient, and which are good for another century, if the coach-builder is worthy of belief. The boxes of the wheels are nearly two feet in diameter, and the spokes are secured with round oak pegs, invisible from the outside. It was by these signs that the age of the wheels was proved; none of that pattern are made nowadays. A peculiarity of the waggon is that it has wooden axles, which run inside narrow liners within the box, and the farmer, who has looked in to inquire as to the progress of the work, says it is the most easily running vehicle he has ever known. He has no waggon less than seventy years old. He still calls the more recently made of them—exactly threescore and ten years in age—his new waggon; a little paint and a few slight repairs are all it has needed up to the present. The coach-builder used to accept payment in kind for his work. At one time he made a new cart for a sack of flour and a side of bacon; at another he exchanged a waggon for a quantity of corn, cheese, hay, or straw, and so helped the farmer out of a difficulty.

The local squire was noted for his eccentric behaviour. It is said that when he had done anything amiss privately he used to walk about the streets wearing a halter around his neck, with the rope trailing on the ground, as a token of self-abasement and humiliation.

THE CHAIR OF GOLD

On one occasion he lent his half-peck measure to a neighbour, who omitted to return it. Thereupon the waggish squire paid a visit to the town crier and had the matter published abroad. The next day the townsfolk were startled to hear the following announcement:

"Lost! Mr. Crowdy lent his half-peck measure to an unknown man. This is to give notice that if the said unknown person doesn't bring it back, Mr. Crowdy will never lend it to him any more."

At that time there was a "wise man" of Highworth, who was given to star-gazing and fortune-telling. Meeting him one day, the squire thought to have a joke at his expense.

"Well, and what have you been dreaming about now?" said he.

"I dreamt I was in hell," the other soberly replied.

"Ho! Ho! And what was it like there?" asked the squire.

"All they that had most money sat nearest the fire," the dreamer answered.

"Is that all?" the other inquired.

"Not quite," said the dreamer. "I walked about and found a beautiful golden seat and was going to sit down when somebody took hold of my shoulder and said: 'You mustn't sit there! You mustn't sit there.' 'And why not?' said I. 'That's reserved for old Crowdy of Highworth,' the other quickly answered."

When the squire died his spirit returned and continued to haunt the drives, as is seriously believed by the townspeople. Sometimes he appeared holding the shafts of the coach and drawing that noisily up and down the yard and before the house; at other times he walked the streets at midnight, with the halter around his neck, and struck fear into those who happened to be abroad at that hour. At last it was decided to lay the ghost. The Vicar, bailiff, and jurymen were approached, and one dark night they set out for the squire's house—locked up and deserted—and attempted to carry out the rite. But it proved a difficult matter, for the spirit was sulky, and resisted the efforts of the parson to pacify it. Finally, however, it consented to be laid on one condition, namely, that it might be allowed to enter a barrel of cider and remain there. So they proceeded to the cellar, where stood a large barrel full of apple juice. Someone took out the bung, the spirit entered, and the hole was securely stopped up again. Then the mason and his men were fetched out of their beds and the door of the cellar was bricked up; that was the last ever seen or heard of the squire's spirit.

"Peggy" Tawnley, accounted a witch, was believed to be half-man and half-woman. She used to be dressed in a tight-fitting black jacket with big green buttons and a blue gown, and she wore a quaint little bonnet on her head. A good many folks discredited the tales told about her, but her strange and sudden disappearance seemed to confirm the report of her being a witch. One Saturday night a rustic saw "Peggy," who stopped him on the road and tried to bring him under her spell, but without avail. He accordingly left her there and went on up the hill; but when he got to the town, behold! there was "Peggy," down on her knees, scrubbing her doorstep. By that he knew for certain that she was a witch, so he ran up to her, and was about to give her a good kick, when she coiled herself up like a football and went rolling down the hill and was never seen after that night.

THE COBBLER COBBLED

Another local " character " was the old apothecary. Every Lent he used to sit on the step of his door, clad in sackcloth and ashes, doing penance for his sins committed since the last Easter.

John Drew, the shoemaker, was a religious man, and a Methodist preacher. He had a big business, and employed several apprentices, whom he kept at work till a very late hour at night. At last the apprentices became dissatisfied and contrived to find means of redress.

Once every week the shoemaker went to Hannington to preach in the little chapel at night; his way back lay beneath a dense avenue of elms that made the road very dark. They agreed to wait for him there and accost him out of the darkness. Accordingly, as the old man was coming home late at night and passing beneath the avenue, he was suddenly hailed in a loud, deep tone of voice from the trees above his head.

" John Drew ! John Drew ! "

" Speak, Lord, for Thy servant heareth," replied he fearfully.

" Don't keep your apprentices at work so late nights," said the voice.

" No, my Lord ! I won't, never more," he answered, and, proceeding on his way, reached home in safety.

The next afternoon, before tea-time, he called his apprentices together and told them how, as he was coming home from chapel the night before, the Lord spoke to him out of heaven and told him not to keep his apprentices at work so late nights. " And now, henceforward, all you young men will go home at six o'clock," said he.

Another Highworth preacher was giving his congregation a few points on geography.

"This earth of ourn," said he, speaking in a solemn tone of voice and clutching the pulpit rail, "is as round—let me see, what shall I say?" "As round as a 'oss's 'ed," shouted someone at the rear, very irreverently. "Aa-a! as round as a 'oss's 'ed," repeated the preacher. This caused the congregation to smile, when someone on the other side quietly interposed with: "You couldn't mean 'is 'ed, could 'e, John?" to which the other promptly replied: "No; I meant as round as the *eye* in a 'oss's 'ed."

CHAPTER III

The Avenue—Shrivenham Village—" Admiral of the White "
—Court Leet—Beckett House—Weather Signs—Local
Tales—Lord Craven and the Farm Boy.

EAST of the town the road enters an avenue of elms planted along the greensward and continuing for a considerable distance, refreshing the traveller with pleasant shade and cooling sweetness on the hot summer days, and affording a refuge from the heavy autumn showers or biting blast that blows across the vale from the north-east in the winter. The heavy branches overarch and interlace with graceful symmetry and almost architectural exactness, producing a noble effect, like that of a cathedral aisle. However hot and blinding the sun's rays and calm the air without may be, there is yet a gentle motion beneath the trees—a soft breath of the clover blooms in the field, or the fresh, invigorating scent of the young leaves. Along the banks and around the bases of the tree-trunks the fragrant violet peeps forth in earliest spring; in autumn the open spaces of the roadside are beautiful with the pure gold of the fleabane, St. John's wort, or yellow bedstraw. In the field, on the sunny side, is a pen for the sheep with the shepherd's house on wheels adjoining; here and there is a disused stone quarry overgrown with bushes and protected with a wooden fence—a welcome refuge for the rabbits and pheasants that stray from the plantations and coverts.

A short way down beneath the trees a second branching of the road takes place. Here, also, is the entrance to another and more magnificent avenue, half a mile long, leading to Warneford Place, out of sight behind densest foliage of elms and beeches. The entrance to the avenue is barred with a high gate, for the road is private. The huge brown trunks of the trees dwindle in size and finally lose their individual shape down the avenue, assuming the form and aspect of masonry at the far end, with a vault of richest green and a shade of umber above.

Immediately within the gate is a pretty lodge with quaint windows, porch, and tiled roof. The high elms provide perpetual shade and overarch the wide road to the far bank, where stands a tall grey stone, and informs the traveller, and whoever else cares to learn, that he is seventy-six miles from London. The under-keeper lives at the lodge. Here he is close to the preserves and breeding-pens and the woods at the rear, and is able to see all who pass that way and prevent trespassers from encroaching upon the plantations or crossing through the avenue.

The grand avenue has been planted for about two hundred years. The trees are of a gigantic size, uniform in trunk and limb, and general growth. A very few out of the whole number have been lost; in their place others have been planted, but they will never overtake the rest in growth and match with them in venerable stateliness. One of the large elms by the roadside was recently struck by lightning, which left a perfectly formed groove, an inch wide and two inches deep, running from the topmost part of the main limb down the trunk to the roots beneath the ground. A large oak, similarly struck in a field some distance away, fared much worse. There a piece of bark, twelve feet long and one and a half feet wide, was torn off, but the tree withstood the shock and thrives apace.

The roots of the elm are very shallow; they are seldom more than one or two feet deep in the earth. Over in the field a large limb recently broke away from an elm by its own weight, which could not have been less than five or six tons. The wood was old and very brittle; the wonder is that such a ponderous mass of timber should have remained so long projected at full length from the trunk of the tree.

Below the lodge gate the road drops steeply down into a winding dell through which the small river Cole flows on its way from the towering downs to the Thames near Lechlade. A small wood of beech and poplar covers the slope on the right-hand side, and extends beside a rich green meadow rendered luxuriant with the waters of the river, that overflows its banks every winter. Across the river, on the opposite slope, is a large rambling farmhouse, and, by the water's side, a stone cottage, all that is left of the ancient mill. The water, through being bayed up to form the mill-head farther down, is almost motionless. Some of the pools are deep and swarm with roach, but there are shallower parts to which the old heron delights to come, watching in silence for hours by the bank, by and by to seize on his prey and carry it off to eat in the open field. The edge of the river is fringed with mint and hemp agrimony. White sneezewort grows in the meadow, and the old stone wall by the roadside is adorned with the pretty and diminutive flowers of the rue-leaved saxifrage.

Shrivenham, or "Shrinam"—as it is called by the rustics—lies a little outside the actual Thames Valley. The river, with its broad sunlit face, deep shady pools and currents full of silent whirling eddies, is seven miles off, and the blue line of the Cotswolds is effectively shut out behind the lofty avenues away back on the road. Southward rise the graceful, sweeping downs, with their hues of green and yellow, gold, crimson, or purple, varying according to the season of the year, the time of day, the light or shade, the cultivation of the slopes and the arrangement and disposition of the crops. To the right is the exquisitely shaped Charlbury Tump, and, east of that, the Russley Down, looking like a mighty heave of the sea or a huge green wave for ever about to break upon the shore, with the "One o'clock bush" showing against the skyline. Straight in front is the mysterious-looking beechen clump surrounding Wayland Smith's Cave; to the left is the towering hill of the White Horse—the classic spot of the neighbourhood—with the graven outline showing clearly on the western slope and the huge fortifications frowning over the wide vale beneath.

The village is ancient, and, besides being of great beauty, it was noted for the sturdy characteristics of its population, from the fighting Lord of the Manor of Beckett adjoining, down to the old archdeacon of the church and the hardy farm labourers. While Lord Samuel Barrington, "Admiral of the White," in command of H.M.S. *Achilles*, was battering the French and sinking their ships at St. Lucia, and the archdeacon, in his capacity of local magistrate, was giving practical advice to would-be litigants at his house, the village teams of gamesters, trained to perform creditable feats with the single-

THE IMPRISONED WITHIES

sticks, and great in the wrestling contests, were slashing away at their inveterate enemies and breaking their heads at Ashbury, Uffington, or Stratton St. Margaret. The large tattered white flag (captured from the French battleship *St. Florentine*), discoloured with age and full of shot holes and rents, hangs in the roof of the chancel at the church, and the village gamesters are immortalised in Judge Hughes' account of the White Horse Revels of 1857.

At the entrance to the village are the remains of the pound, formerly used to confine lost or straying cattle. The rival inhabitants of the neighbouring hamlet reproach the Shrivenham people for something that happened in respect of the enclosure. A couple of newly felled withy trees were one day discovered within it, and it was promptly noised abroad that they had been put there as being guilty of a serious offence. What the fault really was is not known, but it is suggested in the taunt levelled at the inhabitants by outsiders, who declared that "Tha shet thum withy trees up in the poun' 'cos tha 'oodn't swer to the parish." In the early part of the nineteenth century an Act was passed requiring all paupers to swear to their parish in order to facilitate the granting of relief, so that probably accounts for the jibe. The ancient stocks, the terror of evil-doers, stood near. The last offender to sit in them was a carter of the village who had stolen saffron to give to his horses.

The church stands back from the street. Its style is "debased classic," and it is almost square in shape. The interior is chaste and pure. The inner walls are of chalk—obtained from the downs—beautifully prepared and shaped into squares. This is of a soft milky white, and, though it has stood for centuries, it looks clean and new. The chalk stone receives and reflects the light from the numerous great windows; the interior is never dark or dull while daylight lasts. Several fine brasses, including one to the memory of Disraeli, adorn the walls of the aisles and chancel, and a tablet records, in a poem, the virtues and fame of Samuel Barrington, Admiral of the White and General of Marines, who died in the year 1800.

> " Here rests the hero, who, in glory's page
> Wrote his fair deeds for more than half an age.
> Here rests the patriot, who, for England's good,
> Each toil encountered and each clime withstood.
> Here rests the Christian, his the loftier claim,
> To seize the conquest yet renounce the fame.
> He, when his arm St. Lucia's trophies boasts,
> Ascribes the glory to the Lord of Hosts;
> And, when the harder task remained behind,
> The passive courage and the will resigned,
> Patient the veteran victor yields his breath,
> Secure in him who conquered sin and death."

The archdeacon was a tactful man, very courteous to and popular with the villagers. Besides being magistrate he was skilled in the laying of spirits; it is still told how he laid a notorious one single-handed. The parson at a neighbouring village used always, in walking, to jerk his heels up so as to touch his thighs behind, and he urgently advised all his parishioners to do likewise, in order to exercise the muscles of the legs. Another habit of his was to walk backwards, which he sometimes did for a mile or more; and he often lay on his back on the floor of the cottages and gave an exhibition of acrobatic feats before the astounded villagers.

The quaint old sexton, with wooden leg and piercing

eye, knew every stone of the church tower and could tell the names of nearly all the dead buried in the churchyard. He was noted for his aristocratic tendencies and lack of sympathy towards the poorest of the villagers. When they were filling in the grave of one well-to-do the earth was thrown down lightly, but when a pauper came to be interred he hardened his heart against the corpse, and, setting the example himself, told his mates to " Hit it in ! "

The village, though small, can boast of a fair. This falls in April, and though it is insignificant now, it was once a more considerable event. Any cottager, by placing a thorn bush outside his door, could sell ale on fair-days. When the rustics had been served with a short measure of ale at the inns they bit the earthenware cup into small pieces. Brandy was periodically smuggled into all the villages around the downs by " commercial travellers " and packmen. They carried the spirit in bladders concealed in their bundles of calicoes and woollens, and regularly sold it to the cottagers.

After the fair came the feast and revels, which lasted a week. Every cottager, to start the feast, on the first day of the week cooked a quantity of food in the boiler—a gammon of bacon and ten or a dozen plum puddings—so as to be in a position to entertain his friends and kindred from the villages round about. The revels began on Monday. There were skittling and bowling, grinning through the horse's collar, dancing, boxing, back-swording, wrestling, cock-fighting, and prize-fighting. It was not uncommon to have a fatal accident at the games, but that was looked upon almost as a matter of course, and the law concerning a death was not as stringent then as it is now. Though the inhabitants of a village seldom interfered with one another they banded themselves together against outsiders; thus the men of Shrivenham, Watchfield, and Highworth met and fought every week on the Sabbath.

Bull-baiting was also indulged in from time to time in the village and throughout the locality. First a strong rope, six yards long, was fixed to the ring in the bull's nose and the other end secured to a stake driven into the ground. Trained dogs were now set to worry the animal, that went nearly mad with rage, leaping from side to side, while the owners of the dogs stood near to catch them as they fell after being tossed by the bull. Sometimes the bull broke the rope and fiercely charged the crowd; more than one spectator met his death at the game. It was the rule to " bait " a bull before slaughtering it for food. It is even said that the baiting was required by law, but for what reason is not evident, unless it was to ensure a better bleeding of the carcass.

It was customary to hold a public harvest-home at Shrivenham. This was kept in the park, after all the corn was gathered in. Lord Barrington and the local farmers contributed and provided food, tea, and ale. There the rustics regaled themselves and afterwards indulged in sports and games. Before hiring a man the local farmers used to take him into the barn and require him to lift a sack of wheat from the floor standing in an empty bushel measure. Many of the labourers could accomplish this feat with one hand.

Besides the ancient whipping-stocks, the village had a place of incarceration called the Blind House, used for shutting up offenders until such time that they could be removed to the central stations and gaols at the county towns. The "blind houses" were dungeon-like places, built without windows, having merely small apertures secured with stout iron bars for admitting air and light. The prisoners were usually relieved of their handcuffs and allowed the liberty of the cells, though sometimes they were kept chained and only permitted to lie down on a straw bed upon the floor. If a villager had indulged in too much of the nut-brown liquor and became troublesome he was quickly placed in the "blind house," there to stay according to the pleasure of the local magistrate. It was a common practice for the prisoner's friends to visit the "blind house" after dark and carry ale in a pot. This the inmate was able to drink by sucking it in with a long pipe or straw through the aperture.

Drunkards were also put in the stocks and made to sit in them from sunrise till sunset, exposed to the jeers and laughter of the rest of the villagers. Though the prisoner was under the supervision of the constable, he was not debarred the privilege of receiving food from sympathisers. In the afternoon the cottagers' wives brought provisions—bread and butter and a mug of tea—but alcoholic drinks were forbidden. If the boys had been guilty of stealing apples and were taken they, too, were put in the stocks and given a few stripes. Sunday nutting in the copses by juveniles was also punished in the same manner.

The Manor of Shrivenham is one of the few that still hold annual Courts, in accordance with an ancient custom, to do homage to the Lord of the Manor and to grant Surrenders and Admissions of Copyhold property by the old symbol of "The Rod." Six Copyholders are required for "The Homage," and twenty-four nesciants of the Manor are summoned by the Court Bailiff to constitute "The Jury." The attendance of a full Jury was at one time imperative, and if a member failed to appear he was fined, or a part of his goods was confiscated. We learn, for instance, that one John Mills, shopkeeper, refusing to attend as Juryman, had his scales seized from the counter, and others suffered penalties of different kinds.

In the case of transference of Copyhold the vendor surrenders the property to the Lord of the Manor by handing the Rod to the Steward, who then admits the purchaser by passing it to him with the customary formula, comprising the Oath of Fealty : " You shall swear to become a true tenant of the Lord of the Manor of Shrivenham for the estate to which you are now admitted. You shall from time to time bear, pay, and do all such rents, duties, services, and customs therefore due and of right accustomed, and you shall from time to time be ordered and justified in all things at the Lord's Courts to be holden in and for the said Manor as other the tenants of the said Manor, and you shall in all things demean yourself as a faithful tenant ought to do. So help me God." Taking the oath is optional now : it may be avoided on payment of the sum of 6s. 8d.

On the death of a Copyholder or surrender of the property heriots are due to the Lord of the Manor, that is, the best beast or goods belonging to the tenant. In times past, failing payment of the heriot, the beast or piece of goods was actually seized. Now, however, a monetary payment is made, varying in amount according to the position of the parties. After a repast, the health of the Lord of the Manor is drunk from a silver cup, and the Court dissolves.

RAPACITY OF THE PIKE

The business of the Jury now principally consists in appointing the annual officers and in the formal observance of the old feudal rites and traditions pertaining to the Manor.

A modern mansion, Elizabethan in style, occupies the site of the old manorial residence. This was built by a former Lord Barrington, one of whose ancestors, the Honourable Daines Barrington, is celebrated as having been the intimate friend of Gilbert White, the naturalist, while another was the victor of St. Lucia. An inscription on a monument in the church informs the stranger that one John Wildman formerly held the Manor of Beckett. He, in company with his father, suffered a long term of imprisonment in the Island of Scilly, consequent on his devotion to the Royal cause at the time of the Commonwealth. Being a believer in the Roman form of adoption he disowned his relations and appointed a stranger to be his heir and succeed to his estate.

The lake before the house contains a small stock of fish—roach, perch, pike, and a few eels. The greedy pikes play havoc with the other occupants of the water. They devour everything they meet with in the pool, and finally prey on one another. Besides eating other fish, the pike devours frogs, rats, snakes, eels, young ducks, moorhens, and other wildfowl. One reason why moorhens and wild ducks leave the lake to breed in the spring is in order to be out of the reach of the voracious jaws of the pikes when they begin to move; half the broods of little ones would otherwise be swallowed as they swam about in the water. Accordingly, if the tame ducklings stray into the lake, the keeper, or one of his men, gets into a boat, and, armed with a large wooden spoon made for the purpose, lifts them out of the water and carries them ashore.

A few widgeons and teals visit the lake in the winter, but do not stay long. Rare birds are not often seen in the woods; they prefer to dwell upon the slopes of the downs in the south. An otter recently had her litter of five on the shores of the lake and was allowed to go unmolested. She had travelled up the small stream from the Cole, making her way under cover of darkness. The green woodpecker nests in the fir plantations; the local name for this is " the gallibird."

The inhabitants of every locality have special means of foretelling the weather, and are able to make a fairly accurate forecast without having resort to barometers and to the studying of meteorological items in the daily papers. The condition and location of mist at morning and evening are common indicators of what the weather is likely to be within the following twelve hours; by a careful observation of this the farmers know how to provide for the day's work about the fields. Alongside the Thames it is held that a fine evening with mist denotes fine weather, and a dull evening with mist denotes wet weather. The condition of mist on the downs, and especially around White Horse Hill, indicates to the occupants of the country below what the weather is likely to be. If the morning mist hangs over the hill that is a sign of wet, but if the summit is clear and the mist is drawn along in lines about the base, that is a sure sign of a fine day.

" When the mist goes up the hill,
  Then the rain runs down the drill,"

the ploughmen say. " Now, chaps, the owl' White Oss is a-blowin' 'is bacca off this mornin'. We shall ae't wet afoore night," cries the carter, and before the afternoon is over the rain pelts down in torrents and drives the toilers home from the fields. After a heavy drenching rain in summer—in otherwise clear weather—when the downpour has ceased the hollow spaces of the wood on the hill are filled with dense mist — fragments of clouds that were entangled by the trees and detained when the main body had gone by and was dissipated.

"Missis," said old Ike Giles of "Fyas" to his young wife one day—who secretly kept her mother in food—"I caan't make out why our mate bill is so high. A gets 'eavier aitch wik. Whatever becomes an't all?"

"Why, our Jack"—the under-carter who lived in—"is sich a one to et," said she.

"I'll jest ev 'e in to dinner along o' I to-day, then, an' see what a does wi't all," the farmer replied.

This frightened the good wife; so she saw the youth and explained the situation to him, and urged him not to have any lunch, in order to be the better able to eat an extra big dinner.

"Lar, missis," said he, "if I don' 'ae no lunch I shaan' want no dinner!"

When dinner-time came he was brought into the kitchen and placed next to master: a mug of ale was set beside his plate. He fell to and devoured three platefuls of meat and vegetables, to the consternation of old Ike.

"When bist gwain to drenk thi beer?" inquired he presently.

"I never thinks o' drenkin' till I 'aaf finished mi dinner," the other responded.

A neighbouring squire was a notable "character" and much given to out-of-door sports, especially hunting and hare coursing. He was a giant in stature, and he weighed thirty stone. According to local accounts he was a thorough blackguard, proficient in the use of oaths, but very good-natured. No one ever applied to him for help and was refused, and he made many generous gifts of food and clothes to the poor round about the neighbourhood. A farmer dwelling near detested the squire, and often took him to task for his uncivil behaviour, but he laughed loudly and passed off the other's remarks good-humouredly.

" Whenever you die you'll go to hell," the farmer insisted.

" Bent gone to hell yet! " said the squire, with a laugh, meeting him one day on horseback.

" But you're on the way, right enough," replied the farmer.

By and by the squire fell sick and was like to die. When the end seemed to be drawing near he went into a trance, and all thought he was dead. Thereupon the usual offices were performed, and the old woman of the village began laying him out. Presently, however, the supposed corpse revived, and the squire sat upright on the bed. He cursed and raved and ran off, just as he was, and, seizing his gun, shot hard at the old woman, who quickly scrambled out of the way and barely escaped with her life.

It is said by the villagers that when the squire died and came to be buried the coffin and body were so heavy they had to be removed on rollers.

Farmer Jonson used to bet heavily and attend the principal race meetings in the country. He was tall and square-shouldered, with big, round belly and fat, chubby head, and he always wore a suit of

AN ARTFUL STRATAGEM

big check and carried two crab-sticks, one in each hand. Being pestered with rats, he periodically hunted them indoors with ferrets and shot them in the kitchen and dining-room, ofttimes shivering the crockery ware to atoms and filling the house from top to bottom with the reeking smoke of the powder. His temper was not of the sweetest. There was a near neighbour to whom he had not spoken for thirty years. One day, however, on approaching the farm, the horse shied and overturned the high cart, and he was thrown into the ditch and pinned beneath. His inveterate enemy happened to pass that way at the same time, and, seeing his condition, went and released him from his unfortunate plight.

" So you thawt you'd pull me out then, Robbut ! " said he, laughing.

" Aw, aa ! thawt I'd better spake to tha to-day, maester," the rustic replied.

The Lord Craven lived at Ashdown Park, situated over the hill to the south of Shrivenham. One day he was walking down the hill into Ashbury and came upon a short, fat farm-boy lying on his belly in the road, and working his arms and legs about like a frog. When the noble lord drew near the youngster began :

> " As black as a rook,
> As black as a raven,
> As black as the devil,
> And so is Lord Craven."

" Ho ! Ho ! What's that ? What's that ? " cried Craven, stopping short and raising his stick to strike the youngster. Then the artful one began again :

> " As black as a rook,
> As black as a raven,
> As bright as the sun,
> And so is Lord Craven."

"Well done, boy! Well done, boy!" cried Craven; then, taking a crown piece and a half-sovereign from his pocket, he laid them on the palm of his hand and said:

"Here, boy! Have which you like."

"I wunt be covechus, I'll 'ae the little un," the youngster replied, and promptly pocketed the golden coin.

On another occasion the old lord addressed his valet, who also acted as jester, after being dressed previous to coming down to dinner.

"How do I look?" said he.

"As noble as a lion, mi lord," answered the valet.

"You've never seen a lion," said Craven.

"Yes, I have, mi lord," replied the other.

"Where did you see it, then?" said he.

"Down in Stubbs's yard," answered the valet.

"You fool! That was not a lion. That was a jackass," replied Craven.

"Can't help it, mi lord. You're just like him," the valet answered.

After the line was laid to Hay Lane a rustic went on the platform in smock-frock and top hat, wanting to go to Shrivenham. When the train came in he saw it was crowded with "fine folks," and came to the conclusion it was not for him: he could not think he had to ride with such grand people. After the train had left he quietly asked the porter when the next would be in.

"To-morrow morning. Why didn't you get in this one?" answered he.

"I didn't like to get in wi' the fine gentlefolks; but s'pose you'll let me walk!" returned the rustic.

Stronger is the story told of the Irishman—a navvy—who came to the local railway station one

Saturday night wanting to travel to Bath, and found the last train gone.

"Well," said he, with an oath, alluding to the line or the train, and turning to depart, "I thramped it before he was born and I'll thramp it again."

CHAPTER IV

Watchfield — The Stolen Church — Blackbirds — Tales and Gossip—Coleshill—The Luck of the House—The Lord Radnor—Anecdotes—" Mose " and the Farmer—" Old Polebrook."

WATCHFIELD lies to the north of Shrivenham, on the edge of a large tract of open country that extends beyond Faringdon to Abingdon. The village is small and compact. Of its past history very little is known, though it is held by the inhabitants that a great battle was fought on the site in olden times. They say that the modern name of the place originated in the battle, and that from the military injunction, " Watch the field," the present name was derived.

It is not often that a church is stolen, but that was most certainly the fate of the ancient church of Watchfield at some time during the latter half of the eighteenth century. It is said that the small building, left in the care of the parishioners, and sadly needing repairs, was sacrilegiously pulled down at night by the churchwardens and the stones carted off to make cowsheds and to fill up the farmyards. It is also related that the impudent churchwardens continued to report to the bishop that the church was in good condition for twenty-two years after it had been demolished. By and by, however, the truth leaked out, but before steps could be taken to punish the guilty churchwardens each died a violent death. One was found below a bridge with his neck broken, and the other was struck with a "thunderbolt" in the hayfield.

Beyond the village the road is open, and the way lonely. Here we are on the stone, as is evidenced by the colour of the cornfields and the great profusion of wild flowers. Immediately we leave the clay for chalk, or brash, we are made aware of a complete change in the flora and vegetation. There are fewer flowers upon the clay than are to be found on chalk and brash, though certain kinds, such as celandine and crowfoot, are seldom found off the clay. On the chalk and brash there is less vegetation, a smaller quantity of leaf and stem, and more blossom. The corn, also, yields less straw but a heavier ear. The elms are richer and tougher grown upon clay. They appear to thrive very well upon brash, but the wood is short and brittle.

No birds ever venture to eat the berries of the bryony, for they are poisonous, though the village children obtain both the long green vines in summer and the chains of brilliant ripe berries in autumn and make them into wreaths or wind them about their bodies. The bryony is also known as the mandrake, and its roots are still sought by herbalists and used for medicinal purposes. It was formerly held that the mandrake uttered a loud shriek on being taken from the earth, which belief was related by Shakespeare in *Romeo and Juliet*:

> "And shrieks like mandrakes' torn out of the earth,
> That living mortals, hearing them, run mad."

The singular phenomenon of a shrieking mandrake was probably met with in what the rustics call "them old witchcraft times"; the plant has lost its vocal powers in our day.

The root of the bryony is thought closely to resemble the human body; it is common for a rustic to dig one up and exhibit it to strangers.

"Yellacks! dist ever zee arn like that afoore? Yer's 'is yed an' body, arms an' legs, navel an' all an't, as plain as any mortal thing you ever zet eyes an. A oni wants life put into 'n an' a'd walk about."

"Code! en 'e naeterral! As naeterral as I be, that 'e is," the other replies.

Underneath the hedge are two cock blackbirds fighting furiously, though the nesting is over for this year and the young birds are grown up and scattered abroad, each one to look out for itself. Jealousy, no doubt, is the cause of the combat, either by reason of some present vaunting or trespass, or something remembered from the past season; or they are already looking forward to the next spring, both intent on obtaining the favours of the same delightful mistress. Begone! uncivil creatures. How dare you stab at each other with those beautiful gold daggers of bills? Inhabit the hedgerow peaceably together, or—— But they have taken to flight, one this way and one that, uttering indignant cries of protest at being disturbed in their duel.

Is there another bird in all nature more engaging, amusing, and generally delightful than the blackbird? Better singers there may be—in sustained effort, at least—and there are many of a more brilliant plumage, but for richness of form, luscious sensuousness, voluptuous movement, and exquisite pertinacity it certainly has no equal. The blackbird's appearance is best in early spring, in the courting season, and especially in the early morning hours and in showery weather. Then the male bird puts on his most glossy coat and studied feature, like a young beau seeking to engage the attentions of the fairest of the fair and triumph over all competitors and rivals. Lazy, indolent bird! with delicious curve of head and neck, breast and back, whose whole form is of inexpressible sweetness, whose motion suggests the rustling of silks and the scattering of the richest perfumes, whose life is one perpetual round of joy, ease, and idleness, and whose flute-like notes are purer than gold and mellower than the mellowest autumn fruits—for thy beauty I love thee, for thy roguish cunning I condemn thee, but for the liquid outpouring of thy melodious soul I forgive thee and wish thee safe of thy feathered foes and the fowler's nets, ever to dwell in the beautiful fields, secure among the thickets and stoles of the heavy-blossoming hawthorn.

The blackbird—though to a less extent than the thrush—is a frequenter of the haunts and habitations of men. Like the chaffinch it is fond of the highways; there is often a pair of birds to every eighty or a hundred yards of hedgerow by the roadside. Much food may be gathered with little effort upon and near the roads, but there is not the same security for the eggs and young, though the old birds manage to rear their offspring and keep the hedgerows tenanted. They utter their song for the most part from a low position, perched in the hawthorn, on the bottom boughs of a tree, or on a rail, though they are not very particular as to the site they choose. Sometimes they sing from the roof of a house, or sitting upon the telegraph wires, or they may warble their notes on the wing as they fly from hedgerow to hedgerow. For ten weeks during the spring of this year a blackbird sat in an elm-tree over the road and repeated six notes, corresponding to the chimes of the church bells near, daily, with great accuracy till towards the end of spring, when it became careless and confused the scale.

Near the wall of a farm on the roadside is a large board containing the words:

NOTICE

Dangerous Bog

warning off pedestrians and others who might be led on to the greensward where they would be swallowed up in a pit of bluish mud concealed from the eye with a covering of treacherous green turf. Higher up the dell are several other of these bog-pits which are probably relics of the primeval swamp, witnesses to a condition of things once general in the hollow of the valley. In depth they are nearly twenty feet. No draining would carry off the water, for that is far below the river-bed, and the hottest summer has no effect upon the surface of the pits.

One Sir Charles Wetherell formerly resided at Warneford Place. He was noted for his eccentric behaviour and especially for his slovenly attire. It was said that no Jew would have given five shillings for his wardrobe. He had a seat in the House of Commons, where he debated with energy. He never wore braces, and while he was addressing the House he kept pulling up his trousers at the waist, that promptly slipped down again, to the amusement of members present.

While walking in the grounds of Warneford Place one day he met a tramp going to the house, who stopped him and asked him if he thought it was of any use to try the place.

"Oh, I should go and try. You might get something," said Wetherell, and, walking round the house, he met the tramp at the door and gave him a sovereign.

At another time his butler asked leave to spend an evening with a friend.

"A friend. Ah! Then I think I will come with you, for that is what I have never had in my life," said Sir Charles.

Many ridiculous things happen in the villages and are talked about and laughed at by the rustics, but are unknown to the outside world. There is the tale of a villager whose wife sent him to the little shop for needles, cotton, and thread. The old fellow, being unable to read, and of weak memory, was forced to repeat the names of the articles aloud upon the way to the shop. As he was passing down the hill repeating the words, "Needles, cotton, thread. Needles, cotton, thread," he stepped on a slide that the children had made in the road, slipped, and fell upon his back. In the confusion he forgot his needles, cotton, thread, and went on his way and burst into the shop, crying: "Rasm, pitch, and tar. Rasm, pitch, and tar."

A few years ago the village choir was out "Christmasing" at the farmhouses. On going across a paddock in the darkness one of the number stumbled and fell over a donkey that sprang up with the chorister on his back and scampered off with him. The choirman thought he was being carried off by the Evil One, and cried: "Please, Mister Devil, put me down. I'm a religious man and a Psalm-singer."

"Maester, maester," cried the farm-boy one day, rushing into the kitchen in a state of great excitement, "the caaf got 'is yed droo the gyet an' caan't get un out agyen."

"Get the zaa, bwoy. Get the zaa, an' zaa 'n out," the farmer answered. Thereupon the boy got the saw and started to saw off the calf's head.

"Dang the bwoy! Why dissent zaa the gyet?" the farmer cried. Then, turning to his wife, he said: "Never mind, missis, we shall hae plenty o' bif now."

John, the carter, is in a desperate hurry this morning, for he has a lot to do, *i.e.* "to shave an' 'ev a nap." Some farm-hands never use a looking-glass for shaving, but lather their face and shave with the razor as they walk about the stable.

"Please, sir, father bin an' killed mother," cried the youngster, weeping, to the old white horse one dark night in the meadow, running up to him with a naked rushlight in his hand.

"Phoo-oo-oo-oo," returned the horse, blowing out the light with a mighty puff of his nose and causing the youngster to scamper off in terror. He thought it was the farmer in white milking-smock.

It is said of an old labourer, who had been kicked by a horse in the back, that his skin was so hard the doctor had to punch holes in it with iron tools in order to get his needle through to sew up the wound.

"Amber," a clumsy young foxhound, was the squire's dog and a great favourite with the village children, though he was clownishly mischievous and committed many depredations. One day he came running up the street carrying by the cloth a large pudding made in a basin, which he had taken from the table of a cottager. At another time he stole a baby out of the cradle and was making off with it, carrying it by the waistband.

A DARING OUTRAGE

Sometimes, when a young calf dies, novel means have to be adopted in order to induce the mother to change her domicile or to get her to market. Recently, when the dead calf had been skinned and the carcass disposed of, the cow refused to budge, and the boy had to put the skin over his head and shoulders and walk on before; then she followed him. On another occasion the boy had to ride concealed in the high cart and cry "Bar-r-r," now and then, before the bereaved cow could be prevailed upon to leave the farmyard.

"Martha, our Jack"—the donkey—"bin an' jumped over the girt 'igh wall an' got out o' the pound. Fust a put 'is far fit up, then a draad back a bit an' over a come, right into the road," said the villager to his wife one day. But the donkey did not leap over the wall: it was lifted over by a couple of yokels intent on a little amusement. Perhaps the jest is of a more senseless, or even of a cruel kind, as when a pair of villagers raided a cottage one Sunday at dinner-time, seized the pot, full of food, and hung it high in an elm-tree and left it dangling there at the end of a rope.

Belief in ghosts dies hard in the hamlets and out-of-the-way places of the countryside. Besides the spirit of the hunting squire, laid in the fish-pond at Sevenhampton, there was another notable local one that refused to be laid without the sacrifice and offering of human blood. This is reminiscent of the earliest times, for did not the ghost of Achilles refuse to be laid without a human sacrifice, and was not the beautiful Polyxena slain by the superstitious Greeks to appease his clamourings?

The village of Coleshill, which bore the proud title "THE FLOWER OF BERKS," lies along the western slope of a graceful hill immediately opposite Highworth, two miles away on the skyline. To the foot of the hill comes the river, winding round the small dell, as though it knew in the beginning that there would be work to do and a mill to turn at some future time.

Coleshill House, visible for many miles in its setting of elms and beeches, stands near the top of the hill overlooking the vale towards the faint blue downs. This is a moderate-sized mansion, built in the year 1660, to the plans of Inigo Jones, and representing that architect's skill at its best. A mysterious and jealously guarded tradition is associated with the house, though particulars of it have leaked out and are known to the villagers and others in the locality around. It is said that, concealed in a secret chamber in the inner parts of the house, is the embalmed body of a baby or of a young woman, which has been preserved there for several centuries, and upon the preservation of which the luck and security of the house depends. So long as the embalmed body remains, the house and property are assured to the family in possession, but should it ever be stolen or removed from the room in which it is concealed, then the luck of the house would fail and the estate would pass into other hands. Some, eager to shatter the romance of the embalmed child, say it is a wax doll, and not a human body, that is concealed in the secret chamber, but the belief of the villagers on the point is not to be shaken.

The villagers are very proud of their church, and consider it to be of great antiquity. "Sir," says the sexton enthusiastically, "this church is one of the howldest in the land. Why, the Romins builded this church, sir, when they was about 'ere, as I've hallus bin told bi they as hought to know." Doubtless there are those who would not be inclined to favour the view, but village people cling to their cherished opinions.

The sexton of nearly every village comes in for attention, and it is well-nigh impossible to overlook him. Sometimes he is made the subject of a rhyme, or he is famed for his shrewd wit and humour, or he may be remarkable for his oddness, or for the sharpness of his temper. In a village close at hand the sexton was a cobbler, and was celebrated by the cowman in the following lines :

"As I walked along and looked over the wall
I saw the sexton diggin' a hawl,
A left-handed cobbler just backwards at work,
He wore his waistcoat a-top of his shirt.
Between the living and the dead,
That's how the sexton got his bread."

Another used to sleep and snore loudly during the sermon, and sometimes he woke up and shocked the worshippers with irreverent expressions, or disturbed the service by hurling the coal-hammer across the church at the children talking and laughing in the gallery.

On one occasion the board containing the numbers of the hymns was inadvertently placed hind-before, and after the clerk had several times called out, "Hymn number — hymn number——" waiting to proceed, he cried loudly to a worshipper near : "Jest turn that boord round, young man, wool 'e ?"

Here at Coleshill the sexton—whose name happened to be Sexton—used to imbibe too much of the home-made liquor, and when he came to church he was incapable of performing his duties and made inexcusable blunders. Accordingly he was dismissed and the village blacksmith preferred for the post, but he was soon afterwards removed. A carter near Coleshill bore the nickname of "Blackbird," which he received in consequence of his having fallen asleep at church one Sunday morning. Half-way through the sermon he began to snore, and very soon the people were startled with a loud cry of "Come idder, Blackbird!" The carter was dreaming that he was in the field ploughing up the wheat stubble.

There was never an inn at Coleshill, so the villagers were forced to provide ale for their own use. Accordingly, they grew their own barley, threshed it out at home, or in a barn lent for the purpose, made their own malt, gathered wild hops from the hedges, and brewed their own beer in the cottages. This they did in a large copper pot of twenty gallons hung from chains over a wood fire. The vessel—named the "Parish Kettle"—was given to the villagers by the Lord Radnor, and was used alternately by the cottagers. His Lordship also paid the duty on one sack of malt per annum for each labourer on his estate.

The ancient game of back-swording was practised at the feast. At one time two heads were broken simultaneously, which was a very rare occurrence, and a notable event. A swaggering professional back-sworder, unbeaten with the sticks, used to visit the feast and overawe the local men with the "cocksureness" of his attitude and behaviour. At last a young carter determined to make a supreme effort to humble his pride and carry off the prize of thirty shillings offered by the champion. Accordingly, when the swaggerer cried out: "Will any young gamester come upon the platform?" the carter responded: "Yes, I ool," and leapt nimbly upon the stage. Seizing the single-stick firmly, he

THE GAMESTER HUMBLED 73

turned to the crowd and cried : " Well, gentlemen ! What be I to do wi' this owl' man ? Be I to break 'is 'ed or no ? " " Ef 'e ool be obstinate, go at un," they cried, whereupon the young carter began fencing, and presently broke the head of the old gamester, who wept at his disgrace and never more showed himself in the neighbourhood. After that the carter was pressed off to fight against the French at Waterloo, and on returning to the village he introduced the game known as " Prisoner's Base," or " Crossing the Line," which was for some years popular with the youths of the countryside.

Several amusing tales are told of the old Lord Radnor, who, although a stern man in some respects, had the welfare of the village at heart, and did his best to provide employment for the workpeople and keep them in a prosperous condition. The clothes he wore about the farms and grounds were extremely plain, and his old white top-hat and threadbare coat were more fitting for a beggar than an aristocrat.

He was rather eccentric, and he caused some amusement around the neighbourhood by reason of his singular behaviour and his weakness for wanting to know how he was regarded by his workpeople. On the passing of the Reform Bill he entertained the rustics to dinner at Coleshill House and feasted them on the lawn to commemorate the event. He ran about in the marquee carrying the plates of meat and shouted loudly to the carvers to cut thick slices " Now, Pinnegar," cried he to a farmer who was carving, " put that knife into it, and give the men some victuals, and don't be frightened of a bit of meat."

He had a bullock killed once a fortnight and five sheep every week for use at the house, and he gave the inferior parts and gallons of good soup to the villagers.

It greatly amused old Angel, the rustic, to learn that his lord and master sat in a chair on runners in front of a fire on the hearth and had a long staff with a spike and "cruckle" (crook) on the end of it to push himself farther back or draw himself nearer to the fire.

One day he came upon some men sorting over a pile of stones.

"That's a nice little job, men. I think I could do that," said he.

"Come on, then, an' have a go, if you wants to," said an unsuspecting workman, who took him to be a stranger at one of the farms.

Thereupon Radnor threw off his coat, and began to load the wheelbarrow with stones. Very soon he began to question them. "What sort of a man is this old Lord Radnor?" said he.

"Oh," said they, "ther's two ways to take un—the right way er the wrong way. If you takes un the right way you'll find he yent much amiss."

"Oh, I'm glad to hear there's a bit of good about him," he replied, and, giving them half a crown each, he put on his coat and departed.

While he was presiding at Faringdon Police Court a case came forward in which a poacher was the defendant. He pleaded not guilty.

"What were you doing in the wood?" asked Radnor.

"I only went in to cut a stick, my lord," replied the defendant.

"How would you like me to go into your garden and cut a cabbage?" promptly returned Radnor.

While he was talking to two labourers one morn-

A SHOCK FOR RADNOR

ing, several others, dressed in Sunday best, went by on their way to Highworth Fair.

"H'm! Looks as if they are going to enjoy themselves," said he. Then, putting his hand into his pocket and taking out a crown he gave it to the men and continued: "Well, you go and enjoy yourselves, then, but don't drink too much of that beer."

He used to declare to one of his tenant-farmers that every pheasant reared on the estate cost him a pound, and he was furious when a party of young sportsmen, whom he had invited to Coleshill Woods, went out and shot nine hundred birds in one day around Badbury Hill.

His desire to know how he was regarded by the villagers exposed him to certain dangers, and he did not always escape scot-free. Meeting with an old woman who was gathering wood in the field one day he addressed the usual questions to her.

"And whose field might this be, my good woman?" inquired he.

"Aw! this belongs to owld Lard Radner," she replied.

"Ah! And what sort of a man is he?" asked Radnor.

"A crafty, covechus owld bagger, as ull never be satisfied till 'is mouth's chock full o' dust," she answered spitefully.

"Ah! Is that so? Good-day, my good woman," said he, and went his way.

The next morning the old woman was sent for to the house, and was met at the door by Radnor, who gave her a sovereign and a bundle of clothing. "I'm very sorry to hear such a poor account of Lord Radnor. I didn't know he was quite so bad, and I hope you'll think a *little* better of him in the future," said he to the bewildered dame.

Notwithstanding Radnor's fair reputation he was severely handled once or twice at the Cricklade elections; the last time he appeared there his carriage was smashed, and he was fortunate to escape without injury.

One of Lord Radnor's tenants was a rich farmer who was noted for a remarkably keen eye in looking up and down the drills. He was driven everywhere in a small carriage drawn by two horses, and he crossed the rough ploughed land or young crops at any time of the year. If he found a small portion of land missed by the drill he discharged the carter and put him on again within the hour.

One day he was arranging with Moses, the day man, about the hoeing of a patch of beans.

" Now, Mose! What ca'st do this for ? "

" Aw! I don' know, maester. What can you gie ? "

" I'll gi' tha 'aaf a crown "—*i.e.* an acre.

" Aw! Aaf a crown. Well, I'll show 'e 'ow I can do't for 'aaf a crown. Like this, look ! "

Here he put the handle of the hoe between his knees and dragged it behind him up the drills.

" Daal! That wunt do. " I'll gie tha sixpence more," said the farmer.

" Must still trot wi' the 'ow, maester," Mose replied.

" I'll make it another shillin'."

" I'll gie one blow yer an' another ther'," Mose answered, indicating his meaning with the hoe.

" S'pose I must gie tha five shillin's," said the farmer.

" Tha's more like business, maester. Now I can do't, an' do't well," Mose replied.

The village of Coleshill was unmolested with

THE TABLE RETALIATES

witches, but it is said that one Robert Polebrook, who lived not far off, was in league with the Evil One. Robert had been cowman for the greater part of his life, and when he got old he left the herd and did a little odd work on the road. He it was who went to Longworth Lodge, that was haunted and deserted of its tenants, at midnight, and attempted to carry off a table for use in his cottage. Clutching the table, and hoisting it upon his shoulders, he succeeded in getting it outside when a terrific contest began. The table struggled violently and overthrew Robert, who got up again and tried hard to master it, but the table hopped and jumped about around him and struck him on the head once or twice and finally overpowered him, and he was constrained to carry it back to the Lodge and replace it in the room. The operation took him all night to perform; he just managed to get it over by daybreak and met the shepherd coming to work on his way back home.

But the old fellow was cheerful at times, and sang merrily as he pushed his wheelbarrow along the road or clipped the edges of the green turf:

"My pack at my back, and they all wish me well."

Often in winter, when it was bitterly cold and the snow fell, he would be out at work, whistling cheerily, with no hat, and only half dressed. One morning, when the snow was falling in thick, heavy flakes, Robert was out stone-breaking, with his hat tossed in the hedge, full of snow, and his clothes nearly buried on the ground. Then Brown, the fogger, came past on his way back from breakfast.

"Good morning, John Brown! Very muggy warm this morning, John Brown!" said Polebrook.

"Aa, 'tis, Robbut, an' thee't very zoon be buried

out o' zight, 'ammer, stwuns, an' all, if thee dossent lave it an' get along whum wi' tha," the cowman answered.

When at length the old man became very sick and felt that death was drawing near he addressed a final entreaty to his lifelong friend and neighbour. "Betty," said he, "plaaze to put the owl zythe an' shart-'andled hoe into the coffin wi' ma, for I dwunt know what tha'll put ma at when e gets to t'other country. I'll lose a bucketful o' sweat wi that owl' hoe."

After he was dead his two sons, who lived afar off, came with a waggon, put up the coffin first, then piled the furniture of the cottage, the garden tools, wheelbarrow, and clothes-props on top and carted them all off together.

CHAPTER V

Crossing the Ford—Discoveries in the Field—The Hawk and the Blackbird—Inglesham Church and Village—The Round House—The " Grand Old Man of Inglesham "—Steam-ploughing—A Storm in the Vale.

BEFORE the days of the old Lord Radnor the Cole was crossed by a ford and the road was diverted from its original course in order to approach the bridge. Even after the bridge was made the carters continued to use the ford. The horses were accustomed to wade through the river and to take a drink of water, while the carters liked to wash the wheels of the waggons or to soak them if the weather was hot and dry.

Fording the river at deep water was dangerous, however, and accidents occasionally happened. One day a Cheap Jack with his stock of jewellery was being driven in a coach to Highworth Fair and came to the river, that was swollen with recent rains. The driver thought he would take the ford and drove his horse into the river, but the current was strong, and the coach was washed downstream and smashed against the bridge. The Cheap Jack escaped by climbing through the window and clinging to the roof of the battered coach. " I'm a ruined man, but save my life," cried he to the villagers who had assembled to give assistance on hearing of the accident.

When the workmen were clearing a flam out of

the river in order to make the bridge they found embedded in the sand several human skeletons, probably the remains of gipsies, which had been disposed of secretly. The old Lord Radnor's French valet is said to have been buried on the roadside. This was in accordance with his private wish : he objected to being interred with the Protestant villagers.

While the carter was at plough one day near the river the front mare of the team stumbled and her fore-legs sank into the earth up to her knees. Upon examination it was found that she had stepped into a stone coffin buried just below the surface ; though the field had been in cultivation for untold years no one had made the discovery before. Inside the coffin were the bones and dust of a corpse, and a small urn full of ancient coins, which were claimed by the bailiff of the farm, while the carter received the bones for his share of the booty. These he carried home with solemn care and reverence, intending to keep them, but the house was immediately disturbed with ghostly sounds and unaccountable happenings, and the carter was compelled to leave the cottage.

Many attempts were made to unearth the coffin but to no purpose ; even the two strongest horses on the farm could not move it from its low bed. Then the carters were doubly assured of the supernatural agency and declared that the coffin was never intended to be moved. Accordingly it was left in the field, where it still lies beneath the yellow wheat stubble. I have been confidentially informed of an old farm labourer—a very quiet and unobtrusive individual—who is said to possess a sackful of ancient gold and silver coins which he dug up with skeletons in one place and another. Whether it is true or not I am unable to say; the whole matter may be no more than a romantic fabrication.

At one time the sermons at the church lasted an hour, and the parson frequently criticised the farmers' methods of cultivating their land and took them to task about the couch. He told them that sin was just like couch, and if any of the congregation did not know what that was they could see plenty of it by just going outside and looking over the wall into farmer Gosling's field.

Beyond the mill the stream, that before had been but a few yards wide, assumes greater dimensions and puts on the dignity of a real river. Here its course is more open and direct. The willows and poplars have been left behind and the hawthorn clumps are fewer and smaller in size than they are farther back towards the head. A great part of the charm has gone, too; the sweet mystery of the pools beneath the boughs is laid bare under the searching light of the open heavens. The haunting spiritual presence is no longer felt and the spell is broken, for we have almost reached the consummation of the river's course and learned that which before was beautifully hidden from us.

As well as the greater beauty of the upper river in the almost continuous lines and massive round clumps of white and pink blossoming hawthorn, and the richer profusion of flowers growing in midstream and along the borders, there is the incomparable delight of exploring all the crooks and crannies, the twistings and windings of the channel, and peering down through the dense bushes into the quiet holes beneath. Very often the high bushes, interlaced together, completely cover the water.

The thick blackthorn, laden with purple fruit, has grown like a wall along the edge. Wild rose and woody nightshade intertangled clamber along the top of this, or hang down to the bottom of the bank, or trail for several yards in the quietly flowing stream. Here a bank of sand, thickly overgrown with flags and reeds, projects out and almost cuts off the current. Beyond this is a pretty pool, with the beautiful ovate leaves of the yellow water-lily calmly floating on the surface, and, a little farther on, a large bed of sky-sweet forget-me-nots softly glimmering beside the dark green bank.

In the spaces between the hawthorns the river is fringed with a luxuriant growth of creamy meadow-sweet and fragrant pink willow-herb, with an occasional spike of purple nettle or tall hemp agrimony. At the drinking-place are sure to be several clumps of brilliant marsh marigold, plants of the water persicaria, and one or two roots of celery-leaved crowfoot growing out of the soft mud and bursting into bloom. Above the stream flits the blue-bodied May-fly, now and then alighting on the reeds and grasses; the dragon-fly, or "horse stinger," whizzes by overhead in the bright sunshine. In the shallows the caddis worm and destructive water-beetle are busily engaged. On the grass, a short way off, is a large roach freshly caught and half eaten by the old heron, whose footprints are visible in the soft mud of the drinking-place and along the shallow stream-bed.

There is more bird-life, too, higher up the stream than towards its end, where it draws near to the Thames. The closeness of the banks, the continuous boughs, and the forests of reeds and grasses give the birds much protection. There the wild ducks and

ON THE RIVER'S BRINK

moorhens build their nests and hatch their young in safety and lead them up and down the shallow waters, or about the silent pools, running over the broad lily leaves expanded on the surface.

If you come to the river's edge when the grass is newly cut in the large field and, falling on your hands and knees, creep quietly along in the shade of the hawthorn or withy boughs, you may see pretty sights on the waters of the stream. There you may easily surprise the wild ducks, motionless under the roots projecting from the bank, or see the mother sailing gracefully along, surrounded with her tiny brood, nibbling at the edges of the lily leaves, and sipping the water with their small bills; or behold the moorhen, with red bill and white tail, and a flock of little sooty followers paddling behind. Occasionally, too, you may come upon the gaunt old heron himself fishing in the shallow, and be nearly struck with his wing as he rises and immediately soars high up, hovering near to see what your intentions may be about the place.

Of fish there are not so many, except in the pools lower down, and where the water has been bayed up for the mills. Being confined with the flams and shallows they fall an easy prey to the heron, and also to the otter, that leaves the deeper water of the Thames and works its way up to the stream's head under cover of the bushes and reeds. The otter also plays havoc with the wild fowls, though it is often discovered and shot by the farmer whose fields lie alongside the river. A favourite lurking-place of the otter, by day, is a hollow withy tree; the farmer's dog occasionally scents out one there. If it is disturbed and surprised out of the water it is easily taken. The shortness of its legs prevents it from running away, though it is very fierce when attacked by the dogs.

Below Coleshill the course of the river is interrupted and the water turned aside and led away at right angles to meet the Thames a mile above the original junction. This is effected by means of a strong wall built across the bed and provided with a hatch to regulate the water for the cattle in the meadows beyond. The bed was dug out and the course so conducted as to procure sufficient fall for the water to turn the wheel of Inglesham mill. This was done centuries ago, when Inglesham—at this time a ruined place and almost deserted, except for the very ancient and interesting church—was a prosperous and flourishing village, proud in its position alongside the undulating Thames. But evil days fell upon the place and brought about its overthrow; only a heap of ruins remains to mark the site upon which the village formerly stood. The site of the mill is marked by a set of hatches and a broad pool —formerly the " whirly hole." The long, spreading branches of the water-hemlock half cover the surface, and the wild rose blooms profusely on the bank and stoops over the margin, blushing to see her beautiful image reflected in the clear depths beneath.

Numbers of eels pass the hatches every year and many are trapped on their way through the gate. The miller used to take eels by means of a " twig budget "; that is, a bent willow wand with a long net attached. This was set through the hatch and the eels fell into it and became entangled. After taking them from the net, in order to keep them alive until such time as they should be required for the table, they were put into a large perforated box, which was placed in the pool and kept there, secured with a rope. Hundreds of eels are taken at the weirs on the Thames and sold at a shilling a pound by the lock-keepers: an eel-pie is a favourite and highly esteemed dish in the Thames Valley.

In the midst of the withy bed alongside the stream —once the site of the miller's house and garden— is a pit-like place, formerly used as a fish-pond. At one time every miller had one, and sometimes several small ponds and wells in which he stored live fish according to their kind. If anyone was ill, or otherwise in need of a fish diet, instead of resorting to the angle he merely applied to the miller, who, with the aid of a net fixed on a pole, obtained a fish from his pond and sold it to the applicant. Now the dry pond, overgrown with dense bushes and reeds, affords a cover for the great old fox that leaps out at your approach and bounds across the meadow, several times stopping and turning round to watch your intentions before he gallops off and disappears through the thick hedge into the green field beyond.

Out in the meadows alongside the river the haymakers are busy. Here the mowing machines, drawn by stout horses, are going round and round the piece, tinkling merrily, while the tall grass, full of sorrel and crowfoot, staggers and totters for a moment and then falls, to be finally disposed into neat rows by the swath-board, that fetches the cut over as the turn-furrow of a plough gives shape to the stubborn soil in the cornfield. The corncrake runs swiftly from side to side of the patch, crying loudly, while crowds of finches, wagtails, and starlings flock behind the machine and stalk proudly over the swaths, gorging themselves with grasshoppers and other insects that had their home in the thick herbage. On the other hand are the machines tedding the half-dried grass or waking up the hay; beyond, the loaders are busy gathering it up from the field and hauling it into the farmyard to place it upon the rick.

On the grass a little way in front of me the shadow of a bird falls with a fluttering motion. Looking up I perceive a hawk hovering in the air on the other side of the brook. Presently he swoops down towards the hedge and is immediately met and assailed by a cock blackbird, that flies boldly at him and buffets him with his wings, at the same time uttering loud cries and a series of quick, chattering notes. Disconcerted with the unexpected opposition of the blackbird, the hawk wheels round and mounts up again, and prepares for a second attack on the hedge. Again he swoops and again he is repelled, and so on till the third time, after which, coward that he is, he flies off and the blackbird sits upon the limb of a neighbouring ash-tree and pours out a flood of triumphant song at the retreat of the enemy. Tiptoeing to the hedge I see a nest of young with the hen bird perched trembling near: great was the danger from which she had been delivered by the bravery of her devoted mate and husband warbling in the tree-top.

The quaint old church lies off the main road, but a few yards from the Thames. The building dates from the twelfth century: in the year 1205 it was given by King John to the Monks of Beaulieu, in the New Forest. Its length is no more than forty-nine feet. It has north and south aisles, with trans-Norman and Early English features, and a little bell-cot at the west end. Part of the original oak of the roof is yet intact. Built into the walls are several crude figures of great antiquity; the old

W. Dennis Moss, Cirencester.

Inglesham Church; date, Twelfth Century.

"A lovely little building, like Kelmscott in size and style, but handsomer, and with more old things left in it."—WILLIAM MORRIS.

hour-glass, used formerly by the preacher to regulate the length of his discourse, is preserved, a relic of days long past and of methods no more to be employed.

Below the church, shaded by a group of Lombardy poplars, is a building called the Round House, guarding the entrance to the old Thames and Severn Canal, which was once a great highway for those trading between the ports of London, Bristol, and Gloucester. Here, too, the Coln, flowing from the stony Cotswolds, is received into the bosom of her lover the Thames, and the two go dreaming away in mystic union towards the eternal ocean. Broad meadows, the home of the fritillaries, and dotted with clumps of hawthorn, stretch alongside the river. The tall spire of Lechlade church rises beyond the grey stone bridge and above the clustering roofs of the houses in the town.

The canal, with its once broad and deep channel and elaborate system of locks, after being in use for over a century, is neglected now. Its construction was formerly looked upon as a great engineering feat. Hopes were entertained of an endless period of usefulness and prosperity for the waterway; but the possibilities of the steam-engine had not then been entertained, nor could any foretell the wondrous inventions and revolutions to be effected throughout the globe within less than a century from that time.

The Round House is much frequented by tourists and holiday parties during the summer months. The very name of the place excites a pleasing curiosity and impels one to go and see it. There is, moreover, the joy of rambling along the shores of the deep, wise river, of watching for otters and kingfishers, or plucking the flowers that bloom on the bank or about the deep-trenched meadows.

Formerly the house was occupied by the lock-keeper, who superintended the traffic passing through the gates and received the tolls. Now the old blacksmith has taken up his abode there and lives in semi-retirement. He still keeps a small tin of borax, begged from the bargeman who piloted the last load through the locks, in memory of that event. Some of this he occasionally uses for welding steel tackle, such as grains of forks and pickaxes.

Spinning and weaving, though not on a large scale, were carried on in the cottages at Inglesham in olden times; agriculture was the principal industry alongside the Thames banks and round about the valley.

Old Elijah, the "Grand Old Man of Inglesham," lives in a house fronting the road and overlooking the Thames opposite Kempsford church, three miles away, the grey tower of which rises magnificently above the dark tree-tops and beats back the strong rays of the morning sun. His widowed daughter tends him in his age—he is nearly ninety-five. The farmer has assured them the use of the cottage at a nominal rent as long as they have need of it: their anxiety for the future is reduced to the minimum.

Seeing the old man outside, I addressed him, standing near the gate.

"I'm come to have a chat with you," said I.

"An' very plaazed to zee 'e. I likes a bit o' good company," returned he.

"Oh, sir, he's very dull of understanding!" cried the middle-aged daughter, appearing in the doorway.

There was no need of the apology. A man of ninety-five, and a rustic, of no school education, who can talk intelligently for hours about the farm, the passing of Laws and Acts, electioneering, historical events, and great national movements, who can explain many of the phenomena of the heavens and describe the equinox, discuss local topics, from the old Priory of St. John to the British village on Badbury Hill and the Hannington "Liberty," and finish up with singing a score of songs remembered for sixty or seventy years, is not dull of understanding.

As a matter of fact—I tell it as a confidence—Gramp thought at first I was a curate come to make the usual call and was inclined to be formal, but when I had discovered myself as a very common sort of mortal he became friendly and familiar. Gramp is really a splendid figure—a delightful and congenial soul. He is of medium height, is broad and well made, and as erect as many a man at sixty. His head is massive and his features are typically English, with heavy brows, expressive eyes, aristocratic nose, and clean-shaven lips and chin. His long, silky, snow-white hair hangs nearly to his shoulders and adds reverence to his appearance. Every day, when it is dry and fine, with his feet inside a pair of large slippers, and gripping a stout stick in his hand, Gramp walks down the road to the old pound and chats with his neighbour. When it is wet and cold he sits by the fire, hat on head, and smokes his pipe, or hums over the airs he learned as a youth.

Until he was over ninety Gramp gathered flags and bulrushes from the river and made baskets, chair-bottoms, and other articles. He also made the hassocks in use at the quaint little church by the Thames' side. He would have gone this year and got more rushes, but his daughter would not allow him to walk so far; accordingly he has to be content with looking over the garden or sitting and thinking about old times. One of the men with whom he worked on the farm as a boy fought at Trafalgar and amused them with his tales of the battle. When the fight was at its hottest a Sergeant of marines was very despondent.

"Oh dear," said he, "we shall never see England nor the old folks any more, for we can't stand this much longer."

While he was thinking of death, a jolly tar came running up from below and shouted: "What cheer! What cheer! Duck for dinner! Duck for dinner! There's hundreds on the water," and, looking over, they spied scores of wild fowls that had got in the way of the guns, being washed against the ship's side and seized by the sailors.

Another local recruit fought at the battle of Waterloo. During the battle he got cut off from his company and was isolated and surrounded by the Frenchmen, but he fought and killed seven of them single-handed before he himself was over-powered and slain.

The scarcity of men and the difficulty of obtaining recruits at that time is well known. The sum of thirty pounds was paid to volunteers, and Gramp had heard it said that a bold sergeant sat before a drum in the market-place, upon which was placed thirty sovereigns in gold, and that every time he beat the drum the coins sprang into the air, which feat was practised in order to attract the attention of the rustics and induce them to enlist. Towards the end of the war local farmers subscribed the sum of fifty pounds and gave to a villager to procure his enlistment. Before he had got far on his journey peace was proclaimed, and he came home with the money and did no more work for two years.

Gramp has seen many great floods in the Vale. " The water ull cut out o' that owl' Thames an' bust out o' the bank, an' be all over everything in 'aaf a' hour, an' zumtimes be gone agyen in forty minutes," he says. He remembers when there were many more weirs on the Thames than there are now, and when the stream was navigable up to Cricklade. " But the sprengs be wakened in thaay owl' 'ills, an' ther yent so much water comes down as 'twas when I was a bwoy," he tells you. The winter of 1788–89 was unusually severe. The frost lasted continually for thirteen weeks, and the Thames, in many places, was frozen to the bottom. This Elijah had learned of his grandfather, and the matter was also celebrated in a short rhyme sung by the fiddlers who came to the feasts :

"The frost began in eighty-eight
And ended in eighty-nine."

Now the summer is over. All the haymaking is done. The ricks have been tucked and thatched. The mowing machines and horse-rakes have been gathered together and safely stowed in the sheds, and the fields are green with the fresh young aftermath. The sun, that looked down day after day from an almost tropical sky, strikes not so fiercely now. In the evening the mists thicken. Purple shades steal up out of the east and creep early around the north and south, dimming the splendour of sunset and putting the glory to flight. Autumn treads on the heels of weary, jaded summer and paints her beautiful image in the earth. The hills, fields, and valley put on their robes of radiant gold and await the sacrifice, when the high priest of the heavens shall have finished his yearly office and delivered up his burning seal into the hands of all-provident Time. Soon the reapers will enter the wheat, and the proud harvest will be laid low. Soon the sheaves will be ingathered, the smooth, clear grain threshed out, and the winter toils begin.

Already the steam-plough is at work in the field, breaking up the dry, stubborn soil and preparing it to receive the seed, when the kindly rain has fallen and powdered the surface of the earth. The huge engines, one on each side of the field, are puffing and panting alternately, rocking, trembling, and straining like giants to draw the mighty cultivator that staggers and stumbles, jumps and jolts, and plunges headlong on its rough course across the patch. How hard the ground is! How fearful the effort required to force a way through it! And how doggedly the green-painted wizard persists in the toil! The dense black smoke and cinders shoot high into the air. The bright, smooth piston-rod shoots in and out like lightning, and the heavy fly-wheel whirls rapidly round, enveloped in a halo of light. The heavy steel cable, well polished with trailing the implement, flashes like silver in the sunshine. At one time this is straight and taut. Now it leaps into the air, now plunges down, lashing the earth furiously; now it sways to and fro sideways, jerking and tugging, and now it lies prone on the earth, half the length of the patch, its glittering, snake-like coil creeping silently along the surface of the ground. A cloud of brownish dust encircles the plough, half concealing the steersman perched upon his iron seat. He holds fast and grips hard on the wheel and pilots the machine skilfully from end to end.

A THUNDERSTORM

Now the first engine stops, for the plough has reached the end, and the other begins, steadily at first; the ponderous implement turns clumsily round and goes plunging back across the piece. Meanwhile the vacant engine takes advantage of the respite to go forward several paces and patiently awaits the plough's arrival on the other side. The driver leaps down from the engine and pours oil into the lubricators, or chats with the farmer who has come out to see the finishing up of the work, for there is not much more to be done. A few more journeys and several half-turns completes the ploughing; then the engine farthest from the entrance turns round and rushes powerfully across the rough piece, leaving the implement to follow behind and plough out the tracks of the ribbed wheels. This is no sooner done than with a bright flash and a sharp clap overhead the heavens break and a light thunder shower falls, causing the heavy wheels to skid round and bringing the engine to a standstill, with the machinery in full motion.

For several hours a storm had been brewing along the Cotswolds. At noon the sun smote down from the hazy sky with a sultry, humid heat, making one feel faint and powerless and preventing great physical exertion. The small wind that blew over the river died away; a deep hush fell upon the fields, broken only by the *kuh-kuh* of the ploughing engines. A few light, copper-tinted clouds, with burning silver rims, sprang suddenly into mid-air, while lower down on the horizon a dense bank of bluish-white vapour arose and spread along the low-lying hills. The storm made no progress, however, but hovered, phantom-like, in the distance, as fearing to approach until the sun should lose something of his fiery strength and glittering brightness. With the sun's decline the cloud advanced steadily, pushing out its armed squadrons into the air and frowning terribly. By mid-afternoon the outbreak was imminent, and the first warning clap came and the first swift drops of rain fell as the ploughing engines finished their work and proceeded out of the field.

Then the storm broke in earnest. To the north, the sky was blue-black. The pitchy clouds came rolling up, over and over, like huge waves underneath. The zigzag lightning flashed and played about the heavens, and the thunder crashed and boomed, rolled and muttered, and crashed and boomed again incessantly. The rain fell in sheets, dashing on the hard clods of earth in the field and causing them to smoke, while the water ran in streams, flooding the roads and ditches and half drowning the pretty orange-tipped ox-tongue blooming sweetly beside the bank.

Southward, towards the downs, the purple clouds hang in heavy folds, like a half-lowered curtain, showing an exquisite sky beneath. There the near hills wear tints of tenderest green, and all behind is of loveliest gold, from deep to pale, showing like an enchanted land, surpassing the imagination. Now the storm wheels, drawing over the White Horse, which is soon obliterated with torrential rain. Charlbury Hill is ink black, while Liddington Hill, but a mile away, is still robed in unspeakable gold. This lasts not long, however. Presently that, too, is enveloped. The whole heaven is as dark as night; everything is blotted out and the deluge is incessant.

CHAPTER VI

The "Ha'penny Bridge"—Buscot—Squire Campbell's Works—The "Water Gardens"—Herons—Visitors to the Lake—The Woodman Naturalist—Eaton Weir—Floods at Kelmscott.

THE straight-as-a-line raised road, bordered with deep ditches full of meadow-sweet, loose-strife, and valerian, that runs down to the picturesque steeple town beyond the river, has not existed for much more than a century. Formerly a bridle-track through green fields led to the Thames, wide and deep at this point, and travellers and others wishing to go by that way were ferried across into the Gloucestershire town. At length, on the completion of the Canal, the inhabitants decided to build a bridge over the stream and to construct a hard road in place of the green track. Accordingly, after many difficulties, the work was completed. The huge span of the bridge was made and a pike house built to take tolls from those crossing into the town. The amount of the toll was fixed at a halfpenny, and the bridge came to be known far and wide as the Ha'penny Bridge. There is a local tradition to the effect that when the bridge was about to undergo the first severe test the master mason ran and climbed one of the high poplar-trees at the Round House and declared that if the bridge gave way he would leap into the river and be drowned.

Below the bridge the river, that was flowing serenely

down the deep green fields, suddenly turns and forms a double loop, sweeping majestically round and afterwards resuming its course between lines of silvery willows. Running beneath the road is a long tunnel to assist in carrying off the water in flood-time; several other shorter arches, made for the same purpose, support the highway. Pools of stagnant water, half concealed with tall flags and rushes, lie around and below the arches throughout the summer and afford a secure refuge for the water-fowl. Here also the otters love to come and fish in the shallows and chase the half-grown pikes that were borne out of the river during the floods and left behind when the waters sank.

The frequent rising of the water in the winter has washed the mortar out of the stones in the wall and left many deep holes running within. In these crevices a colony of sand-martins have their lodging and rear their offspring, out of the reach of mischievous boys and others, who are unable to climb down the wall and interfere with the eggs and young. Here also the pretty blue titmice build, and hatch their numerous brood, darting in and out of the wall like sunbeams and becoming extraordinarily excited and impatient if you chance to remain near the mouth of the nest for a few moments. In the lower boughs of the large withy trees projecting over the river the moorhens roost; the old heron perches in the scrub at the top of the trunk and sleeps during the night, ready to leap up at daybreak and take his prey, watching patiently beside the pools in the glistening meadows. The graceful swans float beautifully beside the reeds, plunging their long necks deep down into the bluish water, and retire with dignity to the farthest shore in the bend to escape the boat that with much knocking and splashing of oars shoots into sight from behind the tall flags at the curve. The pink flowering-rush shows beside the shaded hemp-nettle; sneezewort and loose-strife, with spikes of blossom often sixteen inches in length, grow along the edge of the water. Tall bulrushes, round and smooth, with a tuft of rich brown blossom growing near the spear-like point, stand amid the pools and along the river-bank, motionless, or gently swaying and stooping beneath the weight of the little sedge-warbler that hops to and fro and perches sideways on the quivering stems.

The village of Buscot, though insignificant in size, is famed throughout the Upper Thames Valley. This, in the first place, is owing to the beauty of its surroundings, its woods and grounds, and, secondly, by reason of the remarkable energy and prodigality of a former occupant of the mansion in the park, whose name became familiar for many miles around. The doings of Squire Campbell, of Buscot Park, were told far and near, and many people came to the little riverside village in order to obtain employment at one or other of the great works he took in hand. He brought into cultivation hundreds of acres of land that before had been useless, dug lakes and reservoirs at the cost of many thousands of pounds, and turned what had been a wilderness into a beautiful and fertile paradise. Money flowed like water, and the workmen were as the squire swore he would have them to be, *i.e.* "as thick as flies"; there was no limit to the outpouring of gold till the Crimean War arose and ruined the well-intentioned but imprudent speculator.

Formerly Buscot had its medical practitioner, who did something for suffering humanity, as is proved by his records unwittingly left behind, in which we read the frequently occurring and significant phrase: "For bleeding old Betty Martin, one shilling." With the doctor's records is preserved a leather label formerly nailed to a package consigned to the Vicar from London, and which is reminiscent of other days:

> To ———
> Burscot Parsonage,
> Near Leachlade,
> Gloucestershire.
> By Waggon to Oxford. To be forwarded by Caravan No. 1.

The road through the village is one of the chief highways from Gloucester to London and was regularly traversed by the heavy lumbering waggons and stage-coaches before the railways were made.

The grey silent church stands but a few paces from the river's brink, upon a small terrace sufficiently high to prevent its being flooded after the heavy winter rains. The building dates from the twelfth century, though no part of the original survives, with the exception of the trans-Norman chancel arch, resting upon its clustered pillars, and this was altered to a pointed shape and spoiled about the year 1180. The interior is simple. The walls and roof are cemented over and there is little of interest besides the east window—painted by Burne-Jones during his sojourn with the poet Morris at Kelmscott—the old Spanish lectern, and an oak pulpit, with three panels painted by the Flemish artist, Mabuse. The centre panel, representing the Adoration of the Magi, is remarkable in that the black king is painted with white legs. There is a legend that the black king's knees were worn white with kneeling; a more probable solution is that the king's legs had to be made white before he could adore the Saviour.

To-day the church is strewn with cuttings of flowers and leaves and is generally untidy, for it is being decorated for Harvest Festival. All the morning the farmers' wives have been employed arranging fruits, flowers, and vegetables in the windows and twining the golden corn around the pulpit and choir-stalls. In the corner is a sheaf of wheat with heavy ears; here the pure white or bronze chrysanthemums mingle with the modest Michaelmas daisies, or the great gold-faced sunflower smiles broadly upon the richly coloured dahlias. Village maidens pass noiselessly to and fro, disposing the bright-tinted leaves and inter-setting the blossoms and fruits, while others arrive with offerings of various kinds—oats and barley from the field, and the largest apples and vegetables from the garden. The vegetables are piled upon the floor, while the orchard fruits are set in the windows; a large home-made loaf is fixed conspicuously upon the lectern. One thing alone is wanting to the picture, that is, a large shock or stook of a dozen or twenty sheaves set up in the middle of the church or a heap of threshed grain, such as the Greek poet Theocritus tells us they had at their harvest festival held in honour of Ceres, with the great winnowing shovel thrust down into it, while the goddess, crowned with garlands and holding handfuls of wheat and poppies, looked benignly down upon them at the celebrations.

A water-wheel, twelve feet high and sixteen feet wide, stands on the river. The weight of this is over twenty-five tons, and it has a driving capacity equivalent to twenty-one horse-power. It is fitted with a number of iron shell-like blades; the water, flowing swiftly down a chute beneath a heavy cast-iron plate, rushes upon these and forces them round, enabling the wheel to revolve four or five times a minute. Alongside is a shed containing powerful pumps which are operated by means of a system of cogs and gear. The teeth of the cogs around the great wheel are worn as thin as pennies, for they have been in constant use for twenty years. A special Act of Parliament was needed to sanction the building of the wheel on the Thames; upon its continued exertions depends the success and welfare of all the farms on the estate, which would be deprived of water if the pumps were stopped.

A spirit factory stood on the bank of the river above the lock-gate. This was the largest and most expensive of all the experimental works undertaken by the squire, but though it cost a hundred thousand pounds to build and equip, and was superintended by French experts, it was doomed to failure after ten years' working. The villagers who worked at the distillery say that excessive duties killed the industry; whatever the cause of its demise there was no lack of energy on the part of the squire to make the concern profitable.

Nevertheless, in spite of his failures, the squire was a remarkable man. Whatever he attempted was on a grand scale, and if one scheme failed he immediately embraced another and was undaunted by difficulties, however great they might have been. The men on his estate worked nine hours a day and received fair wages. He staggered all the other farmers and landowners in the neighbourhood by reason of his profuseness, his unheard-of experiments, and his tremendous energies.

Beet was the material from which the spirit was

PLOUGHING BY LIMELIGHT

extracted. A system of artificial irrigation was contrived to fertilise the hill ground; the water was pumped up from the river by the wheel. The squire manufactured his own manures for growing the beet, grinding up immense quantities of coprolite. Besides this he had quarries opened and limekilns built to produce lime for dressing the land. The hauling was done by steam-power. The whole countryside throbbed with life, and the earth quivered beneath the iron wheels of the heavy traction engines.

To cultivate his land he had several sets of steam-ploughing tackle of considerable dimensions. The engines were of thirty horse-power each, and each weighed thirty tons, that is, more than double the weight and three times the power of those ordinarily in use to-day. They ploughed night and day throughout the autumn and winter, until the whole of the land had been well broken up and cleaned ready to take the seed in the following spring. To enable the steam-ploughing to proceed by night a system of limelight was installed on the plant. If the ground was very wet the engines moved on timbers. The squire visited the field at all hours of the night, and provided relief gangs; he could brook no delays in getting forward with the work of cultivation. The squire's wife was as energetic as her husband. She was often to be seen striding through the fields with the tail of her skirt drawn through her knees and buckled to her waistband in front.

The first method of steam-ploughing differed from that followed in our own time, or even in Squire Campbell's early days. Then only one engine was employed. This was a portable machine, and was drawn out to the field by horses. If the field was of a moderate size the engine stood on one side, but if it was very large it was set in the middle. Near the engine was a heavy double windlass, with which the cables were wound, and which was driven by means of a belt from the engine. Situated at several points about the field were "porters," containing small pulley wheels through which the cables ran. These were attached to a large iron anchor which dug deeply into the earth as the engine was pulling from the windlass. When the plough reached the end of the field the cable was switched off on to another pulley and the implement went plunging back across the piece. The anchor was released from the earth and shifted with levers; several assistants, besides the engineman and steersman, were required to look after the tackle.

When the traction engine first made its appearance on the road it was provided with a set of shafts fixed in front and a horse, as it were, to draw the machine. This, curious as it may seem, was compulsory, in order not to frighten the horses attached to other vehicles on the highway.

A notable feature of the great house is its scheme of water-gardens. They are a series of fountains and their basins, constructed in terraces and connected by a tiny stream that flows down the centre. Lines of tall trees stand back from the arcade. Alongside the fountains are garden plots adorned with statues, sculptures, and massive carved Italian urns and pottery ware. Beautiful wax-like water-lilies float on the surface of the pools beneath the fountains; clumps of iris grow along the margin of the stones. In the open pools the goldfish sport and play and float with languid ease, or stand on their heads above the stone bottom. Big, lumbering carps wriggle about and hide beneath the lily leaves and

A UNIQUE ARCH

among the gauze-like weeds, out of sight of the stranger.

At the end of the terrace garden is a curious arch made of the jawbone of a whale, and which is said to have been standing in its present position for more than a century. The length of the jaw is fifteen feet, by twelve feet wide at the base, and six feet near the nose—the swallowing capacity of the animal must have been enormous. In eastern maritime countries the ancient peoples, in building their houses, used fish-bones instead of timber, which must have been a valuable substitute. Although the arch has stood for a hundred years in rain, frost, and sunshine, it is practically unimpaired, and the bone is almost as hard as iron.

Besides the few carps kept in the fountains there are large numbers in the waters of the lake. They have their homes in the deep pools, and are seldom tempted to take the deceitful bait of the angler, though now and then one may lose its wariness and become fixed upon the sharp hook. Carps live to a great age, even for as long a time as a hundred, or a hundred and fifty years, as has been proved by trustworthy evidence. Carps will live longer out of their element than will any other fish. They have been kept alive out of water for a month and fed with bread and milk during that period.

Many small birds dwell in the wood under the protection of the keepers, who have charge of the lake and fish. Here also, in the lofty spruces and poplars, the herons rear their young close to the shallow waters of the lake, where they may be seen watching patiently beside the bank ready to stab their unsuspecting prey when it swims near. The nest of the heron is large and rather flat, resembling that of a pigeon, with this distinction, that it is provided with two deep holes, one on each side, for containing the legs of the bird when sitting upon the eggs. From this it is seen that the heron does not sit upon the nest with folded legs, as do other birds and wild-fowls, but while its body rests above the eggs its legs are in the holes. Accordingly, when a heron rises from the nest its legs are seen to be suspended and are folded afterwards, while other birds rise with the aid of their wings, being cramped in the legs with long sitting.

The heron lays from five to seven eggs, and takes great care of her offspring, bringing home large quantities of fish from the shallow waters. The heron's plan is to conceal itself on the bank, or amid reeds, and wait the approach of a fish. Immediately one comes into view the heron stabs it behind the gills and stuns it, and the fish, rising to the surface, is quickly seized and thrown out upon dry land. The heron is highly destructive; it is estimated that one bird will destroy nine or ten thousand fish in a year. One way of taking it is with line and hook, baited with a minnow. By noting a regular haunt of the bird and carefully setting a line, it may be caught in this manner. The Romans were acquainted with the heron, and, with characteristic resourcefulness, turned it to some account, making musical pipes out of its leg bones.

The lake has recently been cleaned out and freed from mud and weeds that had been steadily accumulating for nearly a century. This was done with steam-engines, and it took a year and a half to complete the work. First the water was drawn off and the fish removed into other pools. Then a platform of timber was made to enable one engine to enter

THE RESERVOIR

the bed of the lake, while the other took its position in the meadow opposite. The two engines were connected with a steel cable, to which was attached a large scoop capable of holding five tons of mud. One engine drew this empty across the bed of the lake and the other dragged it back, when it automatically adjusted itself and scooped up the mud, lifting when full, and being then drawn to the bank. The engines engaged at the task worked from daylight till dark; eight hundred or a thousand tons of mud were removed in one day.

The reservoir, into which the water for the farms is pumped by the wheel on the Thames, stands high above the lake. This is of twenty acres in extent, with an oval bed seventy-five feet deep in the middle. The digging of the reservoir was an expensive undertaking; its construction is said to have cost the squire between £80,000 and £90,000. This is looked upon, and justly so, as the most valuable work he did; the farmer declares bluntly that " the 'state wouldn't be worth tuppence without the reservoy." To make the basin the entire side of the hill had to be removed and carried back a quarter of a mile in order to form the outer bank and the two ends. These had to be built up firmly from the bottom and the inside " puddled " with clay to make them watertight.

The lake and reservoir, by reason of their remoteness and privacy, form an ideal retreat for the waterfowls. Pleasure-seekers on the river frighten away from there all but the brazen-hearted moorhens and a few dabchicks; the rarer kinds flock to the reservoir, where they are encouraged and protected by the gamekeepers. Most wild-fowls are on the lakes in the winter, though during the summer there are many visitors swimming about among the reeds, and on the middle of the broad pool. Here, besides the more common kinds, are to be found widgeons, teals, grebes, wild geese, tufted ducks, muscovy ducks, shelducks, golden-eye ducks, sea-swallows, seagulls, divers, jack-snipes, summer snipes, a winter bird of passage locally called a "kerr," and, now and then, a bittern.

The woodcock and the peregrin falcon nest in the plantations. Woodpeckers are in great evidence; the large green one, elsewhere called the "ya-ha," and "eke-aw," is here named the "yaffel" and "yukel." The seagulls, driven inland by stormy weather during the winter months, become comparatively tame and sometimes follow the plough in the field, feeding with the rooks and starlings. Not long ago a farm hand found one with its wing broken and took it home. The gull became very tame and fond of its protector, eating out of his hand and perching upon his shoulder.

The little sea-swallow is a daring bird. This dives into the water for five or six feet, seizes on its prey, and darts up and into the open air again. In appearance it resembles the land-swallow, the chief difference being that one branch of its tail is shorter than the other.

The reservoir on the hill is fringed with a growth of dark green bulrushes, standing in the water, and concealing the straight, artificially formed banks. Both bulrush and flag come into bloom in late summer. The former puts forth a small cluster of purplish brown blossom a few inches below the point; the latter unsheathes a long green head which soon becomes a deep rich brown, showing conspicuously among the tops of the graceful sword-like leaves. Bulrushes, gathered not later than the beginning of September, are used for weaving baskets, seats of chairs, and mattresses. They are also used by the coopers, who lay a rush between the sections of wood to fill up the crevices and keep their barrels watertight when the iron hoops are put round.

At the woodman's house many curios are to be seen. He is an enthusiastic student of birds, and, though unable to read or write, he has collected many rare specimens which he has stuffed and sold to naturalists. In addition to this he has been a breeder of moths and butterflies. These he hatched in thousands, by means of glass cases built against the walls of his cottage, and afterwards sold them to students and collectors. He has often taken the eggs of the kingfisher and reared the young, feeding them with minnows from the brook. The tiny birds eat from three to six minnows a day, though the old ones devour many more than this.

Of late years the woodman-naturalist has been afflicted with rheumatism and is prevented from following his vocation as taxidermist, but the cottage still contains a few specimens of rare birds, though they are not treasured as formerly. The splendid peregrin falcon, shot with a pigeon in its claws, is fixed upon a post in the garden to frighten the mischievous sparrows from the peas and cress, and the badger skins are nailed over the roof of the pigsty to prevent the wet from dropping on the swine beneath.

A narrow track branches off from the road and leads through a plantation of spruces and black firs. Within the plantation, half concealed with the dark boughs, is a notice-board containing the words, in large letters—TO EATON WEIR. Farther down, in a small opening, is a pretty lodge and, below that, a tiny stream winds down to the calm-flowing river, half a mile distant. The old village of Eaton Hastings stood close to the river's bank. It has now disappeared, with the exception of the small church and several cottages, though its site is indicated by the enclosure called Town Meadow.

There is no lock alongside the weir, for the fall of water is no more than two feet. Consequently, small boats coming up or going down stream have to be drawn over the barrier on rollers, and large craft, such as steamers and barges, have to " shoot the weir." To enable them to do this the paddles on one side are taken out. The sinking of the water on the high side and the rising on the low side produce a level, and the boat passes through on its journey. Immediately the paddles are again fixed into the stout frame; the water is dammed back and flows over the top in a pellucid sheet.

The weir, officially named Eaton Weir, is called Hart's Weir by the local inhabitants. Thus, if you inquire of a rustic the way to Eaton Weir, he looks at you in silence for a moment and exclaims : " Eaton Wire, sir ! You means Hart's Wire, don' 'e, sir ? " This came about by reason of the inn upon the bank having been kept for several generations by a family named Hart. In time the name Hart's Weir was adopted as being shorter, and, perhaps, because it afforded more ready and significant means of identification.

The innkeeper, according to the account of the villagers, was a notorious smuggler. He obtained his kegs of spirit from the bargemen who came up from London and concealed them in the bed of the river. To the kegs he attached ropes or chains;

when he wanted one he took a long-handled iron rake and groped on the bottom till he struck the chain and so got it ashore. Whoever wanted whisky or brandy came down to the Weir after dark and was supplied by the innkeeper. The spot is lonely and difficult of access in the winter; there was little fear of being surprised by the Customs officers.

Over the wooden bridge above the weir a footpath runs through level fields intersected with a dike full of forget-me-not and loose-strife. On one side of the dike is a bank, three feet high, constructed to contain the water at high flood and save the country round about from being inundated. The wild rabbits, by continually tunnelling in the soft mould, have impaired the bank, though it still serves to hold back the bulk of the water. While digging for gravel recently in a field near the river the men unearthed several skeletons and a number of silver buttons. They were probably the remains of soldiers or officers slain either in the year 1387, when Robert de Vere was defeated by the Earl of Derby, or during the fighting between the troops of Cromwell and King Charles.

So deep were the floods at Kelmscott before the construction of the bank that the cows swam over the tops of the walls bordering the road, and the inhabitants were compelled to live upstairs for six weeks at a stretch, where they were served with loaves handed up to them on pitch-forks by relief-men in boats.

The average quantity of water leaping through the weir paddles every twenty-four hours is 203 million gallons. In dry weather the amount of water falls considerably below this figure, and the average daily flow in September—which is usually the driest month of the year—declines to 79 million gallons. During the heavy flood in January 1915, on the highest day approximately 1760 million gallons of water passed Eaton Weir.

The greatest flood in the valley in modern times happened in November of the year 1894, and the greatest summer flood on record took place in the June of 1903. Then the hay crops were totally destroyed, and the youthful population of the village amused themselves with diving above the hard road from the ancient market-cross standing before the inn.

CHAPTER VII

The Journey up the River—The Rat and Kingfisher—St. John's Bridge and Priory—Lechlade "Flea Fair"—Holders of the Manor—Curious Items of Church Expenditure—Local Witchcraft Tales.

AT the weir a boat is waiting ready to proceed up the river to St. John's Bridge, passing on to the steeple town beyond. Accordingly we take our place at the oars and push out gently from the small landing-stage, avoiding the suction of the weir current, then lie to and creep along some distance beneath the low bank and so into the open.

To-day the river is glorious. The sun, looking down from the cloudless blue upon the quivering fields, has touched them with radiant beauty. Ahead the surface of the water is dazzling silver; behind, above the weir, it is as blue as the empyrean, broken only by a bunch of tangled weeds or a large yellow dockleaf that floats down soon to be carried over the paddles and pitched into the seething whirlpool beneath. Up from the river to the south along the ridge lies the dark fir-wood with the delicate green of the smooth beeches and poplars beyond; on the other hand, level cornfields stretch away to the gently rising Cotswolds. The foliage of the elms is so luxuriant it seems as though the boughs must break with the weight. The lines of pollard willows, the long rakish tops of which are lightly clad with silvery leaves, look cool and unperturbed standing alongside the reedy margin of the river. Behind the hawthorn clump lurks the fisherman, rod in hand, and with cap stuck full of artificial flies, hoping to take the wily trout or great chub basking in the sun's rays at the top of the water. Another is angling in the deep pool for perch and tench, or whatever may chance to be attracted by the wriggling bait impaled upon the barbed hook. Half-way up the field are two hares at play, running round and round and doubling to and fro amid the withering grasses. A fine cock pheasant, straying from the wood on the hill, has flown across the river and now struts proudly and confidently upon the short green turf of the close-cropped meadow.

Smoothly and easily we glide upstream, winding round between walls of high reeds and beneath the green and grey willows. At every dip of the oar a tiny sedge-warbler or reed-bunting shoots out of the flags along the margin; the moorhen, suddenly startled from her late-built nest, flies above the stream, her feet dipping in the water till she settles again higher up. Little waves push out on each side and tremble to the shore; the floating leaves of the water-plants lift gently and sway up and down as the frail barque, prow high and stern low, cleaves a way through the limpid water. Deep down the bed of the river is now and then discovered by means of the grey sand or a cluster of wrinkled lily leaves. Here a large pike, sunning under the bank, swirls round and shoots out of sight, or a great trout or chub, swimming heavily, makes its way beneath the dense weeds.

Alongside a shallow backwater, grown round with flags, and overhung with ash and willow boughs, is one taking up a trap that was set for an otter. This is a large iron gin with sharp steel teeth and stout spring like those of a rat-trap. The presence of the animal was discovered by its tracks. Three times the gin was set and left through the night; on the fourth night the unhappy animal was gripped by a hind foot. By dint of hard struggling, however, the otter succeeded in getting free at the expense of its limb, which it left in the trap. Doubtless it will seek other quarters now, though it will certainly be hunted again, so great is the antipathy of anglers and others to this beautiful and interesting but destructive creature.

Here we pass two lovers in a small boat moored to a torn withy-tree that stands in a tiny recess, half concealed with meadow-sweet and loose-strife, and soon after a brilliant kingfisher flies out of a hole in the bank and darts like a flash of light along the face of the stream. There it probably has its nest made of fish-bones, or of the rib-bones of rats, which, from their curved shape, are well fitted for the purpose. The rat is the deadly enemy of the kingfisher, and is perhaps the chief cause of its comparative scarcity. The nests, built in holes along the bank, are almost sure to be found by the rats that swarm near the river. They devour the eggs, or the young, and very often the parent bird, too, sitting closely over her brood in the dark night. Snakes also destroy the eggs of the kingfisher and play havoc with the young water-fowls, before they have become sufficiently large to take care of themselves. Thus, the kingfisher eats the fish, the rat devours the kingfisher, the pike and eel swallow the rat, and the balance of nature is to some extent maintained. Perhaps the instinct of retaliation prompts the kingfisher to line its nest with the rib-bones of the rat, as though it took delight in sitting above the remains of its most persistent and dreaded enemy.

St. John's Bridge is one of the most ancient on the Thames and has existed for seven centuries, though a more modern arch has been built upon the old foundations. Previous to the opening of the thirteenth century there appear to have been no stone bridges over the rivers in England. At that time the Thames was spanned by wooden structures. Huge rough piers and piles were fixed in the bed, with baulks of timber overlaid, and the road was conducted above them. The bridges were often destroyed or seriously damaged by the terrible floods that befell in the winter, which was a source of great inconvenience to travellers and expense to those upon whom devolved their upkeeping. At length deliberations were held and it was decided to build stone bridges over the rivers. The old wooden piles and piers were doomed; a new era was dawning. In the year 1209 London Bridge was built, and St. John's Bridge at Lechlade was soon afterwards constructed. King John encouraged the work and contributed twenty marks towards the cost of the Lechlade bridge. The old wooden structures disappeared and the bed of the river was cleaned and improved, though the devastating floods from time to time still swept the vale, washing away the crops and buildings and drowning the cattle alongside the banks.

A nunnery, and afterwards a Hospital or Priory, stood near the bridge in olden times. Nearly every town had its Hospital, at which the aged and sick were tended and poor travellers entertained and relieved in their journeyings from place to place. The Hospital of St. John seems to have been originally founded in order to shelter the workmen building the bridge, some of whom afterwards settled and remained there for the rest of their days. In course of time the Hospital or Priory undertook the care of the pile, and was endowed with lands and empowered to take tolls for that purpose.

The rules of the Priory were quaint and curious. It was imperative that the brethren should be dressed in russet-coloured garments, and that no one should possess anything of his own or have a locked chest. All clothing, food, and drink were held in common. The beds were in one dormitory, and the brethren were required to sleep in shirts and breeches. If a member of the community died the others were bound to say five hundred paternosters within thirty days, and one hundred paternosters were to be said for the brethren and benefactors of the hospital each week. After the dissolution of the Priory the building was turned into an inn and called St. John Baptist's Head. Now the Trout Inn occupies the site and is a favourite haunt of anglers that come to exercise the gentle craft and kill time and trout upon the banks of the beautiful river.

The Trout is first and foremost an inn for fishermen. The angling rights for some distance along the river go with the house, so that it is imperative to have the landlord's consent to take the finny inhabitants of the deep waters. It is furthermore expedient, if you are a stranger, to have taken up your quarters at the inn; then you will be the better treated and admitted to the most likely spots for catching good trouts, perches, chubs, or barbels.

Chubs are very numerous in the deep pools of the river. They interfere with the sport and often disappoint the angler wanting to take better specimens. Accordingly, towards the close of every season, war is waged upon them and their numbers diminished.

In order to do this special baitings are made at intervals of several days, after which the members of the local Angling Associations go out with their rods and take them by the hundred. As the chub is a coarse fish it is seldom cooked and eaten by any but the poorest people.

Poaching for trouts and eels with nightlines is common throughout the summer. The poachers set their lines about midnight and take them up before dawn ; many of the finest fish are taken in this manner. As a farmer was walking beside the river, where the water was shallow, his spaniel, seeing a trout, leapt down upon it for a space of five feet and brought it to shore. The fish was a fine specimen and weighed four pounds. Thames trout grow to a large size ; they have been taken up to ten pounds in weight.

To-day the steeple town is full of bustle and excitement, for it is September Horse Fair. This is usually called " Flea Fair," or it should be " Harvest Bug Fair," because about this time harvest bugs disappear from the grass and stubble, and the farm hands and gleaners are no longer tormented with the troublesome insects.

The broad market-place in front of the inn and beneath the shade of the spire is packed with horses and people. Farmers and dealers, hands in pockets, stand in groups or saunter round the square, viewing the animals. Here a prospective purchaser opens the mouth of a well-groomed horse to examine its teeth ; another lifts up a fore-foot and scrutinises that, or feels the fetlocks and knees. He is in want of a couple of good horses, for Poppet is getting a little ancient, and Colonel has a nasty limp on the near hind leg, and there is extra work to be done this autumn. But the bidding will be keen, and the farmer is considering whether or not he will be justified in making the outlay, though he knows something must be done.

There are several types of yeomen about the square and some individuals who have come from afar off, for the horse fair is attended by breeders and dealers from many of the Western Counties. There is the tall bronzed son of Somersetshire, with highly distinctive dialect; the bluff and hearty moonraker, dwelling near the breezy downs, spruce and clean shaven, or with stiff, bristling moustache and side-beard; the comfortable-looking Berkshire man; the thin-featured, gentlemanly Oxonian, and the short, sturdy, thick-set man of Gloucestershire, whose home is upon the strong-blowing Cotswolds. In addition to them are the loiterers and sightseers—the wooden-legged pensioner rigged in Sunday best; the town tailor, crippled in both feet; and, to be sure, the old blacksmith of ninety years, who has absented himself from the forge to-day in order to note the condition of the horses and the fashion in which they are shod.

Higher up the broad street are vans and vehicles with materials for constructing the merry-go-rounds, cocoa-nut shies, and stalls for gingerbreads and knick-knacks. They stand in lines, waiting for the horses to be sold, which will be by noon or soon after. When the dealers have finished they will occupy the square and the space before the inns, and the travellers will exhibit their wares for the young men, women, and children to buy. The afternoon and evening will be devoted to pleasure. Then the people will flock in from the villages round about and the streets will be full to overflowing.

It was a happy decision that fixed the site of the

church alongside the market-place in the centre of the town. This was most convenient in former days, for the fairs and festivals of the people were then more closely associated with the church than they are at this time. When the strolling players came to act their crude dramas they had their stage built close to the walls of the sacred pile, usually in the churchyard itself, or if the church abutted on the street, there they erected the *scena*, and, assisted by the monks and priests, proceeded to act their pieces. The travelling minstrels and ballad-singers, fiddlers, dancers, and wrestlers assembled and made merry, while the image of the good Saint Lawrence, with book and gridiron, looked down upon the mirth from above the lofty window. The stocks stood near to warn the people to be of good behaviour. The last to suffer the ignominy of them was a tippler of the town nicknamed " Billy the Bold un," he having been duly apprehended and imprisoned by one Robert Constable, constable of Lechlade at that time.

A more important fair was held near the river on St. John the Baptist's day. This was attended by a crowd of merchants, traders, and purchasers, who came, as to a universal mart, to supply their domestic wants for the following year. The merchants were classified according to the wares they had for disposal, and streets bearing such names as " The Drapery," " The Pottery," " The Spicery," and so on, were formed in the meadow. The monks, nuns, and priests of the churches and priories, the Lords of the Manors and their tenants came to buy plate, pottery, armour, cutlery, wine, wax, spices, linens, woollens, provisions, and other necessaries. With the rise and increase of shops in the towns, the pedlars' and merchants' fairs decayed and soon ceased to be held.

LOCAL PRODUCE

Floods also interfered with the emporium in the meadow, and it was moreover said to interrupt the harvest work, for doubtless the rustics were not content to labour in the silent fields far from the noise and hubbub of the fair.

To supplement the fairs there were the regular weekly markets, held within the town from the beginning of the thirteenth century downwards. They began about noon on Sunday and were continued until the following Monday night. The market comprised local produce, such as fresh meats, fish fried or baked, pullets, geese, pigs, green cheeses, curds, cream, oaten cakes, and loaves of bean flour and bran—eaten by the labourers.

The Black Death and the Peasant Revolt brought about a scarcity of agricultural labourers. Much land that had grown corn crops was consequently laid down and converted into sheep farms, and no part of the country was better adapted for this than were the stony Cotswolds, lying high and dry above the half-drained marshes and swamps of the Valley.

During the seventeenth century agriculture improved again and cheese and malt became the chief products of the country between the Thames and the Cotswolds. The channel of the Thames was cleaned out from Abingdon to Cricklade and weirs were made in order to allow the boats to pass freely upstream. Barges with a carrying capacity of eighty tons came alongside the Lechlade wharves, and no less than three thousand tons of prime cheese were brought into the town from the villages and farms annually in waggons and conveyed by water to Oxford and London.

Now all the horses are sold and led away from the market-place, with the halter of each one following fastened to the tail of the near one preceding. A few farmers only remain, chatting outside the ancient inn, in which they have partaken of a light luncheon. Presently they depart, some by motor, this one by the high market trap, or on horseback. The proprietors of the merry-go-rounds and cocoa-nut shies make haste to occupy the square with their paraphernalia and get ready for the afternoon and evening sports. Several aged inhabitants of the town loiter in the locality of the inns, eager to talk of the fair, as it is, and as it used to be.

"What d'ye thenk an't to-day, Anngel?" inquires the old shepherd of the carter standing near.

"I sin better an' I sin wuss. 'Tis a very good lot o' 'ossen, takin' on 'em all together, but the faayer yent nothin' like so good as it used to be, an' Bampton comin' sa nigh 'andy this un 'tis oni the riff-raff yer to-day, like. Tha be a leetle smaller than I 'ev a knowed 'em, but, as I ses, I sin wuss. Tha be tarblish good, considerin' the dry saazon we've hed," the carter replies.

It is tedious to stand and watch the erecting of the merry-go-rounds and booths for the fair, and there is much to be seen and learned around the old riverside town. It is claimed that King Alfred possessed the place and had a university here, which may very well have been, since Lechlade is but six miles from Faringdon, where the great king had a residence, and where both he and his son Edward are believed to have died. Then there was the famous old Manor, with its list of illustrious holders, among the earliest of whom was Richard Plantagenet, Earl of Cornwall, the only Englishman who had the honour of wearing the Imperial purple, and who contributed largely to the building of Cologne Cathedral. After

WEALTH OF THE MANORS

him were Hugh de Spencer, who was hanged and quartered at Hereford; Edward Mortimer, Earl of March; Richard, Duke of York, the father of Edward IV. and Richard III.; and Cicely, his wife, doomed to witness more appalling calamities than are to be found in the authentic history of any other individual. When King Edward was marching with his troops from Abingdon to Tewkesbury, his road lay through Lechlade. Here, at his mother's Manor, he probably rested his troops and then pressed rapidly forward and won the battle of Tewkesbury in less than a week.

The wealth of the De Spencers, Lords of the Manor of Lechlade, was enormous; the following is a list of their possessions at the time of the execution of Hugh de Spencer, in 1326: "Fifty-nine Lordships in Sundry Counties; 28,000 sheep; 1000 Oxen and Steers; 1200 Kine, with their calves; 40 Mares, with their Colts of two years old; 160 drawing horses; 2000 Hogs; 3000 Bullocks. In the Larder: 600 sides of Bacon; 80 Carcases of Martinmas Beef; 600 Carcases of Mutton; 10,080 Galls. of Wine; 2520 Galls. of Cider; 36 Sacks of Wool; a Library of Books; Armour, Plate, Jewels, and Ready Money better than £10,000."

The vast quantity of salt flesh discovered in the larders so late in the year as 2nd May—the date upon which the list was compiled—bears witness to the imperfect system of tillage then in vogue. As there were no enclosures, and no sown grasses, roots, or hay to store for winter use, the cattle were fattened and killed in the summer and autumn only. Those beasts not required for the slaughter were turned out to shift for themselves, and no fresh meat could be had during the winter and spring.

The church of St. Lawrence—known as the "Gridiron Saint "—dates from the latter part of the fifteenth century. The architecture is Early Perpendicular, and the absence of structural decorative work gives to the interior a chasteness bordering on severity. The steeple was added to the tower some time during the sixteenth century. Local smugglers are said to have concealed their spirits and dried their malt upon the leaden roof of the building down to the end of the eighteenth century.

The Churchwardens' books discover several curious items of expenditure, and incidentally recall to our mind a notable occurrence in British naval history.

		£	s.	d.
1795.—Ye Bread for ye Communion	..	0	1	0
Ye Bottles of Wine	..	3	12	0
Paid for Sparrows	..	0	7	4
For casting the little bell and postage of a letter	..	1	6	0
For 3 Pole Cats	..	0	2	0
1797.—82 doz. Sparrows' Heads	..	0	13	8
2 Pole Cats	..	0	1	4
Beer for the Ringers	..	0	5	0
Coal for Man to clean Church Clock	..	0	0	8½
1798.—For two Prayers for Victory over Dutch Fleet	..	0	2	0
1799.—134 doz. Sparrows' Heads at 2d. ..	..	1	1	8
2 Pole Cats	..	0	1	4
2 Weazles	..	0	0	8
1802.—Expenses for Beer for Churchwardens and Ringers	..	1	17	6

Now the busiest time of the fair is fast drawing on, for it is evening in the Thames Valley. The sun has set in a sea of gold beyond the Cotswolds, and the sky has changed from crimson to Indian red and deep purple. Over the Round House the faint young moon reclines on a bed of azure; the stars peep out and are reflected in the still deep waters of the

THE FUN OF THE FAIR

river below the bridge. Down the road a stream of pleasure-seekers continues to arrive, while through the trees and above the housetops the sound of the organ and shriek of the siren, mingled with the shouts and cries of the children, are heard.

A great crowd has gathered in the market-place and along the street in front of the inns. This is chiefly composed of Cotswold people, with a few from the Wiltshire and Berkshire side of the river. The cheerful shepherd from the downs, the carters and cowmen with their wives from the farms, the ploughboys with their sweethearts, and all the youth of the town are there. What matter now the long labours of the field in burning heat and rain, the dark hours of winter approaching, the hardships of everyday life ? All are forgotten amid the noise of the street and the pleasure of meeting with acquaintances. And to-night all are cheerful. The harvest money has been paid; the pockets of all are jingling. Everyone is equipped with means to take his pleasure and to make purchases for personal use, or to adorn the walls of the cottage.

The strangest things are offered for sale by the Cheap Jacks, who dispose their goods on the ground and stand in the centre with smoky, flaring paraffin lamps. Here are gaudy-coloured pictures and painted ornaments, green and blue umbrellas large enough to cover a summer-rick, bright gay handkerchiefs, mufflers and ties, preposterous jewellery, with hundreds of alarm-clocks and cheap watches, all warranted to be the finest obtainable. It might be thought that no one would purchase these articles, but John and William, Jane and Mary, are out to buy, and will not go empty away from the fair.

One wonders what would Shelley have thought of

the strange scene beneath the windows of the New Inn, at which he stayed after his walk through the churchyard in the shadow of the tall spire and the Gridiron Saint ? Standing amid the graves he felt the influence of the Cotswold sunset, the calm beauty of the river gliding through the fields, and the peaceful eloquent evening; when the spirit of Apollo is most powerfully and prophetically awake, the dead speak from their sepulchres, and messages from the dim beyond arrive linking up the invisible universe.

But little change is appreciable in the churchyard since the most spiritual of English poets trod there. The tall elms, in which the rooks build, the yews, and sycamores still stand around the thickly massed tombs, and the fiercely grinning figures of the gargoyles and the Assyrian-like heads on the buttress of the tower yet remain, though they have become darker with the passage of time.

The greatest changes that have taken place are in things pertaining to the river. The wharves are deserted; no barges, laden with produce, ever come to enter the old canal at the Round House and glide away to the Severn and Avon cities. The ancient rhyme:

> " Ai, O, the boatmen row
> Up and down the river O.
> The boatmen dance and the boatmen sing,
> The boatman's up to everything,"

sufficiently appropriate formerly, is not so applicable now, though the river, throughout the summer and autumn months, is crowded with small craft full of those on pleasure bent. During the severe frosts of the winter 1788–89 a festival was held on the river opposite the wharf. A fat ox was roasted upon the ice—protected with sods—and fifteen hundred people took part in the feast and games. At that time the bargemen carried firearms in order to be in a position to protect their cargoes, for thieves infested the countryside and lay in wait at night to steal corn, cheese, or coal from the boats.

The inns are full to-night, and more than the usual good feeling is evident among the ploughmen and farm hands, who beam at each other at the Red Lion, or engage in a long confidential chat on the year's happenings, the crops and harvest, lambs and foals, and draw comparisons between this and that time or season. Meanwhile Jonas and Dobbin, Shadrach and Angel, seriously enumerate how many to their knowledge have met the Inglesham ghost, or tell of Betty the witch who lies buried on the roadside, three miles distant.

Old Betty was famed for many acts and was a sore trouble to the carters, cowmen, and shepherds round about, bringing the flocks and herds and pregnant mares under her powerful spell and working incalculable mischief upon all and sundry. At one time the lambs, calves, and foals were stillborn. The gates and doors would fall off the hinges; the pumps would not draw water and the cream would not set in the broad pans. The cobbler could not work his wax while she was near, and half the people of the countryside fell sick, while she danced in the streets at midnight and spat up hundreds of pins and young crows, as the villagers confidently believed.

Jonas, the ox-carter, had heard of a witch who had tampered with a neighbour's pig and caused it to go mad in the sty. The owner of the animal, a farm labourer, was distressed at the occurrence and uncertain what to do. At length it occurred to him to bleed the pig. Accordingly he took the scissors and snipped a piece out of its ear, causing it to bleed profusely, when, behold! out of her house ran the old woman, grasping her fingers, which were streaming with blood. It appears that when the swine's ear was cut the witch, being in spirit within the pig, was also injured. The pig recovered, but the villagers left the old woman alone, and she soon bled to death.

A witch was in the habit of stopping every team that passed the road near her dwelling. This she did with her magic, simply by drawing a line across the road with her enchanted staff. One day, however, the carter, after stroking his horses and speaking kindly to them, cracked his whip loudly and fell upon the witch, striking her violently. Thereupon she ran and crept into a culvert and died there, and the teams were never afterwards molested.

Then Angel must relate what he had heard from his mother concerning a farm labourer who wedded a beautiful young woman, of whom he was very proud, and who proved to be a witch. Before they had long been married the husband discovered that his bride arose from bed at midnight and left him alone in the darkness. Not knowing how to account for her disappearance, he determined to say nothing but to watch her movements. Accordingly, when night came, he lay very still and pretended to be asleep. A little before midnight his wife arose and dressed, and was going downstairs. Then the husband sprang out of bed, seized her by the arm, and demanded an explanation of her conduct. As she insisted upon going out he announced his intention of accompanying her, to which she agreed, on condition that he should by no means utter a word, for if he did evil would certainly follow, said she.

A GOOD JUMP

Then, without another syllable, like young Hermes, she slipped through the keyhole of the door and drew her husband after her. Two milk-white calves were waiting outside. These they mounted and then flew off in the darkness, unimpeded by any obstacles. The husband thought it was an extraordinary adventure, but he said nothing till they came to the river, dimly seen in the starlight. Surely, thought he, the calves would not leap over that. They did so, however, with a mighty bound, and were just coming to earth on the other side when the bridegroom, who was a cowman, amazed at the feat, lost his self-possession and cried: " That's a good jump for a calf to make!" A moment afterwards the calf shot from under him and he found himself in water up to his waist and alone in the stillness, for the others had vanished. His wife, however, with loving kindness, called for him on her way back and took him out with her on the white calves many times afterwards, but he had the good sense to observe her injunctions and never to break the silence with any incautious remark.

So the hours pass quickly away. Night draws on; it is time to close the fair. The moon has set long ago. The heavens are strewn with countless myriads of stars, and there is a nip of frost in the air. The meadows by the river are covered with a low layer of mist that lies flat on the ground, looking exactly like an inundation of the fields. The light at the Round House glitters brightly across the imaginary waste, like the lantern hung from a ship's mast over the harbour. The tall steeple stands weird and ghostly in the starlight, and the lamps are out in the market-place. Soon the clock in the tower will strike the hour of midnight and the town will be buried in slumber, till the day breaks above the glimmering river and the shepherds and carters leave their beds and trudge up the lane to bring in their horses from the field or attend to the flocks on the open down-lands.

CHAPTER VIII

The Cotswolds near Northleach—Carl the Carter—Valley of the Coln—The Mill-Pool—Fairford Church and Windows—Hard Fare—Gipsies—Harvest Home Healths—Sheep-stealing—" Cotswold Ale "—" Tig ! "

ON the windswept hill overlooking the town of Northleach, with its great church and lofty imposing tower, a noble view of the surrounding country may be had. Here we are in the heart of the Cotswolds, that cannot properly be understood from without but only by penetrating to the interior. For the Cotswolds differ widely from the chalk hills and downs of Wiltshire, Berkshire, and Hampshire. In the case of them the lines and ridges are diversified and distinct, sometimes rising to a height of nine hundred or a thousand feet above sea-level. The ascent of the Cotswolds, on the other hand, is gradual, and the face of the country is more uniformly consimilar. There are no very imposing heights to attract the vision and infix themselves in the mind, but vast stretches of almost level cornfields and sheep downs divided with a network of brown stone walls, with here and there a solitary wood or plantation, or a long row of spruce trees standing out boldly against the skyline. One also misses, on the Gloucestershire uplands, the graceful and harmonious sweep and curve of hill and dale, the terraces and coombs, the warm colours of the chalk ground showing in patches amid the pasture, or gleaming like snow on the cultivated fields of the hillside, the friendly clumps of hawthorn inviting one to rest in the shade, and the fiery intensity of the glittering flint roads.

One is sometimes inclined to wonder at the expenditure of labour that was required to construct so many scores of miles of stone walls in the country of the Cotswolds. Could it all have been necessary? Notwithstanding the abundance of materials everywhere the operation must have been tedious. What need was there of all those millions of stones, quarried, hauled, and stacked in interminable lines, crossing and recrossing, ducking and dipping, and rearing up again to divide mere cornfields and sheep downs? On the chalk downs of Wiltshire and Hampshire a much more simple plan was adopted. Shallow trenches divide the cornfields, and plain low ridges or banks run alongside the roads. Boundaries are not so much fixed as implied; there all is large and open, free and generous.

On coming up from Fairford I was saluted by no less than eighteen persons, chiefly carters and shepherds in company with their teams and flocks, either on the road or in the fields and farmyards adjoining the highway. This speaks for itself, and discovers the warm-heartedness and sociability of the Cotswold peasant folk. Theirs is a lonely life, and doubtless they love to see a fresh face now and then, and take comfort in exchanging a few words with a sympathetic stranger. It is pleasant also for you to converse with these genuine children of the soil. Your pains are not lost; you will gain some little insight into life and character that will interest or amuse you for many months afterwards.

As I was leaning on the wall, chatting with a carter who was at plough in the field, a middle-aged woman, bearing a basket of goods bought in the town, came up the hill and, after a respectful nod to me, addressed the carter in a shrill, piping voice :

" 'Ev you a-yerd from Car-rl ? "

" No," replied he.

" We 'ev ed a letter," she continued. " 'E yent agwain on at all well. A no business to a left Calcutt. A was barn ther' an' brought up ther', an' a'd never bin away afoore till a tuk this fit in is 'ed. But a wunt stop away long. A'll break 'is 'eart if a do. Poor Car-rl ! A cried all the way ther', an' a bin that miserable ever since a don' know what to do wi' 'isself. A'll never finish the twelve months out."

" Poor Carl," as I learned, was a Cotswold carter who had been at one situation all his life and had only recently shifted to another village, with the result intimated in the good-wife's conversation.

But we are out to view the Downs, and to trace the valley of the little Coln that flows from the heart of the limestone region and, taking its final leap from the Cotswolds at Fairford, joins the Thames opposite the Round House at Inglesham.

" Out of the hills of Habersham,
Down the valleys of Hall,
I hurry amain to reach the plain,
Run the rapid and leap the fall.

.   .   .   .

The dry fields burn, and the mills are to turn,
And a myriad flowers mortally yearn,
And the lordly main from beyond the plain
Calls o'er the hills of Habersham,
Calls through the valleys of Hall."

The Chattahoochee, of which the American poet Lanier sang, is larger and swifter than our river, but there are yet many points of resemblance in the two streams. In the case of each " the dry fields burn, and the mills are to turn," and the lordly main awaits both, far from the spring-head, to clasp them finally in its eternal embrace.

The source of the Coln is near Charlton Abbots, about twelve miles to the north of Cirencester. From that point the river runs murmuring past the richly wooded slopes of Chedworth, a little below the famous Roman Villa. Now it takes an easterly course, winding round through the old-fashioned villages of Coln St. Denis, Coln Rogers, and Winson, and presently reaches the picturesque hamlet of Ablington, with its grand old Manor House and the quiet beauty of its farms and cottages.

Bibury is the next village on the stream. Here the river is joined by a considerable spring that leaps out of the hillside, the waters of which scarcely vary, even after the driest summer. Near this is a commodious inn and a trout fishery, at which young fish for stocking the river are hatched and reared. Two large mills stand on the stream, and the ruins of a woollen factory are visible in a meadow not far from the banks.

The upper mill is silent now, but the one lower down, at Bibury, is still active and does a moderate amount of work, though only grist, and no wheaten flour. Twenty years ago the miller employed four assistants, whereas to-day he has but one, and he usually had fifteen hundred sacks of wheat shot out loose in the great loft waiting to run through to the stones that turned night and day grinding the golden grain into flour for use about the near countryside. The walls of the mill are very strongly built. The beams within are as large as trees, which was necessary to enable them to carry such a great weight of corn and plant.

INQUISITIVE TROUTS

The large "under-shot" wheel that turns the stones is half of iron and half of wood. The beautiful water sings sweetly at its task, and the tame trouts come close up to the mill-head and thrust their noses against the iron grating, as though curious to see the wheel at work and to know what is going on within the cavern-like place.

The poet Morris considered Bibury the prettiest village in England. The scenery is Swiss in kind, though it has a softness and tenderness which are quite English. On one side of the small valley the road runs down gently for several hundred feet; on the other side the steep bank, clothed with beeches, elms, and spruces, rises almost perpendicularly, overtopping the Court, the church, the gabled farmhouses, and cottages. The tiny Coln, after running parallel with the street for a quarter of a mile, leaps down a cascade and curves round in the centre of the dale, showing like a band of silver between banks of sweet forget-me-not and willow-herb.

Presently Coln St. Aldwyns is reached—what a beautiful name!—and then, winding below the walls of Hatherop Castle, we come to Quenington, famed for its quaint Norman Church and Refectory, and, formerly, for its paper-mills, driven by the spouting river. From Quenington the Coln runs rippling in and out among the shadows of high elms, till, passing a green hill, it widens into a crescent-shaped lake, and then pauses, as though to gather strength, before it rushes down the cascade into the broad mill-pool behind the church at Fairford.

Above the noise of the plashing river, where it leaps and foams adown the cascade, a silvery note is heard echoing through the tree-tops:

"Ting-tang, ting-tang, ting-tang."

This is the small bell in the tower ringing for vespers. Immediately one thinks of Moreau's poem, "Le Tocsin," and its haunting refrain:

"*Tintin, tintin, tintin, rlintintin,*
Tintin, c'est le tocsin."

By the richly adorned porch the worshippers enter and pass up the aisle, with the colours of sunset—crimson, golden, and amethystine—streaming through the gorgeously stained windows, emblazoning wall, floor, and pillar with the image of prophet, saint, king, and hero. There are not many going in. Doubtless the evening is too delicious. The sweet sky, the fragrant air, and the cool river rippling through the fields, the beauty that is felt, as well as seen, are irresistible, and the silvery note of the bell sounds very far away and pacifies the soul, rather than stirs it up to any sense of religious duty.

What is that little patch of pure yellow close by the edge of the water there? Why! it is the mimulus, for which I have sought so long and hitherto in vain beside the Coln, though I always thought I must find it somewhere. Beautiful mimulus, that sippest the crystal water from the brink and shelterest the gentle trout lurking beneath thy much-branching foliage, what joy it is to have found thee! I love thee more dearly than the rose, for thy beauty is rarer to be met with, and thou wilt thrive nowhere but by the purest streams and fountains with thy companions the graceful flowering-rush, noble loose-strife, purple hemp-nettle, and sky-sweet forget-me-nots. But no sooner do I pluck thee than, lo! thou art fled, fallen from thy stem for very modesty, fearing to be sullied with the rudeness of hands, when nothing but lips would have tenderly touched thee,

Though the great church were full to overflowing and the organ should peal forth never so loudly, or utter its " Linked sweetness long drawn out," bringing all heaven before the eyes of the worshippers, I would not leave the river to-night. The sound of the water rushing down the mill-stairs, the whisper of leaves, and the tiny linnet and black-cap piping in the tree-top, have filled me with an unspeakable joy. The sound of the water becomes fainter and fainter. I am borne out of the world to a land of beauty and rest, where the crimson sunset swims over vine-laden fields, the ocean breezes blow, and every care is forgotten.

What noise was that? A trout, that rose under the wall, close by my side here? Yes, and there is another, and now another. The water seems alive with them as they come from their lurking-places among the stones and weeds and snap at the flies that skim along the surface of the pool. The shadow of the elms and poplars is darker on the river. The grey tower is fading in the twilight, and the tall, slender trunks of the silver birches are becoming indistinct. The few worshippers have left the church and filed out into the street, yet here I lie—and would lie — beside the foaming river, watching the last light fade and the twinkling stars showing through the spaces of the poplar boughs above me.

Nearly all interest in the tiny town centres around the grand old church and its splendid windows, some of the most perfect specimens of Christian art extant. The church was built by John Tame, about the year 1500, and is considered to be a nearly perfect structure in Tudor Gothic. Throughout the summer and autumn visitors arrive from all quarters of the country, and from this and that continent, to view the

> " Storied windows richly dight
> Casting a dim religious light,"

and to dream upon the glory and solemnity of long-gone-by but never-to-be-forgotten things.

Several interesting traditions pertain to the windows. One is to the effect that John Tame took them from a prize ship that was on its way to Rome. This probably originated in the fact of the glass having been brought from abroad in merchant vessels. Another account declares them to have been the work of the famous artist, Albert Dürer; and a third states that at the time of the Commonwealth the glass of the windows was removed and buried in a field at some distance from the town and replaced after the Restoration. The truth seems to be that John Tame bought the windows, or had them specially made, during his visits to the Netherlands; that they were painted by a Flemish artist named Aaps, and that, notwithstanding anxieties entertained for their safety during the disturbances of the Puritan period, they were not materially damaged at that time, though a great tempest in 1703 severely shattered the most noble of all—that of the west front.

Responsible critics differ in their opinions as to the supreme quality of the windows, and the visitor who is not a veritable enthusiast may feel disappointment on first entering the church and standing face to face with the seemingly bewildering confusion of images and allegorical details. It is difficult for the inexpert, and more so for the inartistic, to determine their most excellent beauties. They are neither mediæval nor modern, but stand midway between the two styles, lacking the perfect shades and coloration of the former and, at the same time, discovering a superiority over the too striking and " splashing " characteristics of the latter. The Flemish master, Van Dyck, considered the portraiture to be so exquisitely done that it could not have been excelled by the cleverest pencil.

The cottage industries of spinning and weaving, wool-carding, and straw-plaiting, flourished in the town, and supplemented the earnings of those employed on the land. The woollens, when finished, were taken to the various centres for disposal, and the plaited straw was conveyed to London in the road-waggons and there sold to the manufacturers.

The men of Fairford were skilled in the use of the flails, and they travelled for many miles during the winter months, threshing out wheat and barley. When the machine threshers were invented the lively Coln was harnessed to the toil and threshed out the corn as well as grinding flour for the loaves. The Fairford horse-threshing teams also traversed the country around for a great distance. Four horses, attached to as many levers, supplied the power for the thresher. They were outside the barn, while the machine was set within. In the centre, from which the levers radiated, was a cage in which a boy stood to drive the animals; there he must stay in rain or snow, ofttimes drenched to the skin, and half-perished with the cold.

"Many's the time I squat in that owl' cage an' drev thaay 'osses round," the aged carter says.

" Warn thees jest about fancied thiself, dissent ? " his wife replies, with a sly wink and a knowing nod of the head.

But there were hard times around Fairford and in the Cotswold villages during the " Hungry Forties," and the poor found it difficult to subsist even on the rudest fare. With wheaten flour at a prohibitive price and barley meal costing a guinea a bushel, what were the labouring classes to do ? Yet live they must, and it is not to be wondered at if they took to poaching and stole a sheep now and then in order to satisfy the raging hunger within them. Hedgehogs were a common article of food. Badgers, also, were eagerly hunted and devoured, and the nimble squirrel was frequently trapped, cooked, and eaten by the woodmen and labourers. The local squire was surprised at the carter's eating a squirrel. He thought the dish to be unclean, but the carter grinned broadly and replied : " Aa, zur, you don' know the vally of a squirrel. Tha be as dainty mate as ever you tasted, an' good anuff for the king to aat."

As to the eating of badgers, squirrels, and hedgehogs, that is not surprising to those acquainted with village conditions. One sometimes hears of the practice of eating fried mice and snails, and there is a labourer in the village in which I am writing who will eat live mice whole for, or without, a wager. Of the eating of rats I have not heard except when two young ploughmen cooked one in the brew-house, and, by a ruse, induced their mate to eat it. Having formed the plan they caught a fat rat, " cut 'is yed, paas an' tayul off, well weshed un, an' rawsted un an a stick a-vrunt o' the vire." When it was nicely cooked, and they heard Henry coming, they fell a-wrestling and quarrelling as to who should have the " bird," and while they were so engaged Henry quietly took the rat from the stick and ate it with a good relish, grinning at his supposed smartness. He felt sure it was a blackbird, and when his mates laughed at him and asked him how he liked "the rat," he still grinned and said it was "very good mate."

There is a story of two dealers who called at the inn on their way to fair, after an all-night ride, and found the house almost destitute of viands.

"Ane 'e got nar a bit o' mate, mother?" inquired one.

"Lar, no! Who'd a thawt o' seein' you?" replied she.

"Narn a mossel o' bacon, neether, ner it a egg?"

"No! But ther's that peggy-wiggy pie. I forgot that. You be welcome to a bit o' he. I oni made un the day afore yesterday."

"Fetch it along, mother, whatever 'tis, an' we'll pay ya for't," said they.

Accordingly the "peggy-wiggy" pie was brought out and the dealers liked it so well that they ate the whole of it, to learn of the old woman afterwards that it was made of the stillborn young of the long-eared white sow. She had made it for the children, who, she said, were very fond of it: she thought it would be "something for them to get down." Outrageous as this appears, it may have been true. It is certain that stillborn calves were sometimes eaten by the poorest labourers when other food was unobtainable, and the same kind of thing is done to-day, though people generally are not aware of it. More than one farmer, when his cow is delivered of a stillborn calf—provided it has not been too long dead—skins and dresses it, blows up the flesh with a pipe-stem, and hurries off with it to the nearest butcher to exchange it with him for a choice cut or a joint *from another beast.*

Gipsies swarmed about the Cotswolds during the fore part of the nineteenth century. They lived chiefly by poaching, stealing, and fortune-telling. In the summer and autumn they cut rushes and flags from the Coln and plaited them into baskets, or obtained withes and hazel-wood from the copses and wove them into wickerwork for chairs. To take the trouts they made " hoop-nets " and set them in the stream, and then stirred the weeds with light poles and drove the fish into them.

One cold day in January a dark-looking gipsy hailed the shepherd, who was attending to his flock near the wood.

" Hey ! owld man, ood 'e like a basin o' sup ? "

" Don' mind if 'e do. 'Tis a cowld blow this mornin'," the shepherd replied.

" Come on, then," answered the gipsy, and poured out a basin of liquor from the smoky pot.

After the shepherd had swallowed the broth, the gipsy addressed him :

" Do you know what you've had ? "

" No, I don't. But 'twas uncommon good, whatever 'twas," replied he.

" That was house-rabbit, generally known as cat," the gipsy returned, walking away to the camp beneath the high oak-trees.

A gipsy funeral was an interesting event and attracted crowds of visitors to the grand old church. The gipsies often concealed a death in the camp. They buried the corpse in a wood or withy-bed, where the bones would not be disturbed, but when the Burial Laws came to be enforced they were compelled to inter their dead more decently. The last gipsy funeral at Fairford took place but a few years ago. There were about a hundred mourners, the majority of whom came clad in odd suits of black which they had begged, borrowed, or hired from the townspeople.

At the funeral of a true gipsy the corpse was dressed in its best clothes. Coins of copper and silver were placed in the coffin and bread and meat were set beside the dead person. It was the custom to have a hole bored in the lid of the coffin, in order to allow the spirit to have free access to its old abode. The next of kin to the dead person, carrying a bottle of wine, headed the procession. When the coffin had been lowered into the grave he poured the wine upon it and prayed in the Romany tongue. On returning to the camp the elders sat around the fire, muttering chants and incantations for the spirit of the departed, and continued so till midnight. For a week they repeated the ceremony; then they held a feast that ended in dancing and singing.

The toilers on the farms—not only on the Cotswolds but throughout the Thames Valley—had four feasts a year, namely, after sowing, shearing, haymaking, and harvest. The seed-feast—called "Sidcyek" (Seed-cake)—was kept at the end of April. This was held in the barn or brew-house, and was only attended by those who worked on the farm.

"Sherrin'" feast was on a somewhat different scale. A select body of shearers was chosen from a village. They took the farms around, one by one, and when they had finished all the flocks they were entertained at a public feast provided by the farmers collectively, who invited as many others as they thought fit. Games and songs followed the feast, and appropriate toasts were made by the shepherds and responded to by the farmers.

Harvest-home was the most important and the best-loved festival. The whole of the toilers—men, women, and children—attended this; the brew-house and kitchen, too, were needed to hold the company. Besides the farm hands, the blacksmiths and wheelwrights came, invited by the farmer. The parson frequently attended, and the village constable managed to creep in and mingle with the rest. Both the farmer and his wife were well toasted, usually in the following rhymes, which were common throughout the Thames Valley :

TO THE MASTER

"Here's a health unto our master, the founder of the feast,
 I hope to God with all my heart his soul in heaven may rest,
And all his works may prosper, whatever he takes in hand,
For we are all his servants and are at his command.
Then drink, boys, drink, and see you do not spill,
For if you do, you shall drink two, it is our master's will."

TO THE MISTRESS

"Here's a health unto our master, our mistress shan't go free,
For she's a good provider, provides as well as he ;
For she's a good provider, and bids us all to come,
So take this cup and sip it up, for it is our harvest-home."

Sometimes the toast to the mistress took a different form.

"Here's a health unto our mistress, prosperity and happiness,
Prosperity and happiness and plenty of store ;
And he that doth refuse the same,
To drink a health unto our dame,
We'll turn him out of doors for shame,
And own him no more."

The breezy carter—of fourscore and five years—has fond recollections of the old harvest-feast. " Ther' was maaster an' missis a-hippin' an't up in front an us, an' owl' Moll Fry a-skippatin' about wi' the cups. Presently all an us fell to. ' Lar'! faather, byent 'e gwain to saay graace,' missis ses. Then maaster stood up, shet 'is eyes, an' put 'is 'ands together an' said :

> " ' O Lard, make us able
> To aat all on the table.' "

' Oh, dad, you wicked fella!' cried missis, an' all the young uns baaled out 'Amen.' The paason purty nigh chokked 'isself wi' a lump o' bif an' 'ed to wesh it down wi' a cup o' ale, an' when tha sung ' Drenk, bwoys, drenk,' a sed 'twas no need to tell 'em that for tha could do that very well wi'out bein' telled. Tha allus reckoned to sip twice when tha toasted, but I chocked mine down at once an' maaster hollered out : ' Make haste an' put Willum out another, else a'll get all behind wi't.' "

Serious rioting took place in the riverside town during the disturbances of 1830. Threatened with the loss of their employment, and resenting the intrusion of the new-fangled machinery, a party of five hundred labourers, armed with scythes, hooks, axes, and sledge-hammers, marched through the town and proceeded to smash up the implements. The next day the military arrived and order was restored. This was effected not so much by a demonstration of force as by an accidental discovery made by the Captain of the Troop. He, on coming face to face with the mob, happened to glance down and perceive that one of his gaiters was only partly buttoned. Thereupon he turned to one of the rioters, formidably

armed with a scythe fastened to a pole, and cried:
"Hi, there! You fellow! Put that thing down and
come and button up my gaiter, will you?" The
rioter, taken by surprise, threw down his weapon
and approached the Captain; he stretched out his leg
and the gaiter was duly buttoned. The incident had
a good effect on the crowd. There was no more
fighting, and the rioters dispersed to their homes.

A story is told of a Cotswold labourer who stole
a sheep and was strangled in the act of carrying it
home. He had the sheep slung at his back and
secured with a cord which he had put round his neck.
On coming to a gate he attempted to climb over it
but slipped, and as he fell, feet foremost, on one side
of the gate the sheep, hanging by the rope round his
neck, dropped back on the other and quickly strangled
him. At another time, a hungry labourer stole a
fat ewe, killed it, and carried it for six miles on his
back and disposed of the carcass, but was arrested
three months afterwards when he tried to sell the
skin, that bore the private mark of the farmer.

In Shakespeare's day it was customary to brand
a sheep-stealer in the palm with a hot iron, as the
slaves of the Greeks and Romans were branded on
the forehead.

"Goo an up the 'ill, else I'll zend the devul aater
'e," cried the Quenington shepherd boy to his flock
one day, not perceiving the village pastor, who was
close behind him.

"And who is the sheep's devil, my boy?" inquired
the cleric.

"That owl' dog yander, locks!" answered he.

"And who is the dog's devil?" the vicar proceeded.

"I be," the boy replied.

" And who is your devil, pray ? "

" Why, mi maester, to be sure."

" And who is your master's ? "

"You needn't ax I that, zur. A yent very fer awaay vrom I, an' the Biship's 'is 'n, an' the Biship's is the very owld un 'isself, fer 'tis what I bin larned ever since I tuk to ship-caddlin'," the youngster replied.

"A Cotswold Shepherd's Scolding," dating from the early part of the seventeenth century, is interesting, though the language may savour more of the skilled writer than of the rustic sheep-farmer.

"Come heere, you idle lubber, you lazie fellow; a rope shall touch thine hyde. Heere be sheep in a trim pickle indeede. Thou commest cloaked and hooded, as if thou didst watch among them day and night, armed for all stormes and tempests, and thou carryest thy Tarre-boxe to dingle and dangle upon thy hooke. The bowe of thy sheeres peepes out of thy script as though thou wouldst do a great act: but look upon these sheep heere, dost not see what a wrigling they make, and how oft they lye downe, byting and gnawing where they are payned. Put off your cumbersome cloake ; you lyther Mharrhant ! lay hands on these poor sheepe ; scrch them well ; shed the wooll, and where thou findest any scurfe, scrape it off ; cut away those dirty dag-lockes with the sheeres, and doe not tarre them as if thou wert afrayde to hurt them, but make it goe to the skinne, and labour by dilligence to save that which is ready to perish by thy negligence."

A pleasant story is told of the Cotswold ale. One day a waggish Oxford scholar proposed, for a noble, to teach the landlord of the Bibury inn how he might draw mild ale and strong beer from the same cask.

The offer seemed reasonably fair and was accepted. Proceeding to the cellar the scholar bored a hole in a full cask and desired the landlord to stop it with his finger. This was for the mild ale. Then, boring another hole, from which the strong beer was to run, he told him to stop that with the other hand. Having the landlord now fully engaged with the cask, the scholar left on pretence of fetching pegs, then, pocketing the noble, he mounted his horse and rode off, leaving mine host a prisoner in his cellar. Thus it was that, in the words of the poet:

> " From the selfsame cask,
> Mild and October flow just as we ask,
> In limpid Coln, where trout and minnow swarm."

" Then tha didn't kip 'e at Fairford along o' the wowardy," remarks grandfather Elijah, with a sly wink and an artful nod of the head. He is referring to the Retreat for feeble-minded, and by the " wowardy " he means the " waywardy." Even of this place the rustics tell a cheerful story. One evening, as a carpenter, with his basket of tools, was coming past the grounds of the Retreat, he saw an inmate climb down from the high fence and begin running towards him. He took to his heels, with the madman in hot pursuit and gaining ground every moment. Encumbered with his tools—there was a large sharp axe, a saw, and a bill-hook among them—he could not compete with the lunatic, and a deadly fear came upon him. At last, after running till he became exhausted, he threw down his basket and, with a groan, sank to the earth. Then the madman, with an exultant yell, dashed up to him, stooped down, and, touching him lightly on the shoulder, cried " TIG ! "

There is furthermore the story of the Cotswold housewife who had never seen one wearing a veil. One day a young lady neighbour, who was dressed for a journey, came in to wish her good-bye. She, happening to be in her garden, was sent for to the house. Seeing the young woman wearing a spotted veil for the first time, she held up her hands in amazement and cried : " Lar', you ! Whatever's the matter ? Thees got a lot o' girt vlies craalin' all over thy vace."

CHAPTER IX

A Cotswold Ploughing Match—Old Acquaintances—The Carter's Criticism—Progress of the Ploughing—The Prize-Winner.

> "For oh, the honest countryman
> Speaks truly from his heart;
> His pride is in his tillage,
> His horses and his cart.
>
> The ploughman, though he labour hard,
> Yet, on a holiday,
> No emperor so merrily
> Doth pass the time away."
>
> *Old Song.*

WHAT means this uncommon bustle and animation in and around the little riverside town, and where are all the men and horses going at such an early hour, for it is scarcely yet breakfast-time? To-day the most fateful of contests is to be decided. For this is the date of the Ploughing Match. To-day half a hundred ploughmen will compete for the coveted palm and will put forth their best efforts and show their greatest skill and pride in the grandest of all trades, and afterwards await the judge's award with a coolness truly admirable, heroic in a simple spontaneous people.

For weeks past interest in the competition has been steadily increasing for miles around the Thames Valley. In the field, in the stable, at home in the cottage, and in the snug little rooms at the Pig and Whistle, and the Red Lion, where the carters assemble

PREPARING FOR THE FRAY

at least every week-end, the talk has been of little but the coming ploughing match. The young men have been making mental lists of all the veterans and those famed for a straight, even furrow they can think of, and weighing their own chances. Similarly, the champions have taken a survey of the field and singled out their most dangerous rivals among the younger ploughmen, and made careful note of fresh-comers to the farms, gleaning whatever intelligence they could of their skill in guiding the plough and turning up the stubborn glebe. In addition to this, the ploughs have been overhauled and put into condition after lying idle during hay-cart and wheat harvest; the favourite and most easily manipulated implement has been singled out upon which to stake the prestige of the farm and its ploughing staff. The horses, too, have been chosen and are being well looked after. The harness has been cleaned and oiled, the brasses brightly polished, the ribbons, rosettes, and ear-caps produced from the carter's private chest or drawer, or new ones bought at the saddler's and harness-maker's shop.

And now the long and eagerly expected day is here. The clock in the stately tower has struck eight. Some of the teams and ploughs passed through the broad market-place nearly an hour ago, and others are still arriving. It is noteworthy that those who were situated at the greatest distance came first, and those whose farms are near at hand will be the last to reach the field. But there is a reason for everything. Those horses that came from afar will need food and a rest before being harnessed to the plough, while the others, by reason of their nearness to the site, will come forth fresh and untired by a long journey on the road. The morning opened dull and close. A heavy thunder-shower fell early in the night, watering the fields. The land lies steaming in the sun that now and then peeps through the clouds and smiles on the rain-sweetened earth and the lively company assembling to take part in or be spectators of the competition.

"That drap o' raain couldn't a come at a better time. It jest mystened the ground fer the shers, an' 't ull 'elp the turmuts farrud. Our'n used to decler sich raain was wuth a pound a drap. 'Tis jest right fer ploughin'. That owl' clawver ood a turned up akkerd else if us 'adn' 'ad a drap," remarks the carter to his near mate.

There are two kinds of ploughing—with the double and single ploughs. The single ploughs are allocated to the clover-patch that has been carefully measured out into plots of half an acre. The double ploughs are given wheat stubble, as being easier to turn, for the clover has not been ploughed for two years, and has been well trodden down by the sheep and the haymakers. The competitors are of two classes—over and under twenty years of age. In several cases father and son, too, are competing, the one in the senior and the other in the junior class. The youthful ploughmen have a portion of the field expressly allotted to them, but adjoining the other, so that they can exchange a few words with their fathers when they come to turn round in the middle of the field.

Jingle, jingle, jingle. Merrily the bells sound and brightly the brasses shine, as the horses, plump and sleek, with tails and manes plaited and interwoven with bright wheat straw and decorated with streaming ribbons and ear-caps, proudly enter the field, nodding their heads and neighing softly at the

THE EXPERT PLOUGHMAN 151

sight of so many of their kind. Surely they must all be here now, for it is past nine o'clock, and it is time a start was made. But no! There is one more team to come, from Aldsworth, four miles away, and it has been decided to wait for that.

At the same time there is no sign of impatience about the field. No one is in a hurry, for it is a holiday. The old carters walk up and down steadily, eyeing the youngsters' ploughs, and giving sundry words of advice. The young ploughman, with silver ring on his finger and surrounded by several mates who have come to witness the match and give encouragement to their comrade, calmly smokes a cigarette, and, with the touch and skill of a trained mechanic, screws up first one nut and then another, and takes careful note of the wheels, to have them secure when a start is made. The skim and coulter must be fitted after the signal is given. They are usually set with the aid of a new horse-nail, and the operation is performed with care, for it is of the utmost importance to have them correctly fixed. If the skim and coulter are not properly set a thin edge of green will show in the ploughing, and this will tell against the competitor. Most of the ploughmen carry an extra share, and some have a spare skim, too, fastened to the frame of the implement in case they should lose or break one. To do so would be a great misfortune, and would promptly settle their chances of winning a prize, and would moreover expose them to the laughter of all the rest on the field.

Here is a young ploughman singing by himself:

> "My owld 'oss died wi' the toothache,
> And left me here a-sorrowin'.
> Good-bye, Kit, and good-bye, Dan,
> I'm just goin' over the mountain.

So I dug a hole and hit 'im in,
Fare thee well, owld dar-ar-lin',
Good-bye, Kit, and good-bye, Dan,
I'm just goin' over the mountain."

Along comes a carter with critical eye.

" Yellocks ! "

" What ? "

" One trace is sharter than t'other, my bwoy."

" Which un ? "

" That outside un yander."

" A yen much odds, is a ? "

" A's a lenk difference. Let un go one. Tha's got un twisted, too, essent ? Tha's better, locks ! "

" Never tried mi luck afore. Can but try."

" Kip thi eye an the flag, and dwunt caddle thiself."

" If I caan't strik out a line straight away, I be done."

" Dwunt go too fast, ner it too slow. Dwunt get steam up too quick. Ther's a lot of stwuns in this piece. If tha dossent kip thi plough stiddy thaay'll uck un out an't."

" Now, Vylet ! Stan' up, Vylet. Woa ! Way ! Tha's more at it. 'Tis no good to odds it when ya got it ready."

Here is a merry-looking little man, with pilot coat, small boxer hat, and stout ground-ash stick in his right hand, and an old blue umbrella with handle broken off under his left arm, nodding to everyone, and examining the horses and ploughs. Seeing the carter, he stops short ; his eyes twinkle, and his face lights up, for he recognises an old acquaintance.

" Good marnin' to 'e, Robbut. 'Tis Robbut, yent it ? "

" Yes. But I dwunt zim to call you to mind."

A FAIR MASTER

"Dwunt you know I?"

"Can't zim to recollect 'e."

"Why, you knows Quininton, dwunt 'e?"

"I was barned ther, awhever."

"To be sure! I know'd you as soon as I sid 'e. An' 'ow be 'e all this time?"

"Tarble well, e s'pose, considerin'. Caan't run awver very many."

"An' 'ow's yer missis?"

"A got the rheumatics. We byent so young as us used to be, narn an us."

"Aa! if 'tis thaay rheumatics, God bless 'e. I be yer for a day's pleasure, I be."

"Warn you jacked out work now?"

"Nat it. Still kips muddlin' on. I bin an one lot o' land fifty year, an' bin wi' our maester forty out on't. 'E's a good un, 'e is. All that time that I worked wi' our maester I never yerd 'e swer once—never!"

"Phe-e-e-e-ew!" There goes the secretary's whistle at last, calling the attention of the ploughmen and preluding the hoisting of the flag for the start. The Aldsworth team was so late in coming that special provision had to be made for it; to that has been accorded the privilege of beginning and finishing ten minutes later than the others.

At the sound of the whistle there is a general movement throughout the field. The young ploughman's mates fall back and stand clear of the implement, while he prepares to fix the skim and coulter as soon as the signal is given. The wise and cautious veteran, with great outward unconcern, gives a last glance round his traces and whipples. The spectators gather in groups and wait expectantly, and the horses, unmoved by the strangeness of the scene and the voices around, stand like statues, ready to go forward at the bidding of the ploughmen. The land no longer steams, for the surface of the field is dry. The mist has lifted from the woods, and the sun shines warm through the fleecy clouds rimmed with brightest silver.

Now the secretary, standing in mid-field, waves the flag and notes the time with his watch, held open in the other hand. In a jiffy skim and coulter are set; the carters take the reins and shake them clear of the harness and, gripping the handles of the plough, point the share and speak to the horses, and the whole phalanx moves forward, some with a smart rush, some with a more dignified pace, and others creeping like snails. These are chiefly the veterans, who never make the mistake of starting off too quickly, but take things quietly at first, while the younger ploughmen, thinking speed to be the first essential, dash straight away and trust to luck rather than judgment to strike out a good furrow.

"You'll zee marks as straight as a arra, dareckly," the merry little carter exclaims.

"Aa! an' as crucked as a anchor, too, from thase young uns," replies another.

One lean, middle-aged carter has met with an accident already, within a few seconds of the start. His skim, that was none too tight, has struck a stone and been wrenched out of place. In less than half a minute it is right again and on he goes, though somewhat behind the rest.

As soon as the teams have got well away a rush is made from point to point in order to see the first furrows. The bow-legged carter runs as fast as he can, stoops down and squints with one eye along each furrow and, with the other, winks at the bystanders.

A FIELD OF CRITICS

All sorts of remarks, accompanied with merry laughter and playful sarcasm, are passed by the youths and old men.

"Yellocks!"

"Ha! ha! ha!"

"'E got a smartish bend ther'."

"What did I tell 'e?"

"'E'll 'ef to pull towwerd a bit. 'E'll 'ev a job to get that out."

"That ull squer up bad, that ull."

"'E'll never get that out."

"'E got to show 'is rudge."

'Matey got a good mark ther', locks!"

"Thase be the two best furras."

"Well, done, Benjimun!"

"If 'e'd a got 'es chestnut along wi' that owl' brown un. Benjimun ood 'ev it."

"Aa! tha's cyapitul ploughin'. Ther's a lot about everything, yent it?"

"That yunt deep anuf."

"Ther's plenty wuss than that."

"That wunt do. Tha's too much of a 'olla."

"Coom-e! Woa-utt! Wug-tt-a! Stand back, ther', an' let the 'osses turn round, ool 'e!"

"Thee bist nervous, owl' man."

"No, I byent."

"Yes, thee bist."

"It don' trouble I which way it goes."

"Tha bist main white about the gills."

"'Tis a pity Benjimun's turn-vurra dwunt shine a bit! A got a new plough an' fresh 'osses."

"That drap o' raayn jest tuk the polish off the rudge."

"'Tis too many stwuns in 't. It makes a difference wer 'tis sandy sile, er claayey, er brash. We ent a bin about all thase years fer nothin', ev us, Robbut?"

"Look at Willum yander! A got a mark like a rip-'ook."

"Dost thee want to get awver to Quininton? Tha bist gwain a long way round at it."

"I got the wrong 'oss. I wanted my owl' Jinny."

"Kip thi eye an that tree yander, an' get that cruk out, else tha't be zumwher' presently."

And so the ploughing proceeds amid the clatter of tongues, the laughter and jests of the young men, and the sage and witty observations of the elder carters. Here and there a youth accompanies his mate the length of the plot, walking alongside the plough to encourage him with his presence, though that will certainly not improve the furrow.

The old carter is very quiet and scarcely speaks to his horses, but they fully understand what is required of them and plod along at a steady rate, leaning slightly towards each other. As he turns round he half sits on the plough handles, halts a moment to tighten the skim and clean the turn-furrow with the paddle, and quietly resumes his way. The polished brasses and turn-furrows gleam brightly in the sunshine; the scene is one of great animation. The field is rapidly turning from fresh green to a rich brown; it is surprising how much land can be ploughed up in a short space by so many teams at once.

"Ther's one man as ull benefit bi the match, if nob'dy else dwunt. 'E'll get 'e's ground ploughed fer nothin', an' that ull save 'e's 'osses a main bit o' labour," a bystander remarks.

Now Prince Erik of Denmark, cousin to King George, a tall young man dressed in a light suit and wearing a grey cap, comes stalking along, chatting with a farmer with whom he is staying at Fairford in order to get experience of agriculture as it is carried on in the Cotswolds, and the spectators fall back a few yards and allow them to pass by. The merry little carter and his friends continue to walk up and down, viewing the progress made by the teams and examining the furrows, giving a word of encouragement, or expressing sympathy where that is necessary.

" 'E yander's 'aein' all the bad luck, simly. A lost one skim an' brawk t'other. The green shows along 'is rudge. That ull tell agyenst un."

" 'E's a good ploughman else."

" Anybody can see that."

" Tha's a girt baffle to the man."

" 'Tis no good. I shall be diskallified. Knows 'e shall ! "

" Chent no use to caddle thiself about it now. Go into't."

" Tha's a good furra, that is."

" Aa ! cyapitul."

" Ther's some good ploughin' yer."

" No mistake about that."

" 'Tis as I ses. Ther's a purty deal belongs to everything, yent it ? I was jest a tellin' Willum, ther' yent a bin a ploughin' match in Fayreferd fer sixty year. The last as was was in aishen tree ground. That was my fust, but 'e never gained nothin'. Was but a young un then, ya know."

" What ! bist thee a minin' ? "

" Minin', aa ! "

" Tha't get down out of zight, 'osses an' all, dareckly. Tha dossent want to deg thi grave yer, dost ? "

All the time there is a steady movement of the

spectators, a continual coming and going, to and fro, and backwards and forwards, around the field. Some saunter this way and some that, these to watch the juniors and see how they are shaping, while those go through the gateway into the adjoining section to view the double ploughs. They are drawn by three horses, walking abreast, and as well as turning up double the space of ground they move much more quickly, for the stubble land is softer and more porous than the clover, and offers little resistance to the keen-edged share and coulter. The soil, as it is brought over with the turn-furrow, breaks to pieces: it is useless to think of getting anything like an even, polished ridge here.

The pretty pimpernel, fumitory, and speedwell are ruthlessly torn up and buried beneath the rough clods of earth, though they have done their work and scattered their seeds, which will come up thicker than ever next spring when the warm winds blow and the sweet showers fall from the April skies. The low hedge that divides the fields has been cut, the ditch and bank cleared, and the croppings burnt. The white ashes, saturated with last night's rain, emit a strong scent which, however, is not unpleasant. This, together with the rich smell of the newly ploughed earth, fills the air around and is carried out beyond on the wings of the faintly fluttering wind. For once the rooks are baffled, and dare not lodge upon the fallow with so many strangers about, though they frequently fly overhead and wheel round in great rings, presently to take their departure and settle in the next field, or in the boughs of the elm trees standing alongside the park.

" 'Ow be gettin' an wi't, Robbut?"

" Fairish, like."

THE TEST OF A FURROW

" Tha's got a good per o' 'ossen ! "

" Thaay owl' stwuns keps ketchin' an in, an' jabbin' an in out on't."

" Wher's our Tom ? "

" Up a t'other zide. Go up yander you can zin."

" What do you do now, then, sonny ? "

" I be awver at Castle Acton at it."

" An' 'ow's young Maester ———? "

" Aw ! 'e's a larnin'. 'Evin a bit of a flash in the pan. 'E got a lot to larn yet."

" Aa ! 'E got to find that out. You can farm fer the farm, er you can farm fer the pocket. 'E's faather was a good un. 'E looked round the outside an't, 'e did."

" Take that bit off thi turn-vurra, bwoy ! Tha bist too wide an' too deep. The 'arra wunt shek the zid down. If the whate yent deep-rooted, the fust bit of a cowld nip ull cut it all to pieces. Tha essent got no rudge at all."

" This owl' man got a good furra. A's as straight as a gun-barrel."

" A couldn't a done't much better ef a'd a-tried at it, could a ? "

" 'E could shoot up 'e very well."

" 'Tis the 'osses as doos it."

So the conversation is maintained as the spectators pass from point to point. All is bustle and animation. The ploughs glide along, and the toil proceeds.

More than half the ploughing is done now, for the match has been in progress above two hours. Some of the younger competitors have made great headway with their plots. A few of them will soon have finished, but then they were bound to hurry ; no matter how hard they had tried, they could not have gone about it steadily. The old carters are more backward and have not done nearly as much, but they are aiming to win. At all events, they occupy the chief attention of the judges and are the only ones in the running in the senior class, excepting the Aldsworth man, who arrived last on the field. He is said to be shaping best of all, though he has not done much yet, for he is extraordinarily cautious and deliberate.

After two hours of hard ploughing in the hot sunshine—for the clouds have melted away and left a clear, delicious sky, such as October alone can give us—the horses foam and steam with the perspiration. Their nostrils are distended with hard breathing, and they require more words of exhortation or reproof from the man at the plough-tail. Some of the animals perspire much more freely than do the others. This may be the result of the day's feeling, of fitness or otherwise, though it usually depends upon what they have had for breakfast, and the kind of food they have been eating during the week previous.

" 'Tha's all accordin' to what ya gies 'em to aat. Ef thaay 'aes nothin' but graas, tha'll sweat like raayn. Put plenty o' wuts into the mannger. That'll mek ther ribs firmer," the carter says.

The brilliant colours of the autumn foliage in the noonday light are very striking. The long line of beeches shows in the distance like a blood-red flame, eager to consume the light green of the ash and the dark coloured elms ranged along behind. The brasses on the harness, the shares and turn-furrows gleam more brightly in the sunshine. Every particle of mist has disappeared above the woods and along the line of the White Horse Down, now radiant in the distance.

There is not much farther to go now. The clock

in the church tower has chimed out the four quarters and the heavy bell has followed and struck one, which was plainly heard all over the field. Another half an hour and the contest will be over and the fates of the ploughmen decided. The prizes will have been won, and, with them, the title to the championship for the ensuing twelve months. One or two of the young men, as heedless now as when they began, are already on their last journey. Starting at a fast rate, they continued the pace right through the match and are finishing up at the same speed. Those whose furrows were out at the start and were not rectified by the time the middle of the plot was reached, find they will have to make one, or perhaps several half-turns in order to finish up. This leads them to think that the plot was not measured correctly and was consequently out of square, but the old carters soon tell them that the measurement was right.

" Ef thee'st a kipt thi eye an that owl' elm yander, same as I telled tha, thee'st a 'ed un right. 'Tis no good to caddle thiself about it now, an' blame the mizhurment. Jest tread that bit o' green in yander, an' kick thaay uts a one zide. Tha bist all up an' down like a dog's 'ind leg."

The older ploughmen are not as far advanced and have quite a wide strip to do yet. The nearer they get to the end the more slowly they proceed, ofttimes stopping half-way up the piece and taking a careful survey of the furrow, before and behind. When they come to the headland they measure the remaining portion with the handle of the paddle, then re-set the wheels, skim, and coulter, to fit in with the reduced width of the strip.

" Ther's two as be a long waay a'ed o' t'othern,

tha's the owl' man in the middle, an' 'e at the fer end yander. One o' thaay ull 'ae the fust," remarks the carter.

"The young uns ane't a done so bad, neether, considerin'. The ground's tarble akkerd fer thaay, wi' so many stwuns in't."

"Wher's Benjimun got to?"

"Essent thee purty nigh done thy bit, Benjimun? 'Ow much longer bist a-gwain to be at it?"

"One more go ull finish it."

"I should thenk so, too. Tha's bin long anuff about it."

"Yellacks! 'E's a-gwain to uck that all to pieces an' spile the lot an't."

"A might a bin commended else, if a'd a gone a bit stiddy, but you caan't tell the young uns nothin'. Tha got to find it out fer therselves."

By a quarter past one all have finished, with the exception of the Aldsworth man. He has several more journeys to make yet, and is exceedingly tardy; even with his additional ten minutes to go it seems that he will have enough to do to finish it in time. But he is cool and collected, and behaves as though he had all the afternoon in which to finish the piece. The other ploughmen have withdrawn their horses from the plots and stationed them alongside the hedge, where they stand cropping the leaves and twigs. The conversation, except for a steady stream of compliments, quietly expressed, on the Aldsworth man's work, has died down. There is little excitement or speculation as to the result, for everyone is agreed that his is by far the best piece of ploughing.

The committee men and judges, pocket-books in hand, take a final survey of the furrows and make notes by the way, then come and take a stand with the rest and patiently await the return of the plough, that has gone to the other end for the last time. Arrived there, the carter unhitches one of the horses and makes the return journey with but one animal. This gives him more room and a clearer view of the furrow; he can both see and manage the plough better with but one horse in front of him. Once or twice down the piece he stops to tread in a rough clod of earth, or to kick a stone aside, then resumes his way and, punctual to time, reaches the headland and draws his plough on to the green and coolly surveys his piece. Young and old view him with admiration and hasten to examine the plough, to ascertain its make, age, and general features, for all feel certain that this is the prize-winner.

"Why! this is a main owl' plough," remarks a committee man to the carter.

"Yes. 'E bin about a few years," the ploughman replies.

"How long 'ev you bin a-ploughin' wi' this un?"

"A bit over a twelvemonth. A led out in the ground a rustin' for dree er vower year till I fetched un out on't."

"Well! 'twas a good resurrection, at any rate," the committee man replies, and all the spectators show their agreement by various remarks and comments, while the carters stoop down and squint round the implement, feeling the skim, the coulter, the turn-furrow, and the whipples, and pat the horses on the neck or hip.

Now the carter boys come to relieve the ploughmen and take charge of the horses, and lead them back to the carts in the next field, where a supply of hay and corn is awaiting them. The spectators depart, and those who have taken part in the competition file off and make their way to the marquee in the park opposite, there to partake of a hearty meal and afterwards hear the speeches and the names of the winners announced. These will also be published in the local newspapers for the edification of all and sundry round about, while the prize-winners' certificates will be framed and hung upon the cottage walls, precious mementoes of victories honourably achieved and an example for the juniors, to stir them up to similar feats of skill and fine workmanship.

All the talk at the inns and elsewhere this weekend will be of the ploughing match and its result, as to the winners and those commended. The veterans will go steadily on with their accustomed toils, while the young men will pay greater attention to skim, share, and coulter, determined to be avenged for their defeat and to turn the tables at the very next contest that comes round.

CHAPTER X

A Cotswold Carter's Cottage—" Chasing the Cock "—Native Wit and Humour—On the Coln—Whelford—The Smithy —The Mill—Old Elijah's Tale.

NOW the match is over and the teams and ploughs and crowds of sightseers are gone, the field seems strangely deserted. Never before had such a lively scene, with so much laughter and merry-making, been enacted there, and probably it never will be again. Next year the site of the match will be fixed elsewhere, perhaps many miles away, and so changed from place to place until the cycle of towns and villages in the area is completed. The carters and farmers, too, would complain if the match were confined to one locality; they count it a great compliment to any village to have the competition decided there.

Everyone was agreed that the prizes were fairly awarded, though one greybeard thought the Aldsworth man was fortunate in not being penalised for his late arrival. " If 'e'd a bin a-ploughin' along o' we in my time, an' 'ad come a minute aater the start, 'e'd a 'ad to a stood o' one zide. Tha'd a diskallified un, right anuff. Tha was moore perticler then than tha be now. But a's a cyapital plough-man, for all that, an' we dwun' know what pervented un on the road," said he.

The carter's cottage may be held as a fair type of the average home of the Cotswold labourer. The house is of moderate size, with two rooms downstairs and two above. One of the downstairs rooms is set aside as a summer apartment, for when the sun shines hot against the front of the house the temperature within is raised to an uncomfortable pitch. The other is the general living-room, constituting dining- and sitting-room and kitchen together. The furniture of the room consists of a large deal table, an ancient sofa covered with faded red cloth, a chest of drawers, and half a dozen chairs, including the arm-chair by the fireside, in which no one else must presume to sit when the carter is at home. Standing within the door is an old-fashioned oak folding table, the envy of the dealers who pass by, who constantly make advances to the carter's wife and implore her to sell it, but to no purpose.

"Do you want to get rid o' that owl' table, mother?" the dealers ask.

"No. Shan't sell 'e. 'E's years an' years owld, 'e is, if anybody knowed the ins an' outs o' that owld table. Ther'd be jest about a 'ow d'e do if I was to get rid on in. 'E was left to mine bi 'e's grandmother, an' I knows 'e'll never pert wi'n," she replies.

As is usually the case in the poor man's cottage, what is lacking in furniture is made up for in pictures and ornaments. There are no less than fifty ornaments on the mantelpiece. They are of all sorts and dimensions, but are chiefly old-fashioned stone figures and pieces of quaint chinaware, many of them interesting, and some highly valuable. Foremost among them are two fine old images of Tom King and Dick Turpin, the robbers, which the dealers have often tried in vain to buy; the modest sum of eleven shillings for the two was not enough to tempt the carter's wife to sell them.

As with ornaments, so with pictures and photographs; there are nearly a hundred hanging upon the walls of the living-room. Of these the most conspicuous are a reproduction of "The Stolen Duchess," in colours, and two old Scriptural prints—"The Finding of Moses" and "Moses in the Land of Midian." The mirror, before which the carter has his weekly shave, is marked with the name of a certain Embrocation, warranted "Good for Cattle," and the covering over the back of the good-wife's chair is a piece of hand-wrought embroidery depicting Joseph's flight with the infant Christ into Egypt. Hanging up are a hempen halter and a great horn lantern for use in the stables; upon the floor are a long brass-handled whip and a flag dinner basket.

The carter is a strong-made man, with broad shoulders, short, thick neck, massive head, and square face, and he has a loud, deep voice, just the kind to terrify the ploughboys when they have been guilty of any misdemeanour. His wife is a portly dame, honest and homely, whose chief pride is in keeping a clean house and having everything ready for her "man" when he comes home at meal-times and in the evening.

Their family is twelve in number—six sons and six daughters—though they are all grown up and away from home now. Of the sons one is a sailor, three are soldiers, and the others railwaymen. The daughters are either married or in situations, and do not come home very often. As neither the carter nor his wife can read or write there is little correspondence between them. The eldest son writes them a letter once a year—at Christmas; then they get one of the neighbours to come in and read it to them and write out a reply. Yet, in spite of many hardships suffered during a laborious life, the carter is bright and cheerful, and is able to tell a merry tale and recount several quaint customs of which he had heard his father speak, but which have been discontinued of late years.

One of these was that of " Chasing the Cock." It was the practice, on New Year's Day, for all the ploughmen to come home from the field at noon and stable their horses. Then the head carter, carrying the plough-spanner and a wooden wedge in his hand, and followed by the under ploughman and boys, proceeded to the kitchen, and laid them on the table before the mistress with the remark, " Now for the owl' cock, Missis ! " or

" Rain or shine, the cock's mine."

After that the carter and his mates went outside and chased the cock round the farmyard for ten or fifteen minutes and then came into the kitchen and sat down to a substantial meal. There was no more ploughing that day. The afternoon was spent in the stables, cleaning the harness. On the morrow they went out, stronger and braver, to plough the regulation acre, provided the weather and land were favourable.

There is a conundrum many carters love to propose to you, if you are on friendly terms with them and have time to give to their simple requests. This is— " How much will it cost to shoe a horse, starting at a farthing a nail and doubling it each time to the end, counting seven nails to each shoe ? " At first sight it seems that quite a modest sum would be sufficient to settle the bill, but those who care to work the matter out will find that a considerable figure will be needed to pay off the score.

FLAVOURING THE BROTH

At one place where the carter worked as a boy the old farmer was very eccentric. When harvest-home came round one year and the fires were burning brightly in the brewhouse and beneath the big copper boiler, he peeped through the shutters and was astonished to see the master throw an old pair of boots into the boiler among the meat and vegetables. Accordingly, when supper-time came and all the men were busy at table, he alone would not touch anything, but pretended to be sick, and lay on the ground during the meal. The next day he told the men what he had seen, and they gave him a good thrashing for not speaking about it earlier.

A rustic, notorious for his appetite, was accredited with eating a monstrous quantity of fat bacon; it was said that he could devour four pounds at a meal. To test the veracity of the report two farmers determined to put his appetite to the test. They arranged for him to go a journey of eight miles; at each end he was to be given four pounds of bacon with bread. It says something for his digestive ability that he ate the whole and then had a good tea on reaching the cottage.

At another time a teamster came home with a load of ashes the worse for liquor. Thereupon the farmer scolded him for his indulgence. Nettled by the master's remarks, the carter seized the bridle, led the horse quickly into the narrow barn, turned the waggon round sharply, and came out again.

"Yellock! Thee coussent do that," said he.

"No more coussent thee, if tha hassent bin drunk," the other replied.

Old Ambrose Archer, of Quenington, had three hoes which he used according to the price he was being paid for the job. One of these was for 2s. 6d. an acre, one for 3s., and the other for 5s. an acre.

"Good morning, David! Raw air this morning!" said the visitor to a rustic.

"Aa, 'tis, you! Dwun suppose a bin biled awhever," he replied.

And again—"Fine morning, John!"

"Marnin's all right cf thee't let un alone!"

So also with the farmer who addressed the labourer one cold winter's morning:

"Mornin', James! Fine mornin', James!"

"Fine marnin's no good wi' no bren cheese in the cubberd, maester," James answered.

A villager was going to the workhouse to obtain relief there, when someone addressed him:

"Good morning, Etherd!"

"Oy! Oy! I'm a-gwoin on yander. Some on 'em got girt sticks in ther faggots, but I got none in mine," replied he, meaning some people had meat in their broth, but he had none in his.

"Now thee zee I knock that owl' cow into tha millbruk," said the foolhardy young ploughman to his senior one day, when they came to a cow standing on the edge of the river. So he took off his hat and rushed straight at the cow. Immediately she shot forward and the inevitable happened—head first went the foolhardy yokel into the stream, out of sight beneath the eddying water.

"Well! 'Ow tha dist knock un in, you. Tha coussent a done't better cf tha'st a-tried at it," his mate exclaimed.

A few evenings since John came in early from work and took off his boots, "to rest 'is vit," as he said. It is no wonder they were tired, for his boots weighed over twelve pounds. Asked what he had been doing, he said he had been on Fuzzy Hill ploughing with "one bull single."

A DISPUTED PASSAGE 171

The carter on the farm where John worked as a boy was " a very steern man," and the ploughboys were sure of a thrashing when they came late to the stables. Many a time John had stopped on the road and fought with his youthful mate to see which should " have it first " when they got to the farm.

One carter would never descend to the thrashing business, though the boys were never so late. Instead, he made them sit down till breakfast-time and then loaded them with the heaviest set of trace-harness he could find, and made them carry it to and fro in the stables during the meal-hour.

Another teamster was singular in never using a lantern in the stable, not even on the darkest night. When he went to " wrap his horses up " he felt his way about the stalls. As for his horses, he could recognise them anywhere simply by feeling their tails!

One day a travelling salt, on his way from Gloucester to London, was taking a short cut across Farmer B——'s field. When he was half-way over the farmer galloped up behind him and cried :

" 'Owld on ! Ther's no road yer acraas my land."

" Oh ! Thy land, is it ? And how comes it to be thy land ? " said the salt.

" 'Twas left to ma bi mi faather," the farmer answered.

" And how did he come by't ? " the sailor inquired.

" 'Ad it from 'es foorefaathers afoore 'e."

" And where did they get it ? "

" Why ! fowt for't, 'e s'pose," the farmer replied.

" Very good ! If thee't get off that 'oss I'll fight thee for't, but I shan't go back for nobody," the salt answered.

Hearing the story told of the rustic who stole the

butter and hid it in his hat and was then forced to
sit in the chimney corner till it melted and ran down
his head and face, the old carter grinned and said,
" 'A'd better bi 'aaf to a put it in 'is britches pocket."

This is how John and Harry cured father's pig of
jumping out of the sty when they were boys. First
they took it, one by the fore and the other by the hind
legs, and stood still a moment.

" Gie 'n a swing, 'Arry, an' knock 'is owl' yed agyen
the wall," said Jonathan.

" No! Mustn't do that," Harry replied.

" Come on! One, two, three, and away," cried
John, and with a swing they let go the porker and
dashed it against the wall. For a moment the pig lay
on the ground, shaking its forefeet convulsively;
then it became very still.

" Bin an' done for'n now. We be in for a dreshin'
dareckly," said Harry. The porker was only stunned,
however, and it soon revived, but it never climbed
out of the sty afterwards.

The carter had been seriously told by a waggish
blacksmith that the foundations of Fairford Church
were built of bricks made with stubble by the
Israelites in King Pharaoh's time and brought from
Egypt to England in the days of the Romans, which
account he sincerely believes, notwithstanding the
laughter of his wife and family.

From Fairford the crystal Coln, leaping merrily
over the large stones that lie along the bed and
shelter the wily trouts, flows down to Whelford,
where it pauses a moment to turn the machinery of
the mill and then hurries off beneath lines of graceful
willows and aspens. At about every half a mile is
a foot-bridge, made of stout planks thrown across
the stream, with a small ash or withy pole affixed

as a hand-rail. They are constructed chiefly for the convenience of anglers, in order to allow them to pass from side to side, though they are also used by the rustics to cut off a corner, or to attend to the hatches placed at intervals to flood the fields in the winter and spring of the year.

At the division of the fields a barrier is usually set to prevent the cattle from wading through and trespassing on the adjoining lands. In several cases the barriers are made of parts of an old steam-plough cable, drawn across from side to side and fixed to posts at a height of about two feet above the face of the water. If the heifers standing in the river should place their heads beneath these and lift them up, they might easily enter the next field, but they never do so, preferring to stand with their heads held over and the wire pressing hard against the dewlap.

Water-meadows extend to a distance of a mile from the stream. The land lies low, while the river, supported by banks of earth and gravel, is conducted at an elevation, with the object of forming a bay and obtaining sufficient fall to drive the machinery of the mill half a mile farther down. Trouts—they may be of a good size—occasionally escape through the hatches and work their way to the extremity of the field in the winter, when the meads are flooded. This is their spawning-time and the close season: they would not be able to get through the gates at any other part of the year.

Every autumn, while the springs are low, the coarsest of the weeds are cut, the gravel flams dragged out of the river-bed, and the materials piled along the banks to strengthen them during the winter floods. In order to sever the weeds scythe-blades are riveted together and a rope is affixed to each end. Two men, standing one on each side, manipulate these, drawing them backwards and forwards and proceeding steadily up-stream. Sometimes a trout, heedless of the commotion in the weeds, and slow of movement, is cut in two by the sharp blades and becomes the prey of the workmen, though this does not often happen.

Otters, though not uncommon in the Coln, are seldom taken with gin or trap upon the banks. Moving as they do for the most part in the night, and concealing themselves by day in hollow trees and inaccessible places, they easily escape the notice of passers-by.

Otter-hounds come and beat up the Coln and Leach, and work round the small brooks three or four times a year, and usually kill a few animals. Occasionally, when the hounds are hard on the tracks of an otter, they start a hare out of the long grass or rushes and leave the otter to chase that through the fields. Though constantly diving in the sharp clear water and brushing through reeds, flags, and grasses, the otter is yet tormented with parasites ; there are usually several large tics clinging to the back of its head and neck when it is captured by the dogs in the river.

Snipes and wild ducks frequent the water-meadows. Kingfishers are numerous and may be seen flying up and down the village street among the houses at almost any hour of the day, or watching for minnows in the feeder that runs parallel with the road. Another bird, a little larger than the bullfinch, with white underparts and rump, occasionally visits the banks of the Coln and Upper Thames during the winter. This is locally known as the " ossmatch."

AN ORDERLY BLACKSMITH

The auriole is another visitor; this I have seen at Inglesham, in the summer-time.

Whelford lies a short way back from the Coln. The hamlet, never very lively—for the population is small and the situation is on a narrow by-road—seems more than usually quiet to-day. The teams are all afield, getting ahead with the tillage; the shepherd is busy with his flock among the sainfoin; and the cowmen are gone to milking. The good-wives are indoors, kindling the fire and preparing the evening meal against the return of the toilers, and the children are not yet come from school. Every few minutes the brilliant kingfisher darts across and disappears through a gap low down in the hedge, and the pretty dace shoot to and fro, or make little rings on the surface of the rivulet. Only the sound of the blacksmith's hammer on the tinkling anvil, the hum of the mill machinery, and the musical rippling of water beneath the river-arch are heard.

The village smithy, though small, is not pokey within, as is sometimes the case with the rustic forge. This is because of the blacksmith's sense of order, and his dislike of having things in a muddle. He likes to see everything in its proper place and neatly arranged, so that he can find his tools and uses on the shortest notice, and not be compelled to turn out several corners and rummage among heaps of rubbish in search of them. But it is remarkable what self-possession most blacksmiths have, and how patient they are under circumstances that would drive many people to distraction. No matter in what frenzied haste the farmer may be to have his horses shod, or the traces mended, he must abide the smith's own time and not attempt to hurry him.

If he does, he will only hinder matters. The man with the hammer has one pace at which to work, and will not be hustled, but is calm and unmoved and master of the situation.

Conspicuous in one corner is a stock of old bicycle wheels, spindles, cranks, and brake levers, and a bunch of cones held on a wire suspended from the wall. These testify to the variety of work the country smith is called upon to do nowadays; he must be prepared for anything that comes his way. Sometimes the ploughing engines stop to have a chain welded and the gear set right. Perhaps the motor lorry is out of condition and wants seeing to, and, though the chauffeur of the rich man's motor is usually able to keep his own machinery in order, he is sometimes glad of the blacksmith's help to heave the car out of the deep ditch at the sharp corner just below the forge.

Another interesting collection is half a hundred keys, of all shapes and sizes, threaded upon a long wire and hung from a nail in the wall. These the blacksmith keeps in case of emergency; it sometimes happens that a cottager breaks or loses the key of his door and cannot get inside the house. In such a case he goes to the smith and searches among his stock of keys till he finds one that will fit his lock, and so saves himself further trouble and expense. To him the woodman brings his axe in order to have it tempered and a new shaft fitted; the quarryman fetches his picks to have them pointed and hardened; the churns and milk-pails come from the farm to be soldered, and the cottager's fender, fire-irons, or bedstead are brought along to be welded or riveted. In future the local blacksmith will be required to exercise his skill upon yet more complicated machinery, of which some are beginning to be aware : I recently stopped before a jobbing establishment in a neighbouring town to take a second look at a notice board fixed high upon the roof, and containing the significant words, painted in big letters :

AEROPLANES REPAIRED.

The Greeks did not shoe their horses, nor do very many farmers in our own country to-day if they can get along without it. Very often they have the fore-feet shod and leave the hind ones, especially in the case of horses that only work on the land, and have no occasion to use the hard roads. This is a sign of the times, and is done to curtail expenses, though it is an experiment that often fails and one that may cost the farmer double and treble in the end, through injury to the feet and subsequent lameness of the animal.

Not all horses like being shod. Very often it proves both a difficult and a dangerous proceeding to supply a new set of irons to a mettlesome animal; but the smith is used to their behaviour and usually finds means to finish the task. A tripod stands beside the anvil : upon this the hind leg is set while the smith fits the shoe and drives in and clenches the nails. "If you treats the horses well they'll treat you well; but if you're rough wi' they an' knocks 'em about, you can be sure they will kick out an' land you one on the sly some day or other," says the smith.

Here the conversation is cut short by the arrival of one who has an urgent job for the smith to do, which is to come to his premises and ring a couple of young pigs. They are just beginning to throw the troughs about and are become otherwise troublesome with their snouts, and so much nasal activity must be checked ; there is no other way of doing it but by presenting each with a ring.

  Who would have thought the fire had gone out in such a short space of time ? But it is a small matter to light it ; a bit of newspaper and half a match-box will kindle it again. Accordingly the smith rakes away the dead coals from the nose of the bellows, lights the paper, and covers the whole with half-burnt cinders. Now he grasps the handle of the bellows—a large curved cow's horn worn very smooth—and puffs away : in a moment he has a bright fire burning. To make the rings he takes two new horse-nails, heats them, flattens the heads on the anvil and makes them concave. Then he rounds off the stems and files them smooth, holding them in the vice and making the tips nice and sharp to accelerate their passage through the gristly snout. In less than ten minutes the rings are ready, and the smith, after damping the fire with a mop, takes a stout rope provided with a slip to hold the pig by the mouth and departs with the cottager. In the evening after tea, he will come back and hammer out a few new shoes by fire-light, or do a little soldering, not that the job is urgent, but because he is happy in doing it, for he is his own master, and independent.

  The mill is of ancient foundation, dating from before the time of the Domesday survey. In years past a monastery stood at one end and was inhabited by the friars, who had charge of the grinding : monks and mills seem to have been very closely associated during the Middle Ages. Four hatches bay back the stream. Behind are four conduits, fitted with iron

AN UP-TO-DATE MILL

gratings, which are raised by day and lowered by night. They serve to catch the slippery eels that sometimes come down the stream and swim over the hatches. Once over the doors and on to the grating there is no chance of escape for them: down they slide clear of the water and fall wriggling into the trap, to be taken out by the miller in the morning.

To-day the trouts are very busy in the shallows, where the water is not more than several inches deep now that the stream is low. They are preparing to spawn, and are leaping and wriggling about, with their backs and tails out of water, lying first on one side and then on the other, and making such a merry splashing noise as to astonish the pert-looking blackbird that has come on to the flam yonder to pick up a few sweet mouthfuls. The redbreast and wagtail keep him company on the flam and gather up the insects; there is no lack of food for them at any time of the year.

The machinery and fittings of the mill are modern and up-to-date. The old wooden water-wheels have been removed, and in place of them a turbine is installed. This is altogether better; it turns more rapidly, wastes less water, and it occupies considerably less space. In the case of the two old wheels, nearly the whole of the ground floor was taken up with gear, which was necessary in order to obtain the requisite speed for the stones. Now, however, one upright steel shaft from the turbine, fitted with a single cog at the top, is sufficient.

The mill has been in the occupation of the same family for more than two centuries, and is one of the busiest in the locality of the Upper Thames. When every other mill-wheel for miles around was stopped at the end of a hot, dry summer those on the

Coln could still go merrily round, so inexhaustible is the supply of water that leaps from the heart of the stony Cotswolds.

> "It is an amusing thing
> To see a mill in full swing;
> The wheels they run so fast,
> And they caught a *miff* at last."

This is a rude rhyme told me by old Elijah when we chanced to be discussing the subject of the mill, sitting before a piled-up fire at his house one wintry night. I was bound to confess that I could not see the point of allusion in the lines, and as for a "miff," I had never heard of such a thing before. That was just what Gramp wanted me to say; afterwards he set about an explanation of the matter.

Down by the river, in a cottage not far from the mill, lived the cowman, his wife, and grown-up daughter. It chanced that the miller, a man of nearly forty years, fell in love with the young woman, who frequently went to the mill in company with her mother for a gossip and stayed late. Then the husband and father, a senseless clown, fell into a fit of jealousy and breathed dire threats against the miller, and abused his wife and daughter, who nevertheless continued their visits to the mill. One day he overheard his daughter say, "Mother, I shall never forget the miller." Then he denounced them both, and said he would go and see the miller himself.

He accordingly went to the mill and began to bluster, but the miller easily beguiled the rustic. "I can soon tell you what they gets at," said he. "If you knows anything about a mill, you know as there's a big wheel in a little house, and then a door, and some steps going up to a loft. In that loft there's another big wheel, and a roller fits the cogs, and your two women likes to get hold of he and hae a good swing all round un." Then the yokel went up the steps—he had never been inside a mill before—and when he saw the big wheel he thought he, too, would like to swing round it, which he attempted to do and got his hand crushed in the cogs. Immediately he put his fingers in his mouth, and, bolting out of the mill, made for home. His wife and daughter between them tied up his fingers and condoled with the victim. Then he said *he* should never forget the miller. That is what is meant in the rhyme by catching a " miff " (fool) at last.

CHAPTER XI

The Fatal Jackdaw Nesting—Hannington Wick—Kempsford—" The Lady of the Mist "—The Boatman—A Trip by Water—The Home-made Loaves—Rustic Medicines—Rhyme of the Shorthorn—Tales at the Inn.

OLD Elijah's cottage at Inglesham commands a pleasing view of the Vale above the Coln, looking west to Kempsford four miles distant. The scene is one of considerable charm, calmly and quietly beautiful. The winding river bordered with hawthorn clumps and the water showing in silvery patches, the broad meadows beyond, and the stately tower of Kempsford Church rising above the tree-tops in the distance form a delightfully harmonious landscape. Some things we admire and others we love. Grand mountains there are whose tops threat the sky, and whose broad bases form extensive valleys and give birth to many a cataract and mighty river; but the summits are stark and cold, the slopes and bases, where little or no life exists, are often barren and unbeautiful, and the rivers, foaming amid shattered rocks that look like the ruins of a world that has passed away, and strike terror into the heart of the beholder, are fierce and rude, icy, sterile, desolate and dangerous.

"My visit still but never my abode."

Gramp, though admiring the outlook as well as any, has his appreciation of it marred by the re-

THE FATAL ARGUMENT

membrance of something that happened when he was a boy. "I allus thenks o' the jackdaas when I ketches zight o' that owl' tower," says he. Then he goes on to relate how two farm boys climbed to the top of Kempsford tower in search of young jackdaws. When they reached the top—a hundred feet high—they looked over and discovered a nest in one of the gargoyles. Being unable to reach it by leaning over, one boy took the other's hand and supported him while he got through the battlement and stepped down to the nest, which contained six young birds. Then, in that perilous position, they began to argue over the division of the spoils.

"'Aaf an 'em be mine. I shall have 'aaf an 'em," said the one above.

"I knows tha ootn't have 'aaf an 'em, neether," the other replied.

"If I don' have 'aaf an 'em I'll let tha down," said the first.

"Let ma down, then, if thas likes, but tha ootn't have 'aaf an 'em," answered the other, and his crazy mate, not realising his crime, loosed his hand and he fell and was dashed to pieces on the hard stones beneath.

A bridge spans the river at Hannington Wick. Up to this point the stream is both wide and deep, but beyond the depth varies from ten feet to as many inches, and in the summer time "the bruk," as it is now called, is nearly dry in places. Formerly there were weirs at intervals up to Cricklade, but when the traffic in butter and cheese came to an end they were removed. The farmers said they kept the land wet and injured the pasture, and there was no very real need of them after the railways were made and the local trade in dairy produce ceased.

The farmhouses at Hannington Wick are old and picturesque buildings. They lie off the road and are surrounded with pools and dikes that do not become dry in the hottest summer. The deep ditches yield a heavy growth of reeds and rushes which are cut every autumn and used for thatching the ricks, and as litter for the cattle.

The little house martins delight to dwell beneath the eaves of the buildings; last year I counted no less than fifty nests packed as tightly as could be along the front wall of one of the sheds.

Moorhens, ducks, and dabchicks breed among the rushes and flags of the dikes. Here their nests are concealed, and they are free from disturbance by anglers and others who pass up and down the riverbanks and would interfere with the eggs and young. During the winter the birds repair in flocks to the Thames and are unmolested, except by an occasional visit from the farmer. Nearly every little pond has its pair of moorhens that hatch out two broods each year, and yet the birds do not appear to increase in number. A great many of the young fall victims to rats, pikes, eels, and otters that work up the ditches by night, which accounts for their disappearance.

During the floods widgeons, shelducks, goldeneye ducks and divers visit the meadows near the bridge. Not long ago a local farmer killed seven wild fowls at one shot as they were crowded on the shallow water. Shortly afterwards he was witness of an exciting combat between an otter and four herons, which was waged for the possession of a fish. The birds followed the otter for half a mile along the river, repeatedly beating it with their wings and striking at it with their long, sharp bills.

The word Kempsford is derived from Kynemeresford, which was the name of the village in times past. "Kyne" indirectly meant great, and "mere" stood for marsh, so that Kynemeresford probably meant "The Ford of the great Marsh." In the year 800, or thereabout, Ethelmund, King of the Wiccii, who inhabited what is now the county of Gloucestershire, led his army through the river at Kynemeresford to attack the Walsati under Wearistan, who dwelt in the present county of Wiltshire. In the engagement both chiefs were slain but victory fell to the injured Walsati.

The church is a noble structure and is the pride of the villagers from the vicar, squire, and farmer to the cowman, shepherd, and ploughboys that tend their teams in the stables immediately fronting the walls. The building dates from the Norman period and contains, in addition to portions of the original walls and doorways, many specimens of choice workmanship in the carvings and chevron work, the ornamental columns and arches, the lofty panelled oak roof, the lantern of the tower, and the splayed windows.

The amazing tower is of fourteenth-century work, with corner buttresses reaching to the top and terminating in pinnacles ten feet above the leaden roof. It is supported by pillars and arches, and the lantern is richly decorated with the arms of the Earls of Gloucester and Lancaster, and bosses and frescoes, unusual in a village church, and more frequently found adorning the interior of some stately cathedral.

Dr. Woodford, afterwards Bishop of Ely, was for some time Vicar of Kempsford. He was remarkable for his absent-mindedness. It is related of him that soon after coming to Kempsford, being in conversation with a farmer, he heard the word "ewe" articulated for the first time. " I am so glad to know how to pronounce that word. I have always read the passage ' e-wee lamb,' " said he.

Being in need of a horse he timidly approached a churchwarden and asked him to buy one—" A horse quiet to ride and drive and, I think, about fourteen or fifteen feet high," explained he.

The castle of the Duke of Lancaster stood near the river. There is a tradition to the effect that Kempsford was the site of a Royal Palace in Saxon times, and that John of Gaunt also resided here. Before the Conquest the manor of Kempsford was held by Harold; it subsequently came into the possession of the Earls of Lancaster. On the confiscation of monastic properties it fell into the hands of the Thynnes, and the old mansion was rebuilt in the time of James I. Nothing of it now remains but a solitary wall set with a large mullioned window, and a terrace converted into a green walk and believed to be haunted by the " Lady of the Mist," as she has been named by the villagers because she usually appeared floating above the river in the pale moonshine.

Lady Maud is said to have been the beautiful wife of Henry of Lancaster, grandson of Henry III. and nicknamed " The Actor," who came to Kempsford and wooed her in the grand old hall where she had dwelled with her father in the reign of Edward II. On the resumption of the Baronial Wars, Henry, instigated by his brother, and against the will of his wife, joined the Barons and, with him, fought against the king and was defeated in several minor engagements. Day by day stragglers from the beaten army, hungry and destitute, arrived at Kynemeresford, crossed the river at the castle, were

W. Dennis Moss, Cirencester.]
Kempsford Church and Porch; the scene of the fatal jackdaw nesting.

A MIDNIGHT TRAGEDY

helped to food and wine by the Lady Maud, and went their way. At last, one stormy night, her husband's brother, with a price on his head, came and craved food, rest, and concealment from his enemies that pressed hard upon his tracks. His brother Henry, said he, had escaped in another direction and, though safe, would not be there yet. Accordingly the Lady Maud, who alone had recognised her brother-in-law, took him and concealed him in a room at the end of the terrace and visited him with food and drink at midnight. For a while this went smoothly till a jealous guest at the mansion, coming to know of the presence of the stranger, and having tempted the pure-souled Maud and failed in his designs, posted off to Henry and told him of the midnight meeting on the terrace and accused the Lady Maud of infidelity. This brought the Earl home in haste, fierce to avenge the supposed unfaithfulness of his wife. Guided by his informant, one tempestuous night, he came secretly to the terrace and concealed himself in the dark boughs waiting for the supposed lovers. By and by his brother and the Lady Maud appeared. Then he rushed forward, struck down his brother, seized his wife, and hurled her over the ramparts into the deep waters of the Thames. On learning the truth, beside himself with grief, and fearful of being captured, he fled with his brother, put himself at the head of the Barons and was taken and executed at Pontefract, while his brother escaped to France and died in a state of misery and penury.

After that the Lady Maud, bare-headed, her hair floating loosely, her face pale, but clear and sweet, her eyes like stars on a moony night, wrapped in a thin mantle, with naked feet and sleeveless arms folded across her young breast, appeared moving along the face of the river in the grey mist and singing a sad sweet song that swelled over the dew-moist meadows and only ceased a little before dawn. Or sometimes she appeared in full womanly beauty and, springing gracefully upon the wall, with a piercing shriek leapt into the river and disappeared beneath the waters that foamed and raged along the sedgy banks. Her betrayer, haunted by a guilty conscience, became a monk, and when he died he was laid to rest in the chancel of the great grey church and a sculptured tomb erected over his remains.

Affixed to the outside of the north door of the church is a horse-shoe that records an interesting item of history connected with the place. It is said that when Henry of Lancaster, whose castle stood near the church, was leaving Kempsford through grief at the loss of his son, who was drowned in the Thames, his horse dropped a shoe which was afterwards nailed to the church door in memory of him. It is reported that a horseshoe to which is attached a similar story may be found in the centre of Lancaster town itself.

The village of Kempsford is poor in appearance. A single street runs from end to end of the place, and the cottages, many of them little, old dilapidated buildings, stand ranged in rows and groups, with doors opening on to the road. Half-way down the street is the village green, and in the centre of this stands a large elm, called by the inhabitants "stocks tree," and "crass tree," because it was there that the ancient market cross and stocks were formerly situated.

The canal, that cuts across from Inglesham to

Kempsford almost touches the river beyond the church and then continues away to Cricklade. There are several locks of great depth between Inglesham and Kempsford, and others occur at intervals to beyond the Thames Head. They bear witness to the constant rise towards the river's source; if the fall at each lock were carefully ascertained and a table given it would discover a declivity that would not be guessed by merely following the channel of the stream. The stones that compose the bases of the bridges are ready to tumble into the shallow water; the wharves are ruined, the towpaths deserted, and the bed is choked with vegetation.

"The closin' o' this canal was like takin' a link out o' the middle of a chain," says the old bargeman as he sits and calmly smokes his pipe, while his wife stitches away at a new shirt for her grandson, and looks over the top of her spectacles to note the effect of her good-man's words. For more than half a century they had lived in the barges. Backwards and forwards, year after year, they travelled with their burdens of corn, cheese, coal, stone, and timber, at one time frozen in for weeks at a stretch, at another aground for days in the dark tunnel, and again washed out into the mouth of the Severn by the boisterous tide. Yet, though they suffered hardships, they were fond of the life and were never so happy as when gliding through the beautiful meadows, or halting for the night in some secluded spot above the lock, where the spouting water gushes out musically of a warm summer's evening. Both the bargeman and his wife are stout and robust. "It don' look as if it 'urted arn an us, do it?" inquires the dame, with a broad smile, again looking up over the rims of her spectacles.

The most alarming accident that the old bargeman had experienced occurred at Bristol Docks. There he had his barge alongside a steamer that was taking on board sacks of corn, when one of the sacks, raised to a great height by the crane, slipped from the chain and, striking him upon the breast, threw him into the water and carried him to the bottom of the dock, twenty-five feet deep. On reaching the bottom he got free, however, and in less than half a minute from the time of falling he was on top again and was hoisted into the boat.

"Be 'e gwain to Cricklut, mother?" inquired the bargeman, Adam Twine, of the stout old dame who, with basket on arm, took the towpath at Marston bridge on her way to the town one afternoon.

"Aa, I be," she replied.

"If you likes to jump in you can ride. We be off directly," said he.

"Oh Lar'! I never bin aboord ship but I'll come wi' thee. 'Tool rest mi vit an' legs a bit," answered the old woman.

Accordingly she got in and went below and sat in the cabin, and the two conversed on various subjects. Meanwhile the boat had started noiselessly and without a tremor. The boy was at the rudder and the conversation was maintained. By and by mother became fidgetty.

"'Ow much longer bist agwain to be afoore thas starts?" she inquired at length.

"Afoore 'e starts!" exclaimed old Adam.

"Aa! cos I be tired o' waitin' yer. 'E could a got 'aaf-way ther' bi this time," she continued.

"We shall stop in two or dree minutes, mother," said the boatman.

THE HOME-MADE LOAF 191

" Stop another two or dree minutes ! Why essent a telled ma as tha wassent agwain to start afoore, nat kip anybody yer an' make a fool an ma. I could a got ther' bi now if I 'edna looked aater thee," cried she, burning with indignation.

Just then the boat gave a bump—they had come alongside the wharf.

" Yer us be, mother. You can get out now, an' mind not fall in an' be drownded," said Adam.

" Lark a massey! What! be we at Cricklut, then ? An' I didn' know as we'd a started," exclaimed she, stepping out of the boat in amazement.

Although the greater part of the country adjoining the Thames is pasture there is yet upon the slopes and levels a considerable quantity of arable land that produces heavy crops of wheat and barley. At the same time, it is common knowledge that milk is the more profitable investment in this country to-day, though many farmers make the admission regretfully, and think it is a pity it should be so. One old farmer, in order to prove that a good loaf of bread may be made from unadulterated English flour, baked large loaves of flour ground from his wheat, took them to market and set them in the open mouths of the corn-sacks, which were soon surrounded by a crowd.

" What d'ye call this thing here ? " inquired one.

" Well! This is a real English home-made loaf, if you want to know," the farmer answered.

" Why didn't 'e bring some cheese ? " another drily inquired.

" You can allus tell wh'er a man's a good maaster er nat bi 'ow 'is work-vawk stops wi'n er le-affs un," says old Shadrach, who lives in a roomy cottage at the far end of the village. Though this may be accepted as a general axiom there are exceptions to the rule. Many farm labourers have a natural inclination to rove from place to place, and cannot be cured of the propensity. The old system of fairs encouraged this tendency; the habit of going to be hired became ingrained in the men and youths. As the time came round they began to grow restless, as do birds at the season of migration; they were bound to obey the innate prompting and look about for new quarters.

An almost infallible plan of getting to know whether the men intended to stop at the farm or not was carefully to watch their gardens. If they were kept clean and well-stocked with cabbages and winter greens the farmer was persuaded that Bob or Jack intended to stay with him; but if none of these were planted and the plots were allowed to become untidy, that was a sure sign that the men would be on the move at Michaelmas.

Very often, too, the men would stop at a place but their wives will not consent to it; they have the same inclination as the husbands to change their quarters and experience " fresh fields and pastures new." One day, a little before dinner-time, a cowman came to the kitchen door and asked to see master.

" Can I 'ev 'aaf a day off, maaster ? " inquired he.

" Oh aa ! Thee cast 'ev 'aaf a day, Bob, if thas wants one. Anything the matter ? " said the farmer, guessing his intentions.

" No ! Don' know as 'tis, maaster."

" Anything I can do for tha ? "

" Nat as I knows on."

" Anything wrong wi' thi mates, or the cows ?

AN UNACCEPTED OFFER

Dost want more money, or what is it? Bist dissatisfied at all?"

"No! Nat I byent, but the missis is. A dwun' like the 'owse," he admitted hesitatingly.

"Dwun' like the 'owse? But 'tis a good 'owse."

"The rooms be too big bi 'aaf. 'Er dwun' like un."

"Well! I tell tha what I'll do. I'll come over an' 'ev a look round, and put some pertitions up an' make the missis comfortable, an' gie tha another shillin' a wik an' ten shillin's extra at Michaelmas. Think it over an' see 'ow tha's like that."

Thereupon Bob went away, apparently satisfied, and for a week said nothing more about leaving. Then he came to master again and told him it was no good, he did not feel settled, he thought he should go to fair and get another place. The story of his wife's dissatisfaction with the cottage in this case was invention. The roving fit was upon him; he could not resist the impulse to leave and find a new master.

The shorthorn herdsman is a clever little man, with fine features, soft, smooth voice, and merry sparkling eyes. He is quick of perception, is not backward nor yet too forward, with a ready supply of words, possessed of much useful knowledge of birds and animals, rustic work, life and lore, and abounding in fun and gentle humour. In stature he is but just over five feet. His shoulders are slightly bent with age, and he limps a little with one leg, the result of having a contracted muscle caused by an accident when he was a young boy. Naturally sharp and intelligent, his position as caretaker of the prize cattle, which brought him into contact with other people, helped to develop those qualities. Many strangers came to see the beasts, and the long journeys by road and rail taught him much that he would not have learned by staying in the village.

As well as being superintendent of the prize stock, he acted as commander-in-chief of the ox-teams when they were used for ploughing up the fields alongside the winding river.

"Thaay owl' oxen went as well as any 'ossen in the world, an' thaay was as deedy an' knowin' as ever you or I be. When I 'ed my owl' Champion an' Lion I didn't keer for the best 'ossen you could put up o' zide an 'em," says he.

Besides the oxen, Champion and Lion, there was the famous old bull Britain, that weighed a ton, and was equal in strength to a team of horses. When the engine and thresher were to be set, or an extra heavy load of hay or corn brought in from the field Britain's aid was invoked. Though all the others failed, if he was harnessed to the shafts the heavy weight was soon shifted. " Gee up, Britain ! Come agyen, Britain ! " shouted the herdsman, and the patient beast, bowing its neck to the yoke, pressed steadily forward and overcame the difficult task.

The herdsman's cottage stands at the bottom of the street, close beside the tiny inn. Its dull grey walls and roof of thatch, blackened with age, give it a dingy appearance from the outside, but the interior is bright and cheerful, thanks to the good-wife's cleanliness and care, and her desire to have the " old man " comfortable. There are four fair-sized rooms—two upstairs and two down—to the cottage. The furniture and ornaments are above the average for a labourer to possess, and the whole go to make up an interesting lot, though nothing is held in higher esteem than a certificate for rick-building, formerly gained in the local competition. As soon as the herdsman reached home with this he took it to show " missis " and " our young miss," and she declared it must have a suitable frame and paid for one out of her own pocket. A flitch of bacon, wrapped in a newspaper, hangs on one side of the great old-fashioned chimney mellowing in the heat of the wood fire that smoulders beneath.

Many curious odds and ends are poked away in the sideboard and in the old oak drawers—quaint ornaments, photographs, and other things treasured for memory's sake, and last, the cottage stock of medicines, everything prepared of the mandrake, or bryony root, and purchased at the very last cattle show, at which the dealer—a specialist in uses of the root—has a stall every year. Here are boxes of pills and ointment, embrocation to be rubbed in for sprains, rheumatism, and stiffness, tonics for indigestion, a bottle of smelling " salts," and powders for headache and toothache, warranted to cure in a moment.

"Ther' yent no headache stuff ther', is it ? " inquires the good-wife, looking up from her newspaper, that she is reading by the aid of two candles.

" Yes 'tis, fer 'edache an' all an't," the herdsman replies, rummaging amongst the papers in the drawer.

" Oh Lar' ! I wish I'd a know'd that this marnin', then, for I was purty nigh crazy wi't," says she.

" Then thee oostn't a tuk it," the cowman answers, while the mistress smiles benignly and continues reading the newspaper.

Presently the herdsman, after expatiating on the subject of flocks and herds, breaks into rhyme, and delivers the following verses, of his own composition, upon the features and qualities of a perfect Shorthorn beast.

THE PRIZE SHORTHORN.

"He's broad in the rib, and long in the rump,
With a straight and flat back, and never a hump,
Deep in the chest, and thick in the thighs,
Clear in the nose, and mild in the eyes;
Full in the flank, and well up in the chine,
Straight in his joints, before and behind,
With a long silky coat, and thick in the skin,
He's a grazer without, and a butcher within."

This rhyme was composed, without pen or paper, as the herdsman went about his work in the yards and stalls, or as he lay a-bed at night, and was first of all communicated to old Shadrach and the shepherd, sitting in the small room at the little Axe and Compass Inn, at which they delight to meet now and then and talk over the day's experience, and see which can tell the quaintest item of news, jest, or story. By far the greatest part of the talking is done by the herdsman, however, while little Shadrach, with white corduroy suit, clean-shaven lips, and thin fringe of grey beard, sits smiling across the narrow table, proud to be in the others' company and to listen to their "oondermenting," as he calls it.

"'Tis instinct as doos it wi' tha beyassten, else 'ow ood thaay know?" says the herdsman, discussing the characteristics of the animals under his charge in the stalls. "Ther's thaay caaves! I can gie thaay the vly in the middle o' winter wi'out ever touchin' an 'em."

"Gie 'em the vly in the winter? Never yerd tell o' that afoore," says Shadrach.

"Tha's yezzi enuff," answers the herdsman. "I goes out in the paddick an' carrs 'em a bit o' 'aay in one 'and. When I gets to 'em, I jest begins buzzin' like a beg vly—'Z-z-z-z-z,' an' drives 'em silly. As I ses, it must be instinct, cos we all knows as there's no vlies about in the winter."

One day the herdsman is sent for in a great hurry to go down to a neighbouring farm, where a strange accident has happened. A milking cow, in trying to leap a gate, has got half-way over and is hung on the top spar, with all four feet off the ground, and no efforts of the farmer or his men can avail to get her clear of the gate. But it is an easy task for the herdsman. He goes to the cow, puts one shoulder under her belly and gives a good grunt and a heave, and she, straining in sympathy with it, leaps over the gate.

One here relates the Cotswold jest of the town youth who had come to learn dairy work. He, being provided with a stool and appointed to milk a nice quiet cow, went into the yard as directed. By and by the farmer at the top end of the yard heard a scuffling noise and went to see what was the matter. Arrived on the scene he found the youth struggling violently with the beast.

"What b'e got at wi' 'er? Why don' 'e let the cow bide?" said he.

"I can't get the old hussey to sit down, sir," replied the youth.

"Now get ready to yer a good lie, if you never yerd one afore," says the herdsman, with an artful smile, whereupon little Shadrach pricks up his ears and the shepherd pays stricter attention, gripping his staff firmly with both hands and leaning his chin hard upon it.

"Is this a true lie, or a damn lie?" inquires Shadrach, with a wink at the shepherd.

" 'Tis true as I yerd un, but I can't vouch far'n no further than that," replies the herdsman.

"As I was going to Romford, 'twas on a market day,
I saw the finest ram, sir, that ever was fed with hay,
The wool upon his back, sir, reached up into the sky,
And in it was a crow's nest, for I heard the young ones cry.

'Twas there I bought a flock of sheep, the finest ewes and wethers,
Sometimes they bring me wool, sir, and sometimes they bring feathers,
And I swear, by good St. Oswald, at every change of the moon
They bring me a pair of lambs, sir, each one of them full soon.

And there I bought me a little bull, nine yards round or more,
Such a pretty little bull, sir, you never saw before,
But when I drove him up the street he set up such a sound
That all the walls of London came tumbling to the ground."

" 'E was begger than thy owl' Brittin, then," says Shadrach, while the shepherd, tickled with the notion of the fine ram and ewes and the wonderful fleece thick enough to conceal a crow's nest, laughs immoderately and thumps on the table with his fist to summon the landlord with a full cup, at the same time crying loudly: "Thaay was Cotswuls! Thaay was Cotswuls! Ther's nothin' like the Cotswuls fer big jints an' fleeces."

There is a story of two Kempsford men who set out for Ciceter Mop, intending to put up at the inn the night before the fair and spend a full day among the games and shows. Arriving there early in the evening, they drank too deeply of the home-brewed liquor and the landlord put them to bed, over the stables, where they slept all through the next day and night till the following morning and woke up to find the mop over and the streets deserted.

"Faather," said the cobbler's son to his sire one night, on seeing a half moon in the heavens high above the grand old tower that stands by the river, "what is it when the moon channges? What do thaay do wi'n? What becomes an in, I should like to know?"

"Damn tha! Tha byets un up inta stars, dwun 'em," the irate parent replied, hammering away at the sole and leaving his offspring with a look of great stupidity depicted upon his countenance.

CHAPTER XII

Squire Archer, of Lushill—The Vanishing Stag—Castle Eaton—Tragedy of the Roach, Heron, and Fox—"Darby and Joan"—Queen Victoria's Coronation Dialogue—The Trout Stream—The Landlord and the Farm Boy.

JOHN ARCHER, of Lushill, was the best known of all the worthies of the Upper Thames Valley.

Men of stronger individuality than he possessed there certainly were. Squire Campbell, of Buscot Park, was a vigorous and indefatigable farmer and experimentalist. His chief qualities, however, had a commercial bent. He was essentially a man of business and was lacking in the picturesque. Lord Radnor, of Coleshill, though a well-known figure, was a stern and trenchant politician, and was never on terms of real intimacy with the farmers and villagers who were his neighbours alongside the Cole. Squires Calley and Akerman, of Blunsdon, were of a different order. They quarrelled, pulled up each other's fences and caused the cattle to stray, and strove to see which could squander most money and gain the greater reputation for liberality, but their estates and influence were small, and their fame never travelled far beyond the actual village.

Squire John, however—the people invariably called him "Jacky," which name he acknowledged good-humouredly and often applied it to himself—combined most of the qualities usually found in the sporting lord of the manor. He was courteous and

THE VILLAGE SQUIRE

amiable to farmers and labourers alike, was possessed of artistic tastes, and a *naïveté* which was refreshing and amusing, and which counterbalanced the few faults he had and at the same time endeared him to the villagers. John Archer was, in fact, a real old-fashioned squire, a little feudal lord, if you like, the father of his workpeople, and the pride of the neighbourhood. Whether at home in the circle of his intimate friends, in the field a-hunting, at market in the town, or about the farmyard, he was the centre of all attention—what John Archer said and what he did was, rightly or wrongly, looked upon as of very special importance.

Squire John sprang from an ancient stock. His ancestors were a hardy race, noted for the excellence of their farming and their passionate devotion to fox-hunting. For four centuries they had occupied lands round about the river, and had successively reaped the harvests of the bounteous old earth and steadily prospered.

John kept between forty and fifty teams of oxen for ploughing and general work on the land, and he paid £3500 in wages every year. He employed nearly the whole population of two villages, besides a small army of casual labourers, or " strappers." Whatever the weather, he desired to have everyone employed at some task or other. When it rained he supplied waterproof coats for the men out of doors, and he used to say in such circumstances : " I wants 'e all to stop at work if 'e can, and remember, if you can stand the weather I can stand the pocket." Farm wages were low at that period, and Squire John paid no more and no less than was the custom in the locality. When his labourers had become too old to work he pensioned them off ; he would no more have thought of sending them to the workhouse after their life had been spent in his service than he would of sending his favourite hound to a dog's home. The system was crude and economically unsound, but it was about the best of its kind at the time.

Squire John was a little, wizened old man, with a clear complexion, merry, inquisitive eyes, and strong white hair—in appearance he was about as shaggy as a terrier. He hunted three and four days a week, riding gaily off on his brown nag dressed in his well-worn familiar pink jacket and velvet cap, both of which, according to local tradition, had served him for forty years. On every other day of the week he rode about his farms mounted on a shambling pony with the reins hanging loosely over its neck, or, wearing the shabbiest of coats and hats, drove a pony and cart through the fields and lanes. He discovered his present mood to the workpeople by the position of his headgear—hat on forehead meant good humour; hat on poll meant ill humour. Though normally of a genial disposition he was " a okkard man to plaaze when a body 'ad 'uffed un," but he was easily reconciled, and it is admitted by the majority of the old labourers that " Jacky Archer was the best man as ever trod in Cassul Aeton." In the evening, after a day's hunting or a ride over his farms, he dressed for dinner in front of a fire of logs in the dining-room, and when the meal was over he propped himself up on the sofa and perused the *Times*, while his daughters played to him on the harp. He kissed all the young girls and pretty women openly and publicly. This he considered to be his prerogative, and he exercised it without taking into account the lady's social rank and position.

The residence of the Archers was at Lushill. Here a survey could be had of the meadows and cornfields with the busy toilers at work in the summer and autumn. Standing on top of the hill the squire could see the hay being gathered, the ripe corn felled by the reapers, and the teams of mottled oxen at plough, and could send out instructions to this or that one as a general, posted on an eminence, overlooks his troops and marshals them for battle on the plain. A certain amount of country house state was maintained, and Squire John received many visitors, among whom was the worthy Dr. Woodward, of Kempsford, who frequently crossed the river in his boat and wended his way to Lushill to take dinner and discuss theology with the farmer squire. John, who was a staunch follower of Keble, was often assailed in the field and the town by local leaders and exponents of evangelicism, but he replied to them boldly and answered all arguments with quotations from a Bible which he carried in his pocket so as to be equipped for any emergency.

The squire was possessed of a keen instinct for farming, which was not at all blunted but rather sharpened by his devotion to fox-hunting : he used to declare that he earned fifteen shillings every time he went out with the hounds simply by looking round other people's farms and studying their methods. " To be a good farmer you must look round the outside of things and try and keep your workpeople satisfied. I pay twenty pound a week for no return, and it's no good for any man to think of getting on without putting his hand deep into his pocket," he would say. He sometimes complained to the blacksmith about the expenses of the farms and the difficulty of making both ends meet, but the man of the forge answered him boldly, and told him he had so much wealth he was unable to calculate it.

Although John was a peaceable subject and a loyal churchman he nevertheless had a long-standing quarrel with the Vicar of Castle Eaton. This was concerning a piece of glebe alongside the river, to which the squire laid claim, but the parson, fortified with documents, stoutly opposed him. By and by the parson took his revenge. In the middle of hay-making rain set in, and the river, overflowing its banks, washed a field of hay from John's side over to the parson's glebe where it lodged, and the vicar, when the water subsided, hired labourers to dry it and had it carted home to make into ricks for his own horses. That ended the dispute of the glebe. The parson had scored a point, and John was content to let the matter drop.

When the squire got old and feeble he grew sad at heart, and felt concern for the welfare of his farms and workpeople. With his companions of the hunting-field long departed this life, the conditions governing agriculture rapidly changing, and machinery displacing hand labour on the land—though he clung to the old methods when all others around him had cast them aside—he became melancholy and despondent. "I'm above the age of man, and when I'm gone I've got nobody to see to it as I like to have it done. No man will carry on my business successfully and keep things together when I'm gone," said he, which remark, though it might have seemed impertinent at the time, was justified by subsequent events. "Give my love to my people," were the squire's last words as he sank breathless upon the pillow. His mortal remains were borne from Lushill to Down Ampney, by roads which he had travelled for upwards of eighty years, and the bells that rang at his wedding, sixty years before, sounded a muffled peal as he was laid with his forefathers of ten generations.

A century and a half before old David Archer, John's ancestor, bought the estate the house at Lushill was occupied by one Squire Parker—a forbear of Archbishop Parker—who was a great hunter of deer that used to run wild about the vale and along the hills lying up from the river. There was one stag they often chased but which they never could take. No matter how swiftly the dogs ran, the stag always disappeared very mysteriously, baffling the efforts of the huntsmen. Then one day Squire Parker swore a terrible oath: to-morrow he would hunt the stag again and would not rest until he had secured the antlers. Accordingly the hounds and horsemen went forth early in the morning, the squire in his merriest mood, and all the others intent on the chase. All through that day they ran up and down, and round and round, over the river and back again, plunging through the thickets and scrub, and still the stag was untaken, though the squire swore by all the powers in heaven that he would not desist. Presently sunset came, by which time everyone else, with the exception of the squire and a strange horseman, who rode neck and neck together, had dropped out of the chase. At last, having once more crossed the Thames, they came up with the stag at Lushill, and the squire seized it by the antlers, when he felt a sudden shock and the stag and strange horseman vanished together in a sheet of flame. In the morning Squire Parker was discovered on his lawn grasping the antlers tightly in his hands, but there was no sign of the stag or tracks of the horseman, nor was anything ever seen of them after that day.

The old early Tudor building—formerly the Manor House of Lushill—contained numerous relics of the deer-hunting, and the square hall was embellished with stag's heads—trophies taken by Squire Parker and his companions of the chase.

Castle Eaton is about a mile and a half below Lushill. It is a small but ancient place, very compact, and it lies high and dry of the river. In winter, when the country around is buried deep beneath the floods, the inhabitants of the village are themselves secure, though they were often isolated from the rest of the world. In early times the site of the village was an island, as is indicated by the name of the place. Formerly this was Eiton, or Ettone, made up of the Saxon words " ey " an island, and " ton," a dwelling or village. A later form of the name was Eiton Meysey. Afterwards the St. Maurs and the Zouches held the Manor of Eiton, the last-named of whom built a sumptuous castle upon the south bank of the river, and the village was called first Eiton Castle, and, subsequently, Castle Eiton. The old castle has long since been demolished and its site eradicated. No trace of the ruins exists in the meadows: there the fritillaries and purple orchis thrive and bloom, and the cattle graze quietly amid the rich pastures.

The village, viewed from the Thames' side, shows grey and hoary. The cottages, built of local stone, stand in little streets and squares, and the gardens slope down to the river's brink. The wells beside the doors are shallow, and are commonly surrounded with a low, dry stone wall, the appearance of which is suggestive of the Biblical East.

The church is a unique structure, Norman in design. It dates from the twelfth century and has round-headed doors, a font that is either early English or

Norman, and strong square tower. Above the nave is a fine Sanctus bell turret, roofed with stone, of considerable age. A mixed choir of men and women —toilers on the land—sang in the church and accompanied the rude orchestra. The duties of clerk devolved upon the hoary carter, who stood in the small gallery and announced the hymns and psalms in choice vernacular: " Lat us zeng to the praaze an' glary o' Gaad the 'underd an' vartieth Zaam," or whatever it might have been. A buxom young farm woman, who carted manure and picked stones the workaday part of the week, was the leading treble.

In a big hollow withy tree, below the church, an otter has had her litter of four; they were several times seen by the cowman as he went after his herd in the early morning hours. Growing along the riverbanks are loose-strife, hemp-nettle, and yellow cress; water-pepper and persicaria expand their foliage and float on the water, or push up their heads amid the lush grasses on the margin. About the mead bloom bed-straw and milk-vetch; the purple heads of the great burnet show conspicuous alongside the cream and rose of the dropwort.

Above the bridge the prospect is more open. The hawthorn clumps along the river's course are not so frequent, but the gnarled old pollard willows, bent and twisted, and with grotesque shapes resembling men and beasts, supply the deficiency and mark out the winding channel. Although comparatively near to the river's head there is no diminution in the breadth of the stream: it is almost as wide here as at Buscot, fourteen miles lower down, though the bed is shallower, and the current more swift. At every few dozen paces is a flam of sand and gravel that was washed up by the turbulent waters during the winter. These are cleared out and the tangled masses of weeds and vegetation—water-hemlock, cresses, and brooklime—cut and removed in July, so as to have the course clear and unobstructed against the advent of the floods.

What is that silvery patch upon the ground close beside the steep bank yonder? Drawing near I perceive it to be composed of the scales of a large roach that was taken from the water by a heron and devoured a few yards from a great withy-tree that hangs over a deepish pool. Quarter of a mile farther up-stream I discover a quantity of blue-grey feathers scattered about, which are unmistakably those of the heron. Gorged with its prey, it was seized unawares by a hungry fox that promptly devoured its victim and so saved the life of many another finny inhabitant of the sparkling waters. But a speedy fate overtook the nimble fox and brought it low before it had time to digest the meal. In less than half a mile I find reynard dead, and minus the brush, lying in the midst of the thick hedge where it had been unceremoniously thrown. On the ground, a short distance off, are a couple of empty cartridges that indicate the manner of its death and complete the chain of circumstantial evidence begun with the finding of the fish scales. Whether it deserved the charge or not is another matter: it was really a beautiful animal, with lovely golden fur and glistening teeth.

In a corner of the field, in which a large pile of loose thorn-bushes has been stacked, I chance upon a polecat with a small bird in its mouth. Now a large hare leaps from beneath a scrubby bush and races across the field, and a timid stoat darts out of the hedge and shoots back again. Out from the

IN THE FARMYARD

farmyard in the village, a mile distant, the sound of the thresher is borne, and, floating along in the wind, is an occasional thistle seed that was shaken out with the straw as it left the rear of the machine to fall into the box of the elevator and be hoisted upon the high rick.

For a week the men have been busy with the tackle in the farmyard. Rick after rick was attacked by the sturdy labourers, who first of all cut the tar-cord and pulled out the sprays that held the thatch and uncovered the stack: the machine had been set alongside and coupled up with the engine, about ten paces to the rear. The sheaves, thrown quickly down from such a height, fall on the deck of the thresher with a loud flap, and sometimes strike the feeder on the legs or shoulder, but he takes no notice and proceeds to cut the bond and pass the sheaf into the drum, distributing it as evenly as possible in the short space of time allowed for the operation. The conical top of the rick is soon removed and the height diminished; in two hours, with good luck, it will be reduced nearly to the level of the machine. An ordinary sized rick provides one day's work for the tackle and yields from sixty to eighty sacks of wheat, though John Archer's ricks yielded as many as a hundred and ten sacks. The size of the straw rick afterwards is much greater than that which contained the sheaves, for they were stacked in compactly and were well compressed together, whereas the straws, after passing through the drum of the machine, are crumpled and loose and take up much more room. If the wheat is in good condition a sack of grain will be run out in about four and a half minutes; if the ears are small and inferior the time required to fill the sack will be correspondingly longer. Yesterday the men threshed out seventy sacks of wheat in five and a half hours. This they considered good work; but the sheaves were unusually heavy, and the yield worked out at fifteen sacks to the acre.

The thresher is a prize model, made with the latest improvements of drum, fans, and screens—a simple yet beautiful piece of mechanism, running smoothly and easily under the power of the engine that is transmitted by means of the long heavy belt. A father and son are in charge of the machinery. They take the engine and thresher in turns, each alternately feeding the sheaves into the drum and seeing to the engine fire and boiler. The old man is very proud of the tackle, and tends it with a parental affection; the son is of a different temperament and looks upon it in the most matter-of-fact light, thereby marking the progress of a generation. The farmer frequently comes and stands before the sacks and catches the beautiful grain as it rattles down from the screen, and the workmen continually wheel away the full bags and stack them in the crowded barn near by.

In a cottage opposite the farmyard dwell old Thomas and Jane—the Darby and Joan of the Thames' side—who, though both within one year of a century, retain an active and intelligent interest in the life and work of the village, and especially in the threshing, which they can view sitting before their cottage window. Very different indeed are things now from what they were when these two were first wed. They have seen generations come and go and have outlived their own time, till they have become very strangers to the village in which they were born and to the scenes amid which they have so long dwelt.

TOM "WUTTS" THE BULL

Ninety-three years is a long time for a mortal to remember a thing, yet old Thomas's memory extends back so far. When he was six years of age he used to run into the farmyard to watch the men at work with the oxen and horses. One day, in the presence of old farmer Archer, the men were trying to yoke a big bull to a manure cart, but, try as they might, the animal would not back into the desired position. At last young Tom became impatient and, to the amazement of the men and the delight of the farmer, cried: " Let I 'ev a try, an' see if I can wutt un in." The farmer smiled at the youngster and exclaimed: " Go on ! Let the child try."

Accordingly, young Tom, who was so tiny that a good snort of the beast might have knocked him down, took the halter, cried " Wutt back ! " to the bull, and backed it into the shafts very simply and easily. Then old Archer laughed heartily at the youngster and told him to come into the stalls, and thereupon appointed him master of the bull and gave him three shillings a week in wages, which was double the amount received by the other boys who were older than he.

After that he took the oxen to plough, learned to sow, reap, and thresh, and performed the hundred and one duties of the farm. His wife's father was a maker of baskets and sieves for winnowing the corn in the barn after hand-threshing, and her mother was a lace-maker at a time when the cottage industries had not entirely disappeared from the region of the Thames Valley. A family of twelve followed their marriage; they have between two and three hundred grandchildren and great-grandchildren, and several sons who are in receipt of the Old Age Pension.

Of the two, granny is the more active and energetic.

Clad in an old faded gown, with woollen vest, a pair of knitted stockings, with feet cut off, drawn up the arms, and quaint little cap on the head, she hops to and fro with surprising agility, cleans the grate, sweeps up the floor, dusts the ornaments and pictures, and sees to her housework generally, while the old man grips his fork or spade and toils in the garden among the potatoes and cauliflowers. " I got a goodish spirit an' tha's what kips I up," says granny, while Thomas smiles approvingly, reaches his pipe, half burnt away, from the mantelpiece, fills it with tobacco, and lights it with a spill from the hob.

" I got to master'n now, same as 'e allus 'ed," granny says, with a triumphant little laugh and a knowing wag of the head, at the same time giving her husband a playful cuff. Gramp wears an old pair of trousers with patches half a yard long over each knee, a thick woollen overall, and a little brown felt hat, which he keeps on his head indoors and out.

Their daily mode of living and general routine are as follows: Rise at 7 a.m., breakfast at 8; dinner—a little meat, broth, bread, and potatoes— at noon; tea at 3.30; supper at 6, and retire at 7 p.m. Granny's breakfast consists of a basin of bread and water sops with a lump of butter and a little salt and pepper added. This she prepares every afternoon ready to heat in the saucepan the following morning. For supper she takes a cup of warm beer with bread; to this habit she attributes her long life and good health. Years ago they lived principally on butter, milk, and " skim dick," *i.e.* cheese made of skimmed milk, which form of diet may have been the cause of their attaining to such a great age. Old Thomas says they never felt the

THE CENTENARIANS 213

need of butcher's meat—it made them sick to eat it.

Every Saturday the big living-room in the cottage is subjected to an extra special turn out. The tables and chairs are moved aside, and granny, provided with pail, brush, and house-cloth, scrubs the stone floor and then whitens it with freestone, rubbing it round and round and describing many curious and fantastical figures that resemble a child's first exercise in caligraphy. This is performed early in the morning, before breakfast; then grandfather has to lie in bed an hour later so as not to obstruct the most important operation of all the week.

"Afore I married 'e," says granny, "I used to help missis in the dairy. I can remember 't as well as ef 'twas but isterdi. Maaster used to go to church every wik, an' one Sunday marnin', when us was all set at dinner, a turned to I an' sed: 'Byen you well to-day, Jane?'

"'Yes, I be all right,' I sed.

"'Cos thaay bin talkin' about you in church.'

"'An' a good job too! I don' keer what tha doos,' I sed to'n."

This was when the banns were published. Afterwards master and mistress subscribed and bought her a wedding gown, and made them a present of a side of bacon and a cheese that the cunning little mice had nibbled slightly with their pretty teeth.

Their wedding took place about the time of Queen Victoria's Coronation, which was celebrated in the little Thames' side village, and when several droll compositions were recited and committed to memory by the rustics.

"I say! Mrs. Fairplay, what do you think of our young Queen? I'm told she's going to do wonders in favour of the women. My old man told me he heard a man say another man had told him he heard one read it in a newspaper. There's going to be a Parliament of women. Mother Bounce is to be Prime Minister, Mrs. Grieveling Secretary for War, and Mother Chat-all is going to be Lady Chancellor. Can't make a Lord of her, you know. Every man that beats his wife has got to be locked up in an empty garret till he begs her pardon."

"Won't that be nice!"

"Yes! And that's not all. Every woman in England, Scotland, Ireland, and Wales is to have a gallon of gin to drink the Queen's health—when she can get it. For if the sea was all ink, the fishes of the sea all writers, the trees all pens, and the earth all parchment, it would not be enough to describe the good qualities of the women.

"So maidens, wives, and widows all merrily sing: 'Long life to the petticoats and Heaven bless the Queen.'"

Though October is nearly out, the weather is still delightful. From the heavens the sun shines warm and bright on the fresh meadows dotted with hawkbit, and on broad stretches of corn land and stubbles marked with the wheels of the heavy reaping-machine that levelled the golden waving crops two months since. The foliage of the leaves and hedgerows possesses a hundred tints—warm reds, pinks, crimsons, yellows, and varying shades of brown and purple. Brightest of all are the maple leaves. They fall early and leave their bare crimson twigs that show conspicuous in the hedgerow all the winter. St. John's wort and knapweed are yet in bloom, and willow-herb and hemp agrimony are to be found upon the bank. The flowers of the meadow-sweet have long fallen in snowy clouds and were succeeded by clusters of small green fruits upon which the birds feed.

In the wall of the bridge spanning the trout stream is a wasp's nest. Far advanced though the season be the wasps have not yet disappeared, but still continue to fly to and fro and sluggishly creep through the aperture into their cells within the dark recess. This year they have been numerous and very troublesome, destroying the fruit in the gardens and orchards and working incalculable mischief. Soon after midsummer they attacked the early plums and forced the farmers' wives to convert them into jam before they were fit. Afterwards they set about the sweet pears ripening under the warm walls, and, when they were gone, assailed the orchards and played havoc with the juiciest apples, stripping many of the trees.

In the gravelly stream that flows beneath the bridge a trout shoots like an arrow obliquely from side to side, pausing for about a second between each rush to obtain strength and direction for the next effort, and making a plunging noise adown the brook. Though the water is not deep there would be great difficulty in taking it, and should you force it down to the bay and think to corner it there, it might take a sudden spring and leap over the hatch and so escape on the other side. In and out among the oak-trees the magpies are hopping, and on the left are several teams at plough, creeping with a snail-like pace up the field. Over opposite, moving amid a sea of gossamer that gleams with a bronze tint, are some at drill, planting early wheat that must be up before the sharp frosts come in order to stand the winter and yield a big crop the following harvest.

Now one on horseback comes round the bend, walking on the greensward and taking a careful survey of the fields each side of the road. This looks like a steward of the estate, or it may be the landlord himself riding over his domain, though from the complacency depicted upon his countenance he is in a better way than was the one of whom the villagers speak in the story.

This landlord, as no rent was forthcoming for several quarters, determined to take a ride round and look up his long-winded tenants. He accordingly mounted his nag and trotted from farm to farm, but could not meet with anyone for some time. At last he came up with a boy, the son of one of the defaulting farmers, and addressed him.

" Where's thi father ? " said he.

" Oh ! He's gone to make a bad matter wuss," the boy replied.

" How's that, gone to make a bad matter wuss ? "

" He went to market yesterday wi' a cow, best cow we'd a got. Was in want o' money, an' a means to bide ther' till 'tis all gone."

" Is thi mother at home ? "

" Yes. Very busy bakin' the bread we ate yesterday."

" How's that, bakin' the bread you ate yesterday ? "

" Why ! 'er's bakin' some more in the place on't, to be sure."

" Thees got a sister. Wher's she ? "

" Upstairs, cryin' for want o' calico to make her a milkin' smock."

" Well ! " says the landlord, " if thee can'st come to my house neither daylight nor dark, neither a foot nor a hossback, neither naked nor clothed. I'll forgive thi father the rent."

When the squire had gone, the boy considered and eventually thought out a way to do it. He waited till the sun had set behind the wood, then took off his clothes, wrapped a calf net around him, jumped upon the donkey, rode up to the front door of the manor-house and challenged the landlord.

"Well! well! You've beat me. There! There! Go on about thi business and tell thi father there's no more rent due now till Christmas," said he good-humouredly.

CHAPTER XIII

Source of the Thames—Water Shortage—" Wassail " Song—Thames Head Villages—Cricklade—Election Scenes—" Open House " Expenses—A Local Execution—" Bark Harvest "—" Looking through the Rafters."

ALTHOUGH the Thames source is fourteen miles above Castle Eaton the river, in a general sense, is not recognised higher up than Cricklade. There interest and association, except for the enthusiast, practically cease. Navigation in any form is at present impracticable above the junction with the Churn. The great Roman thoroughfare of Ermin Street forded the Thames at Cricklade. By this road produce was brought from the Cotswolds on the one hand, and the Wiltshire Downs on the other, and shipped down-stream. For some miles west of Ermin Street good roads were lacking; it was therefore convenient that Cricklade should be the starting-point of the river's trade, though the stream was traversed by small barges to within a mile of Ashton Keynes.

There are several ways of accounting for the shortage of water in the Upper Thames as compared with what its supply was in earlier years. The clearing of the woods and forests from the hills around its source was an important factor in diminishing the size of the stream. The thickness of the woods and trees accelerated condensation, and rain fell in greater abundance than it does now. Lack of drainage and the prevalence of cumbersome hatches and weirs, that were almost fixtures, also blocked back the water. In the winter, owing to the impossibility of lifting the hatches, they occasioned terrible floods and were execrated, condemned, and finally abolished through the antagonism of farmers and holders of property on the banks. The Kemble pumps every day divert from the Thames between three and four million gallons of water, and sometimes the river is quite dry at Ashton Keynes, six miles down. This could not have happened in early times, or the buccaneering King Canute and the doughty Alderman Edric would never have got up to Cricklade with their fleet of one hundred and sixty ships to overrun Mercia a thousand years ago.

Though the highest Thames spring is at Coates, the potential Thames Head is at Kemble. The local inhabitants claim that the river really begins to rise in the neighbourhood of Culkerton, five miles to the west of its acknowledged head, and that it is conducted by a subterranean course to Kemble. Culkerton represents one of the highest summits of the western Cotswolds and is the starting-point of two rivers. On the eastern side the waters of the Thames springs are gathered, and on the west smaller springs originate to supply the Bristol Avon. The highest mill on the Thames banks stood a mile and a half from the head. The old house, called Mill Farm, still remains, though the wheel and machinery have been demolished for over a hundred years.

Half a mile below its source the spring was forded by a road, and foot passengers crossed on stepping-stones. By daylight the journey was safe, but at night it was attended with risks, especially when the springs were high. Then most people waded and ignored the stones. Will Darby, the short-sighted old tile-digger, found them by instinct and could usually cross in safety, though once, at least, he came to grief. That day he had been to Ciceter Mop and was returning in a state of mental elevation. " I shall go into the bruk to-night, as sure as the day," he repeated to himself on the road. When he came to the stones he put the wrong foot forward, missed at the second step, and went floundering into the stream.

The Thames is born in beauty and cradled amid scenes of considerable interest. Around its source is clustered a group of ancient villages and hamlets containing many imposing farmhouses and cottages, and rich in historical traditions. The life of the locality was breezy and boisterous, typical of the Western Counties. From earliest times the wooded hills that guard the birthplace of the river were inhabited. To the south-west is the town of Malmesbury—one of the earliest homes of English learning and art ; Cirencester, the ancient *Corinium* of the Romans, and but little less famous, lies three miles away to the north.

The abolition of the local inn has metamorphosed the life of the place, and sports and games have disappeared, though there were many amusements formerly. In addition to the annual festival of Jackiman's Club a village Wake was held at which there was morris-dancing for ribbons, back-swording, and wrestling. Agriculture and stone-digging comprised the principal out-of-doors work ; wool-spinning was carried on in the cottages. Wassailing was the favourite sport at Christmas-time, and the jovial custom was observed in all the villages upon the banks of the Thames streamlet. The wassailers

THE WASSAILERS

rigged themselves out in fancy dress and carried a bowl decorated with ribbons and holly round to the farmhouses, where they sang their merry song and received money and ale. The effigy of an ox preceded the company as they journeyed from house to house. The effigy was formed of the skin of an ox set on a skeleton frame, with the head and foreparts stuffed with straw, and with two bottles for eyes. Two sturdy wassailers crept inside and bore it along, imitating the motions of the beast, to the delight of the rustics.

THAMES HEAD WASSAILERS' SONG

" Wassail, wassail, all over the town,
Our toast is white and our ale is brown,
Our bowl it is made of a maple tree,
And so is good beer of the best barley.

Here's to the ox and to his long horn,
May God send our maester a good crop o' corn !
A good crop o' corn and another o' hay,
To pass the cold wintry winds away.

Here's to the ox and to his right ear,
May God send our maester a happy New Year !
A happy New Year, as we all may see,
With our wassailing bowl we will drink unto thee.

Here's to old Jerry and to her right eye,
May God send our mistress a good Christmas pie !
A good Christmas pie, as we all may see,
And a wassailing bowl we will drink unto thee.

Here's to old Boxer and to his long tail,
I hope that our maester 'll hae nor a 'oss fail !
Nor a 'oss fail, as we all may see,
And a wassailing bowl we will drink unto thee.

Come, pretty maidens—I suppose there are some !
Never let us poor young men stand on the cold stone.
The stones they are cold, and our shoes they are thin,
The fairest maid in the house, let us come in !

Let us come in, and see how you do.
(*Maid*) Yes, if you will, and welcome, too.

Here's to the maid and the rosemary tree,
The ribbons are wanted and that you can see,
The ribbons are wanted and that you can see—
With our wassailing bowl we will drink unto thee.

Now, boteler, come fill us a bowl o' the best,
And we hope that thy sowl in heaven may rest,
But if you do bring us a bowl o' the small
Then down shall go boteler, bowl, and all."

The last inn at Kemble was kept by one " Damper " Adams, who was a maker of wooden ploughs. He sold such notoriously bad ale that a gang of men set upon the house, rolled out the casks, smashed in the heads, and sent the beer tumbling down the hill into the river.

Both Ewen and Poole Keynes together would now make no more than a good-sized hamlet, though Poole has been a famous place. Few country mansions surpassed in stateliness the grand old fourteenth-century house—the home of the Barons Plat—that covered an acre of ground. This was almost totally destroyed by fire early in the seventeenth century. All that remains is one splendid room—said to have been part of the coach-house and now used as a kitchen for the farm that has been built on to it—a fine octagonal stone chimney, and the gruesome attic in which the last of the Plats hung himself in grief for the destruction of his property.

Ewen—pronounced "Yeowin" by the rustics—possessed neither church nor stately mansion, but it has many picturesque farms and cottages and it is backed with magnificent timber. No spot on the Thames is more beautiful, and certainly none is more healthy, to judge from the great age and appetites of its inhabitants. Centenarians were almost as much the rule as the exception, and for a hearty appetite who could excel the redoubtable Cornelius Uzzle that, in the presence of living witnesses, unostentatiously devoured twelve pounds of bacon—six pounds raw and six pounds parboiled—at one meal for a wager at the old Wild Duck inn? The thatched cottage by the roadside yonder has had but two tenants in a hundred and fifty years. The aged occupant's memory extends back through his father for nearly two centuries.

Three mills stand on the Thames near Somerford Keynes. They date from the earliest times and were founded by the Saxons, who built a beautiful church and adorned it with sculptures and frescoes, some of which are still preserved. Agriculture is the staple industry of the village. " Plenty o' 'ard graft an' nat much bezide at Zummerverd," says the rustic, leaning on the stone wall in front of his house. North of the village is the forgotten hamlet of Shorncote with its quaint little Norman church; two miles lower down, we come to Ashton Keynes, the largest village on the Thames above Cricklade.

It is possible that Ashton Keynes is older than Cricklade and that it was looked upon in prehistoric times as the highest point on the Thames for general navigation. When the Romans came to the island and founded Bath and *Corinium*, and, with characteristic energy, surveyed the country and projected the great road from Cirencester to Speen, they decided to cross the Thames at Cricklade, and, by so doing, definitely established that as the starting-point of the river's commerce. Whether there was a ford or not previously mattered little to them. If there were no means of crossing they soon made them, for the Romans seldom deviated in order to avoid a difficulty but overcame it boldly and scientifically.

Whether Ashton was before Cricklade or Cricklade before Ashton may be open to question, but it is impossible not to be impressed with the charm of the place. The little Thames, flowing in several parts, unites in the centre of the village and runs rippling beside the broad street, passing through several stone arches and leaping down a pretty cascade, washing the foundations of the manor-house before it hurries off beneath a line of drooping beeches. The cottages, built on the opposite bank, are reached by foot-bridges. Along the stones of the walls creeps the pretty toadflax; here and there the golden mimulus blooms. This is rare, however; I have never seen it anywhere else on the Thames bank.

Glove-making was for several centuries an important industry on the banks of the Thames brook between Cricklade and Kemble. There were local tanyards for preparing the skins, and workshops for cutting out the leather. This was distributed throughout the villages and the gloves were sewed in the cottages by the women and girls, who earned from five shillings to seven shillings a week at the work. Since the war the glove industry has revived in the locality, though the cutting-out is done at London.

Cricklade is about half-way between Ashton Keynes and Castle Eaton, astride the famous Roman road of Ermin Street. The place is smaller than it was formerly. At the beginning of the tenth century, the Danes, incited by Ethelwold, carried fire and sword throughout Mercia, came to Cricklade, forded the Thames, beat down the walls, and, after seizing all they could lay hands on hereabout, retired by the same way they had come. In those days the town was of importance, and possessed a mint, which continued active throughout Saxon and Danish times till the reign of Henry II. A few of the Cricklade coins still exist in collections, and others are buried about the meadows.

Cricklade is said to date from a period much more remote than that of either Dane, Saxon, or Roman. According to monkish traditions the Trojan Brutus came here with a party of his countrymen as long ago as the year 1180 B.C. and founded a university among the early Britons, who had their fortress upon Blunsdon Hill, overlooking the Vale. What the son of Troy taught, or in what manner his teaching was received by the rude natives in those unenlightened times, does not appear. He could not have brought the *Iliad* in his pocket, nor yet have told the story of Dido and Æneas, for neither the one nor the other had been composed at that time, if, indeed, Troy had been sacked and the eventful voyage to Carthage and Italy made by the son of Venus and Anchises. As for the "university," that was probably founded by Pendà, King of Mercia, long afterwards, namely, A.D. 650. The seat of learning seems to have flourished until it was transferred to Oxford by King Alfred towards the end of the ninth century.

There is another striking tradition attaching to the locality. It is said that Saint Augustine met the Welsh Bishops and deliberated with them in the vicinity of Cricklade. It was formerly supposed that the meeting took place near the Old Passage on the Severn, but it has been suggested that it was held in the forest of Bradon, which extended to the walls of the town. Bede says they met "at a place which to this day is called Augustine's Oak, on the borders of the Wiccii and the West Saxons." From the direction, the relative distance, the site, and the tradition, the conclusion has been drawn that the Augustine's Oak of Bede is the Gospel Oak at Bradon in the Cricklade parish.

The town is an old-fashioned place, rather quaint than beautiful. It chiefly consists of one long wide street bordered with old stone-built houses with roofs of tiles or thatch, black with age. An ancient Preceptory stood near the river. This was built by the Knights Hospitallers in the time of Henry III.; parts of the original building still remain included in the walls of the Priory. Cricklade is a borough "by prescription." It sent members to Parliament irregularly from the reign of Edward I. till that of Henry VI. After that date the returns were continuous till the year 1782, when, by reason of bribery and corruption, its franchise was extended to the freeholders of Highworth and Staple.

The town possesses an ancient Charter, which was granted by Henry II. out of gratitude for the kindness shown by the townspeople to his mother, the Empress Maud, when she fled from Stephen. By virtue of the Charter the people of Cricklade were to enjoy their Tole Book and all customs, be undisturbed in their passage throughout the kingdom, and protected against all molestation under a penalty of ten pounds. It was furthermore granted to them that they should not be arrested nor have their goods seized anywhere unless they were principal debtors or sureties, and they had the right to sell "toll free" in any town in Great Britain or Ireland. This part of the Charter is still effective. Quite recently a Cricklade dealer refused to pay the toll demanded by the market authorities in a neighbour-

W. Dennis Moss, Cirencester.]
Saint Sampson's Church and Cross, Cricklade.

ing town and they threatened to seize his goods. Upon making enquiries, however, they found that the dealer was secure; he was " toll free " by virtue of the ancient Charter of the town.

What the early election riots and fights at Cricklade were like can only be imagined at this time. Doubtless they were serious risings, attended with bloodshed, plundering, and devastation, for Crickladians had the reputation far and near of being a most boisterous and pugnacious people. When a stranger was located the cry went up: " Put un in the bruk," and the suggestion was usually no sooner made than carried into execution.

The " funnel trick " was frequently the cause of fighting at the inns. When a stranger came on the scene the novelty was introduced to him, and it usually ended in an uproar. The trick was played as follows: First a funnel was thrust into the stranger's garments about the waist. Then he was required to hold back his head, lay a coin on the middle of his forehead and, by repeated movements of the brows, to wriggle it down his nose and so let it fall into the funnel. The offence committed against the stranger is obvious. While he, with his head held back, was wriggling the coin someone dashed a potful of ale into the funnel, and the trouble began.

In former times the Cricklade elections lasted for eight days, which were spent by the townspeople in feasting and drinking. Then " open house " was kept at the inns. All voters, and any others who might be able to influence a vote, paid frequent visits to the inns, ate here and drank there, and seldom declared for their candidate till the date of the poll. Canvassing had been on for six months before this. It was usual for the candidates to visit the homes of the poor voters and attempt to buy something or other, offering a fabulous price for it in order to secure the householder's vote. " I'll give you ten pounds for that picture," or " I'll pay five pounds for that canary," the candidate would say, and the bargain was made.

Another practice at the Cricklade elections was for the candidate to lend money to probable supporters without the precaution of a security. The amount of money required in anticipation of the vote was signified by the number of bars in a gridiron which the voter roughly chalked on the outside of his door. The ordinary gridiron possessed ten bars, and a corresponding number of sovereigns was accordingly tendered as a loan to the householder. There is on record but one case in which the borrowed money was repaid. Then the voter, after receiving the money, was stricken with such remorse that he drowned himself in the river, whereupon his widow refunded the amount with interest.

The bill on opposite page for " open house " and general expenses connected with the Wootton Bassett election in 1774 proves the costliness and suggests the depravity of the system. There were four candidates to bear the outlay.

The price of 30 guineas for a vote was above the average ; 20 guineas was the sum ordinarily paid. Occasionally, however, the cost of a vote was considerably increased, and in the year 1807 the local price rose to 45 guineas. The sum of £77, 13s. for cockades is a big item, though the ribbon bill was invariably high. It is said that at one election in North Wilts a candidate was pressed to sell fifty acres of good pasture land in order to pay for ribbons worn by his friends and supporters.

ELECTION EXPENSES

Squire Archer, of Lushill, was to the fore at election times. He stood in the market-place and made speeches in support of his candidate, while the crowd surged round yelling "Jacky," "Jacky," and jeering at his oratorical efforts. Elections proved both troublesome and dangerous to the squire. He would

	£	s.	d.
(For food and drink at the inns.)			
Star	52	4	7
King of Prussia	90	10	0
Shoulder of Mutton	56	10	0
Horse and Jockey	107	4	0
Wm. Henley's	35	0	0
Waggon and Horses	78	11	0
Oak	336	0	0
Three Tuns	54	0	0
Three Goats' Herds	47	0	0
Cross Keys	90	0	0
Hay and Corn	3	16	0
King's Head	76	17	1
For Cockades	77	13	0
First Canvass	152	0	0
Money paid for various expenses	11	11	0
Total of votes, then computed at 135, 30 guineas each	4252	10	0
Money to men deserted or dead	441	1	1
	£5962	7	9
Item	11	0	0
	£5973	7	9

have been well advised to refrain from active participation in them, and especially from speech-making, but he boldly faced the multitude and took all interruptions, and even personal assaults, in good part. Though his politics were distasteful to the bulk of his workpeople they bore him no particular ill-will on that account, though he was often taunted about the low wages he paid to the men on the farms. Thus, when the disturbance on polling-day was at its height and " Jacky " was in the midst of the scrimmage, a witty labourer at the rear cried out lustily : " Dossent go to 'it the owl' man. Dwun' go to 'urt un, cos a'll allus find us plenty to do if a wunt gie us nothin' far't." On one polling day he lost no fewer than three top-hats, and he was finally chased home across the fields wearing the rim of one of them round his neck.

The custom of Court Leet, or Reeve Leet, is observed at Cricklade. It owes its origin to the common lands, and to the practice of letting out some part of them every year for the feed and hay-crops. The tithingmen have the right of turning out their cattle on the common lands from Michaelmas to Candlemas. This privilege does not extend to those living within the borough. They, however, have the right of the North Meadow—a hundred acres—during the autumn and winter. Then every householder of the borough, from the greatest to the least, may turn out nine head of cattle to graze in North Meadow from August to February, and thirty sheep to graze from September to February.

A jury of twelve conduct the Court Leet. They first of all meet and initiate the ceremony, then swear in a hayward, whose duty it is to impound all horses and cattle found straying on the common lands, and to see that all brooks and ditches around the borough are properly cleaned out. From the meeting-house the jurymen march in procession to the inn, where they sit down to a repast. Afterwards bowls of hot punch are brought in and toasts are drunk to the Lord of the Manor of Calcutt and Chelworth.

Clearing the room is not always an easy matter

A GHASTLY SOUVENIR

after the hot punch has worked upon the jurymen. On one occasion, when the time for departure came, the tithingman found a burly farmer making determined but fruitless efforts to get inside a small cupboard in the room. "Come on, old man! You must get out of this," cried the tithingman. "You get along an' let ma alone. I come in this way an' I'm gwoin out this way," the husbandman replied.

Many highwaymen resorted to the neighbourhood of Cricklade and committed deeds of plunder and murder in the Bradon Forest. The last outrage of the kind was perpetrated by one Watkins in the year 1819. He waylaid and shot a salt dealer named Rodway, who had been trading at the farms. Watkins attempted to fix the guilt upon another, but he failed, and was hanged at Purton Stoke. When the body was cut down from the gallows a farm labourer named Matthews ran forward with scissors and cut off the dead man's ear to keep in memory of the event. The labourer was subsequently known as "Crop" Matthews, and his deed was mentioned in a song composed upon the crime and execution of Watkins.

> "This barbarous man, who chanced to be there,
> What a barbarous fellow! he cut off his ear,
> When the rope it was severed and down he did drop,
> And for this same reason we all call him 'Crop.'"

It was while Zechariah Giles was constable that the mail van was attacked and robbed near the borough town. Old Zechariah showed his bravery on this occasion by climbing up a high elm-tree, but the robber was taken, tried, and gibbeted near at hand.

All the old sports characteristic of Wessex—bull-baiting, back-swording, boxing, wrestling, and cock-fighting—were carried on at Cricklade until the fairs were abolished. For those of a more gentle turn of mind there were other amusements, such as morris-dancing, skittling, bowling, fiddling, and flute-playing. At Christmas-time the mummers went about playing *Robin Hood* or *St. George*, or, with a collection of old and new songs, perambulated the town and paid visits to the villages and remote farmhouses, where they were well received and entertained.

It was usual for those engaged at the tanyards to observe a festival at the end of " bark harvest," which fell about the beginning of June. After the bark had been dried, stacked, and thatched, the proprietors of the tanneries gave a supper to their employees. This resembled the harvest-home of the farmers. Food and ale were supplied, and the hours till midnight were spent in mirth and merriment.

Following a discussion at one of the inns concerning the weight of a bushel of corn, one Will Simpson made a wager for a guinea that he would wheel a sack of wheat from Cricklade to Gloucester—about twenty-five miles—within twelve hours. This feat he straightway performed, though the time of year was midwinter, and he had to traverse many miles of unrolled stones upon the roads.

Poulton, the dealer, was an eccentric person, but he was clever and witty in making a sale with the neighbouring farmers. One of them, being in want of a cart-horse, went to the dealer to select an animal. Forthwith a well-groomed half-bred was led from the stable and paraded before the prospective purchaser. " You'll be delighted to see him work," said Poulton to the farmer, who paid down £25 and led the horse away. That delight he never had, however, for the half-bred would not work, which the dealer well knew when he made the remark.

It is said that the parson of a village church near the borough town was famed for boxing and pig-killing. He boxed with the villagers—farmers and labourers, too—and killed the poor people's pigs, gratis, with skill and despatch.

Although civilisation is spreading and a new spirit is pervading the countryside, there yet remain a few old-fashioned folks who will not be reconciled to the present methods of work and travel. It is not many years since Betty Hall, a maiden lady, held the farm at Water Eaton, and, with the help of a horse and a bull, ploughed her fields and afterwards sowed the seed, reaped and threshed the corn, mowed her meadow, milked her cow, and managed her affairs without the assistance of a male. At another farm near the town dwell several ladies, nearly four-score years in age, who have never seen a railway, though for thirty years one has been laid not a mile from their door.

The ancient manor-house was once inhabited by a large family among whom were several maids who, for want of space, were forced to sleep in the attic. The roof, which was of thatch, happening to be in a bad condition, the squire made arrangements for the necessary repairs. The workman arrived early in the morning and mounted the ladder. Before he had been long engaged a portion of the decayed thatch fell through upon the maids. They, in ignorance of what was being done, began to scream and call for help. "It's all right, missis," cried the thatcher, peering down upon them, "I'm only lookin' through the rafters."

CHAPTER XIV

The Upper Thames Valley in the Making—The Youth and the Traveller—The British Camp—"Slan" Feast—"Ratcatcher Joe"—Jack and the Squire—"Joe the Marine"—Moll Wilkins and Tom Hancock—Bet Hyde, the Witch of Cold Harbour.

LONG ago, before the existence of the most ancient of the human race, the Cotswolds extended over Cricklade to Purton, and had for their southern boundary the higher valley of the White Horse. That was ages before the birth of the Thames. Though Nature might have been dreaming out the scheme, she had not yet set to work to fulfil it. By and by, however, she awoke from her cold slumber and started into activity. First of all she loosed the mountainous blocks of ice, breathing into the chasms and fissures with her warm breath, and sent them sliding, for countless centuries the same, taking care to have them all furnished with huge projections like ploughshares, as hard as steel underneath. These icebergs seemed motionless, and they were years passing down the tract of hard rock. The sun glistened gloriously on their high tops; in the moonlight they stood awfully and majestically calm, like an image of eternity. But they passed, and each one, as it went, ploughed the solid rock and wore it lower and lower until it came to its present level and the ice melted. Then Nature turned in her bed, and the water from the ocean rushed back again, covering everything, and

MATERIALS OF THE DOWNS

continued so for many ages, till finally she rose and shook herself and gave to the sea its proper boundaries, only reserving so much water as was necessary to supply the river and beautify the valley, and make the sweet flowers grow.

Both the Cotswolds and the chalk downs of Wiltshire, Hampshire, and Berkshire were once parts of the floor of an ocean, and were formed in the same way, and of almost identical materials, that is, of the minute calcareous shells and flinty skeletons of billions of microscopic insects that abound in every sea. When these little animals die they sink to the bottom of the ocean and form a deposit like that of the Cotswolds. The very flints were obtained from the waters of the ocean and turned into a solid form by countless myriads of animalcules in times past.

The chalk downs were pushed up to their present height by contraction of the earth's crust, and were roughly treated in the process. The same plan was tried with the Cotswolds, but the limestone rocks were stubborn and would not be lifted so easily. Then Nature said: " Since you will not rise, continue where you are, humble and debased, and I will give unto the future White Horse to have dominion over you for ever and ever." The pits and quarries around Uffington and Bishopstone provide abundant evidence of the upheaving of the chalk; there it is piled up in an almost indescribable confusion.

Whoever had stood upon Blunsdon Hill in early times and looked across the broad valley above the spreading expanse of water would not have admired it as he might now. After the mountainous icebergs had ploughed out the hollow and the sea came in, washing the cold stone shores, there was little to please the eye, and the loneliness and solitude would have quelled the most courageous spirit. Even after the sea subsided and the water shrank back north-eastward there was no beauty visible—nothing but a dreary, muddy waste with occasional pools and shallow patches of water, and one broad sluggish stream stretching away in the middle of the valley.

After many years a thick mass of vegetation—grass, bushes, and reeds—sprang up and pushed out from both sides to the centre, and changed the prospect. Great monstrous animals floundered about in the swamps and slimy pools, and crashed through the underwood, preying upon the fish, fowl, and other occupants of the forest, and upon each other. Here the giant mammoth strode, causing the woods to quake; the rhinoceros swam in the pools or plunged through the thorny thicket, and the scaly ichthyosaurus lay concealed in the reed-bed, half under water, waiting to pounce upon the fishes that swam to and fro all too careless of their skins.

By and by strange-looking creatures, like great apes, with round shoulders, and long hairs all over their bodies, armed with sharp stones and pointed stakes, appeared on the scene—from Egypt or Asia—and began to hunt for fish and small game. They made houses of bushes set in the forks of trees, and haunted the hill for many generations, but gradually died out and were seen no more. After this another tribe appeared and took up the trade of hunting in the forest. They were dressed in skins, and they made houses of boughs covered with reeds on the ground. After a stay of nearly a thousand years they, too, disappeared from the confines of the valley, and it seemed as though the new race of beings—whatever they were—had become extinct. Then one day a more numerous band arrived on the hill, equipped with implements of bronze and iron—a sturdy, noisy, cleverish set, with dark features, and of a dauntless spirit. After a few months of hunting and fishing, they constructed themselves a kind of village and fortified it with an earthen wall and palisade. There they dwelt for many generations, and when they were attacked and driven out by a fierce Celtic tribe, the victors took possession of the fortress and themselves dwelt there until they were called forth by one Cassivellaunus to fight against a band of Italian marauders that had lately landed on the shores of Kent.

One day, three-quarters of a century ago, as Farmer Smith and his neighbour Mundy were riding down the hill on their nags to Cricklade market, they saw the poor folks at work enclosing the ground and building cottages. Then Mundy cried: "This won't do, Smith. We must see an' put a stop to this. We must get that hedge shifted back an' knock they walls down. If us don't do summat we shan't be able to get neether up ner down."

"Damme, let 'em bide, an' dwunt interfere wi' 'em. Ther's room enough for thee an' I," answered Smith.

The other, however, attempted to stop the operations, but was unsuccessful. By and by Mundy fell into misfortune, and was reduced to the necessity of working on the roads for a livelihood. Then old Paul Hancock, who lived down the hill, ran out from the cottage and gloated over his downfall, and shouted: "Hello! Hello! Is a wide enough now far tha? A's wide enough now, I'll lay a penny."

"Pray, my good friend, can you tell me how far it is to Cricklade?" inquired the traveller on horseback of a tall, raw-boned youth digging potatoes by the roadside half-way down the hill.

"Dursay I can, gaffer," replied he, with a grin. "It used to be reckoned vower mile, but now tha cut the 'ood away the zun shrivelled the road up an' chent about dree. The vust 'owse as you comes to is a barn, and the zecund is a 'aay rick. Owl' Shammel Giles's 'owse is a good way yon' that. Tha plagues our maester moore ner a bit, thaay do. 'Is zhip yets our turmuts and 'is gels gets into the orcut (orchard). Gaffer zets the dog aater the zhip an' I aater the wenches, an' between us we makes the 'ool an' the petticwuts vlee."

"Ah! and how it is that one of your legs is longer than the other?" inquired the traveller.

"Well! I never 'lows nob'dy to meddle wi' my grass-stranglers, gaffer, but since 'tis you I don' mind tellin' you I was born so at my perticler request, so as when I 'owlds plough I can walk wi' one vut in the vurra an' t'other on the land, zo's nat to lop awver, d'e zee," the youth replied.

Christopher, the carter, had been and married a wife upon the Downs and was bringing her home to Cricklade with the horse and waggon, lent for the occasion. On reaching the brow of the hill Christopher drugged the wheels and mounted the waggon. Then he shut his eyes and addressed his bride.

"Everything that I can see now's mine," said he.

"What! all that yander?" exclaimed his wife.

"Everything," he repeated.

Near the bottom of the hill, for several centuries, stood an inn with a large signboard, upon each side of which was painted a red lion, and a rude rhyme as follows:

>(On the lower side.)
>"Before this hill you do go up,
>Look in and take a jovial cup."

A PREHISTORIC VILLAGE

(On the upper side.)
"Safe down this hill, all danger past,
Call in and drink a jovial glass."

The prehistoric people that built the village on Castle Hill were possessed of considerable tactical skill and judgment, and were thoroughly imbued with the instinct of defence and self-preservation. It is probable, too, that they had a sense of the beautiful, and loved a fine prospect as well as any, though perhaps they placed safety first and made the other a consideration of the second importance. If they had chosen to construct their village upon the highest part of the hill, though it would have been impregnable on one side, it would have been necessary to defend it with ramparts on the other three, and they would not have had such a complete domination of the country round about. But by choosing a site at the extremity of the hill—though the spot was lower the situation was safer, as for two-thirds of the distance around the camp the ground drops sheer, and approach could only be had by the level on one side.

The interior of the castellum slopes considerably towards the vale. It is about eight acres in extent, and it has no raised earthen rampart, since it was surrounded with a stout wall of stones and timber, a supply of which could be obtained on the spot. A number of the stones remained down to a few years ago, when they were dug out to make roads to the farms. At the lower end of the camp, beneath the general level, is a semicircular terrace. Here, no doubt, was some special building, it may have been a prison, an isolation ward, or a place of execution for such as had transgressed the law and defied the august authority of the chiefs in council. Water was obtainable within the camp, summer and winter:

there was no fear of a famine if they should be besieged by an enemy.

The houses were built of stone and wood, and were thatched with reeds obtained from the swamps below. In addition to the dwelling-houses there were a business thoroughfare, a market-place, a carpenter's yard, a smithy, a repository for grain, forage, and pelts, and, very likely, a foundry, since several fine specimens of battle-axes and poll staves have been found in the fields round about. The cattle and horses, goats, hens, and geese were usually kept outside the camp, and only brought within when there was danger of their being stolen, or when they were required to make a feast, or as a gift to ratify some agreement made between members of the small community.

The surprising roughness and disproportion of the walls of many of the old cottages owned by labourers along the roadside is accounted for by their having been for the most part built at night. There was a custom—respected till towards the middle of the nineteenth century—which, under certain conditions, allowed a man to enclose a piece of ground on the roadside and claim it as his rightful possession. If he could manage to start his walls, build the fireplace and boil a gammon of bacon over the hearth he had made himself secure, and no one could deprive him of the holding. Half the old cottages down Blunsdon Hill were built in this manner. At a later time efforts to take the cottages were made by farmers and landlords, especially where the old owners had died and the claim put forward by the new person was doubtful. But if it could be proved that the house had stood for twenty-one years the property could not be interfered with.

RURAL FESTIVITIES

As well as being indispensable, the local blacksmith was otherwise important, and he used to give a supper to the carters and ploughmen every year at his own expense. The custom was also observed by the village carpenter; it was held common throughout the Upper Thames Valley while the wooden ploughs remained in use. The blacksmith gave his supper as having to do with the ironwork of the ploughs, shoeing, and keeping the traces in order; the carpenter because he supplied the woodwork—the whipples, and so on. The ploughshares were of wrought iron and they often wanted a new edge welded on. For this the blacksmith charged 10d., and 1d. for every new link or broken trace repaired.

In the autumn came the church festival, known in the locality as Blunsdon Slan Feast. At that time it was usual for the villagers to gather ripe slans or sloes to make a pudding. The festivities were kept up at the inns and cottages for a week, and while the local gamesters had a bout at back-swording, Bob Kempster and Dick Hornblow, with their followers, stole off to cock-fighting. Gipsy Smith played so merrily and well that the floor at the inn gave way and let grandfather Eggleton, who was dancing, fall through into the next room upon the head of old Moll Phillips, just as she was in the act of drinking a health to her neighbour, Joe the Marine, in a glass of home-brewed liquor.

Not many places possessed such a number of inhabitants noted for sturdy, quaint, or eccentric qualities as did the village of Broad Blunsdon, though it was commonly known and spoken of as " a roughish place," by the people round about. There were Squire Akerman and old Moses Akerman the farmer, Squire Calley, Farmer Snook of Bury Town, Dick

Ockwell and "Leather Breeches" Ockwell, "Ratcatcher Joe," "Joe the Marine," Tom Call the burglar, and Betty his wife, Tom Hancock and his mother Moll, Poll Packer, and, greatest of all, old Bet Hyde, the most famous witch that ever dwelled in these parts.

Squire Akerman was son to Moses the farmer. His birth was marked by a mighty brew of ale at the farmhouse, and casks containing a couple of hogsheads were stored up to remain till his coming of age. When he came to be twenty-one the people on the farms were feasted and the strong ale was served out at the rate of a pint for each individual. When a third of the strong beer had been consumed other ale was poured in, and so the cask was replenished.

The squire, according to the account of "Crazy Dick," was "as tall as a Yankee herrin'," and "not worth a cold fourpence." This description may not be entirely reliable, however, since it was the squire who put Dick's grandfather, "Ratcatcher Joe," in the stocks and kept him there all one Sabbath till the folks went to church in the evening. Squire Akerman was both magistrate and constable at the time, and "Ratcatcher Joe" was overfond of the liquor, and was moreover very disorderly when he had imbibed too much. Whether it was the fact of Joe's having recently come into some property or that he had secured an extraordinary haul of rats in the farmyard is uncertain, but without doubt he was very drunk or the squire would not have taken the trouble to confine him. But Joseph proved to be a greater nuisance in the stocks than as if he had been at liberty, for he did nothing but sing and shout and speak rudely to all who passed that way. In

A COURAGEOUS FEAT

the evening, when the people were going to church, and the squire's wife and daughters were passing, he made more noise than before and shocked them with his rude and irreverent expressions. Then the squire, for very shame, set him free, and no one was afterwards put in the stocks there.

This is one of "Ratcatcher Joe's" feats. First he drank a pint of shoe-oil. Next he ate one pound of tallow candles, two pounds of boiled fat bacon, hot, and a large cow cabbage cooked with it that when cut would not go into a peck measure. Then he swallowed the greasy pot liquor, and afterwards drank a quart of beer, completing the whole within half an hour.

Joe's property was of the kind described as key-hold—that is, he was master of it who happened to be holding the key. Joseph took possession of the cottage by the singular rite of striking an axe into the trunk of a large plum tree standing in front of the house. The tree, though it had never previously borne fruit, was scarcely known to fail afterwards. "Ratcatcher Joe" did not long remain in possession of the property, for a lawyer found means to make him drunk and then induced him to sign away his rights for a song.

In sharp, cold weather Joe used to wrap the newly caught rats around his body, next the skin, in order to keep himself warm.

The squire was noted for many artful devices. He was moreover inordinately fond of his money, but he met his match one day in Jack Sanders, the ditcher. Jack had cut and laid a mound and cleaned out the ditch that twirled and wriggled like a serpent, and came to the squire to settle up the account.

"The mound's two chain long," said he.

"Daal! He's more than that, gaffer," replied Jack.

"Knows a yent! I mizhured un this ten year," returned the squire.

"I wants un mizhured a-new, then," said Jack again.

"Very well! Please thiself. Who'll drag the chain?" said the squire.

"Thee cast drag un," cried Jack.

The squire accordingly took the chain and struck a bee-line to the bottom.

"Yer! That wunt do, gaffer! The ditch is crucked," said Jack.

"I telled tha a was but two chain," the squire cried.

"Damme! Ther's odds between the ditch an' thy chayn. Thee let I 'ae'n," said Jack.

When he had correctly measured the ditch it proved to be nearly as long again as was shown by the previous measurement, and the squire had to own to it and pay the extra money.

When the squire got old he used to play with his money, and he died with a good round sum in gold under his pillow, which circumstance caused the rustics to remark that he had placed it there in readiness to pay his passage down to the lower regions.

Old Moses Akerman, the squire's father, was of a different type. Plain and homely in his dress, manner, and speech, he was nevertheless a fine farmer, was generous to his workpeople and kind to strangers. About the farm he rode a shaggy black pony; when he went to market it was in the old-fashioned gig drawn by one of the plough horses. And what a merry time was had at the harvest-home! There was not another such a feast in all Blunsdon. Old Moses did the carving and the ale was so strong that the very smell of it overcame Moll Hancock and made her intoxicated. Dick Hornblow sang of the Fly and the Grasshopper :

> "Said the fly unto the grasshopper—
> 'Thee bist a hopping dog,
> And let thy mother be what she will
> Thy father sprang from a frog.'"

and Joe Packer followed with an ancient and ridiculous ditty :

(*Solo*) "A fly stood on the steeple-top, the steeple-top, the steeple-top,
A fly stood on the steeple-top——"
(*All*) "Yellacks a is now !"

Several times old Moses Akerman's sheep got through the fence into Squire Calley's field until the squire lost his patience and quarrelled with him about it.

"God love the fella ! I s'pose thees thinks nobody got money but thee. I'll tell tha what I'll do. I'll show money wi' thee an' buy tha up," cried Moses.

"Ah ! Akerman. You can load a jackass with money till he breaks down to the ground, but you'll never make a gentleman of him," Calley replied.

In the end Moses left the farm that his family had rented for a hundred years, because the landlord would not build him a new cowshed, though he afterwards declared that if he had known what he was worth he could have bought the place and put a gold fence round it.

It is said of Farmer Snook and his wife, of Lower Bury Town, that they had twenty-one children twice. This at first appears incredible, but it is explained in the following manner: Their twenty-first child died, afterwards another baby was born, which a second time brought up the number to twenty-one.

The old man possessed several peculiar characteristics. The workpeople called him " Dandy " Snook, because, as he rode about the fields on horseback, at every few paces he stopped, took off his sleeve hat, brushed it, and, with the aid of a small pocket mirror, carefully combed his hair.

He rented three farms situated at a triangle and each about a mile apart, and he shouted his orders for all three from the top of Castle Hill. One morning, as the boy was bushing the field, nearly two miles away, he heard the master shout to someone : " Tell Eggleton to leave the bushing and go to Stanton Mill for some grist."

Without waiting for the messenger the boy unhitched and left the field, and presently met the bailiff on horseback.

" Where are you going ? " inquired he.

" I be off to Stanton Mill," the boy replied.

" Who told you to go there ? "

" Maester zed 'e was to go."

" You young liar ! I'm only just come to tell you now."

" You needn't fret yerself. I yerd what maester zed, plain enough," answered Eggleton.

Notwithstanding the farmer's wonderful vocal ability, and his energy in other directions, he failed in business and soon afterwards died, and it is said that his corpse was arrested for debt in the street at Highworth on the way to burial at the church, and was only released upon one of the mourners undertaking to pay a proportion of the amount due.

REYNARD'S CUNNING

Was there ever one more crafty than Dick Ockwell, who performed the duties of cowman, hen-minder, and egg-collector? It is said of him that he could pick out eggs for a sitting so cunningly that every chicken hatched should be a cock. This he often did for a wager, according to the account of the villagers, whose belief in his powers is unshakable. They say that he was able to do it merely by examination of the eggs—by holding them up to the light.

> "I fancy I can see him now,
>   Down in the old thatched pens,
> Mixing up the barley meal for the cow,
>   And milking the cocks and hens."
>
> *Old Song.*

A cunning old fox caused Richard much trouble and anxiety. Time after time he had tried to take it with a trap, but had always failed. At last, one morning, on going to the pen he found reynard, that had broken in and devoured several hens and could not squeeze through the hole to safety. Upon looking a second time the warden of the roost perceived that the fox was stretched out stiff on the ground, as though it were dead. He accordingly turned to open the door more widely and shed light on the matter, when up sprang reynard, leapt upon his shoulders, and, darting through the door, was gone in a jiffy.

"Leather Breeches" was kinsman to the henminder and was an odd man about the village. The buckskin breeches he wore, according to a carefully preserved tradition, had been in the family for a hundred years, and as well as being wrinkled and withered with age they were filthy with grease. People said that all he had to eat with his barley bread was fat from his breeches obtained by frizzling them before the fire.

Then there was "Joe the Marine," Tom Call, and Betty his wife. The first-named of these was a tinker, while the other two were of no certified occupation, but were known for a precious pair of housebreaking thieves and rogues. The husband was a notorious purloiner of corn, which he stole by getting beneath the floors of granaries and boring holes in the woodwork.

Betty's forte was egg-stealing, and she used to keep a hen of her own indoors so as to be in a position to account for any eggs she might have in her possession. But one day a dozen turkey's eggs were missing, and on a search being made they were discovered at Betty's house.

"Where did you get these from?" inquired the constable.

"Bin an' becas me little 'en led 'em," Betty replied.

About the same time Tom Call was caught in the act of house-breaking, and was transported, and Betty was forced to enter the workhouse, where she ended her days with the paupers.

"Joe the Marine" was a hero of Waterloo, and could testify to the straight shooting of the French soldiers. Five minutes after the battle began he was shot through the calf, and in less than three minutes more another bullet tore through his top lip and carried half that away. Then he was taken to hospital, but when he arrived there, though the fight had only just begun, he was refused admittance, for there were hundreds of wounded men. When he returned to Blunsdon his mates laughed at him and told him it was no wonder he was hit in the head, for that was of such a size that no one could possibly miss it, and as for the other wound, that was entirely his own fault—he should have put his calves out to grass at Bury Town and not have taken them over there to Waterloo. Then Joe grinned and cursed Bonaparte, and said he'd learn tinkering, which he did of Mark the Gipsy who camped in Golden Rose Lane, and came to be a maker and mender of pots and kettles, and constructed a " dandy horse " with which he used to ride up and down the streets of the village. As he grew older he lived like a hermit and was called a " wise man " and a " dreamer," and when the farmers lost anything they would go to him for advice and he told them where to find the missing property. He was also said to have commerce with Satan, who was frequently seen in the shape of a crow perched on the back of his chair in the firelight. A good many deny this tale, however, and say it was Bet Hyde, who lived below Cold Harbour, that Satan used to visit under the guise of a crow.

Moll Wilkins was not so well known at Blunsdon, since she had removed to Cirencester, ten miles off, and there were other witches without going all that distance. But Tom Hancock, " journeyman farmer," of Blunsdon Hill, having need of the services of a wise woman, and distrusting the two local ones—he really owed each of them money, one for information as to the weather when he wanted to gather up his haycocks, and the other for a consultation about his white sow that was soon to farrow—made a special visit to Ciceter and proved the infallible skill of the witch. He had lost a white fustian coat from the clothes-line in the garden, where he had hung it to dry after having been out in the rain ferreting rabbits. Accordingly he put a new fourpenny bit, to pay old Moll, in his pocket, and tramped off to Cirencester. When he arrived there and came to the house, she took him into a little room that was now pitch dark and now brightly lit, as though someone were continually switching on and off an electric light, though such a thing as an electric lamp was unknown then.

" Canst thee see this picture ? " asked Moll at last, opening a little black box and taking out the portrait of a man.

" Yes," said Tom.

" Dost know who 'tis ? "

" No."

Then she showed him another.

" Dost know who this is ? "

" No."

" Well ! wait a bit. Now," said she, producing a third card, " Hast ever seen this fella ? "

" Yes," replied Tom.

" Well ! Tha's the man as got thy coat. Thee go to Ashton Keynes an' ther' thee't see'n werrin' thy jacket."

So Tom gave her the fourpenny bit and went to Ashton Keynes, and the first person he saw was a drover wearing his fustian coat with the big pearl buttons, just as old Moll had shown him in the picture at Cirencester.

Tom Hancock was a " love child," and was born in what was called the " Bastard House " at Blunsdon. Many towns and large villages had one of these houses in which unfortunate young women were detained. When the child was born and the mother had recovered she was taken before the magistrates and committed to prison. Poor labourers could not afford to keep their children in distress. The " Bastard House " was administered under the Poor Law, and the term of imprisonment was a punishment for those who had been forced to accept

THE ENCHANTED ROPE

relief, and a warning to them not to transgress further. When Moll Hancock appeared before the magistrates to answer for her fault she took the opportunity of passing scathing remarks on the practice of sending young girls to prison for such an offence. " And now, gentlemen," she concluded, " you can send me to prison for as long as you like, but I'll have another child when I come out, as sure as you're sitting there."

Poll Packer was an inferior kind of witch, though she was greatly dreaded by the carters and cowmen, whose horses and herds she tampered with, stopping the teams on the road and causing the cows to get loose in the night and jump over the highest gates and fences. She was able to bewitch plates and saucers, knives, forks, and spoons, and even the very innocent slices of bread and butter, and to make them dance upon the tea-table. Her greatest feat was to make a waggon-line stand straight up in the air in the hayfield and so tease the farmer half out of his wits, who wanted to bind the hay on the wain and get it down to the rickyard before the rain came on. But poor Poll was often blamed for what she knew nothing about, and she suffered many a curse and execration that should rather have been levelled at her powerful rival and neighbour, Bet Hyde, who lived in a tiny thatched cottage below Cold Harbour.

Even titled lords and ladies came in their carriages to see old Bet, to ask her advice, and to hear her prognostications. When the crusty old Baron was about to begin a lawsuit against the indomitable Squire Q, who would not have the great grandfather elm-trees lopped, nor yet give up to his Lordship the little field in which he turned loose his favourite hunting nag—to which the Baron laid some sort of claim, though in reality the meadow should have belonged to one of the Hancocks—he thought it best secretly to visit the witch to hear what she had to say about the issue of the suit. Then old Bet, sitting on her low stool by the fireside, after hearing his account of the matter, spat up the chimney back and cried in a squeaking tone of voice :

> " Cuss'd be the hand
> That strikes at the tree,
> And cusséd the meadow
> If it channgéd be ;
> For the grass shall wither,
> And the tree shall fall,
> And the Spirit shall fetch
> Squire, Baron, and all."

It is furthermore said that Satan, in the shape of a crow, came hopping out from beneath the table and perched on the old hag's shoulder, croaking loudly. That was all the witch spoke in reply to the Baron, who hurried off and allowed the suit to fall through and did not further molest the Squire. The big branches—some of them ten tons in weight—have nearly all fallen off the elms, and the trunks are rotten and hollow. The little field has been ploughed up and is now used for the production of potatoes, peas, and cabbages.

Ladies came to see old Bet for various reasons. If one was in love and had a troublesome rival she came to learn the best means of overcoming her. If another wanted to know her neighbour's secrets she came and bribed the old woman to discover them. If this one wanted to get rid of warts, freckles, or sunburn she came to have them charmed away. All things lost, stolen, or strayed were sought for—and that successfully, it is said—at Betty's house.

BET HYDE'S PROPHECY

"I wonder if the old bitch is at home," said Mary Ann to Emm the cook, as they were going to see Bet one Sunday afternoon to have their fortunes told. When they came to the cottage the old woman was standing in the doorway.

"Yes, the old bitch is at home. Walk in, my dears. My pretty black bird told me you were coming," said she, pointing to the crow, that was perched upon the clothes-horse, looking very wicked and cunning. Then she went on:

"You've got a mole on your right shoulder and a strawberry mark under your left breast, and you've got a bad leg that'll never be well. You had a bundle of clothes, a letter, and a purse to take to the housekeeper, but you hid the clothes in the box bush coming down the lane, looked in the purse, and read the letter. There's a new place waiting for you, but the gentleman will die. You will marry the second cowman, and he will run away from you the Sunday after Michaelmas. You will both be widows and cripples in your old age because you despised old Betty and her pretty black bird.

"For the devil shall pinch them and scratch out their eyes,
Plague them with grasshoppers, beetles, and flies,
Strip them and rip them and on their heads ride,
That mock at the wisdom of old Bet Hyde."

CHAPTER XV

Roman Remains at Bury Town—Stanton—Fulk Fitz-Warrene—Burial of the Dead—The Lake and Woods—"Moll Taw's Corner"—"Man-Traps"—The Wood Sale—Tom Fowler's Feat—Tricks and Conundrums.

WHEN Farmer Snook lived at Bury Town—the same who shouted his orders from Castle Hill, and whose corpse was arrested for debt in Highworth Street—he made many discoveries of old forgotten things on his farm, but, like a true barbarian, he demolished them all and so deprived those coming after him of the pleasure of their investigation. In the meadow called Town Close he employed William Gleed, the quarryman, at digging stones for over two years to make a road through the fields to his farm. There he unearthed numerous interesting relics, such as arms, tools, and implements, a coat of mail, coins impressed with the figures of the most august Roman Emperors, rings, trinkets, and cartloads of mosaic stones and "panches," or pottery ware. One day, as they were removing some large slabs of stone the iron bar slipped through and disappeared, and made a noise like thunder when it struck the bottom, which caused the quarryman to quake with fear, and he ran off and would not return to work any more that day. When Squire Akerman came to hear of it he had the stones set in place again and forbade further disturbance of the ground, and no one living now could say where the spot is.

THE SAXON CONQUEST

Less than two miles distant was another ancient Roman or British village. Many of these have been brought to light throughout the Upper Thames Valley, and there are doubtless others yet undiscovered. They were chiefly inhabited by the Britons who had made peace with the conquerors and, in return, had been taught by them some of the arts and crafts of Latin civilisation, as town planning, building and decorating, the manufacture of arms, tools, pottery ware, and so on. A feeling of security was abroad in the land. This is evidenced by the position of the new villages, that were often built in unstrategic and indefensible places. If the founders of Bury Town had been in any way apprehensive of an attack by a foe they would not have built where they did, nor would their near neighbours have chosen a site in a hollow, hemmed in with woods and hills, and from which escape would have been impossible if they should have been besieged by an enemy. But, as the poet says: "We are mortals, and know not the morrow." The greatest happenings recorded in history have usually been those that were least expected.

The long series of calamities that befell the Roman Empire in the East necessitated the withdrawal of the Roman troops from Britain A.D. 410, and the island was left to the mercy of the Low-German tribes. Soon the Jutes, Angles, and Saxons, bent on conquest, came over, and the kingdom of Kent was founded in the year 449. Step by step the half Romanised Britons were driven back or slain by the invaders, and their towns and villages razed to the ground. Many of the German tribes had served with the Roman Legions and were well acquainted with the Latin civilisation. The Jutes,

Angles, and Saxons, however, knew nothing of it, and cared not for its works, but destroyed them as though they had been an abomination. Dearly as we should love to know the names of the British villages in the vernacular, that is denied us; they are blotted out of history.

Although the Saxons were constrained to destroy the village in the hollow they nevertheless fell in love with the situation and decided to found another settlement. They chose a position on the hill, and, setting up a tall stone for the centre, formed a circle of other large stones around it. Then they brought up the materials of the walls they had overthrown and, with them, and with timber cut from the woods, built a new village, not of beautiful and stately houses, as the other had been, but of rude huts and low sheds in which the Romans would have scorned to herd their cattle. Staneton was the name given to the new settlement. This meant the " stone village," either from the fact of its having been built upon a stone hill, or because of its being enclosed with a stone boundary. A few traces of the village still exist. The large centre stone is a greywether, and it was once seriously believed by the villagers to turn round every time it heard the first cock-crow in the morning.

The family of the Fitz-Warrenes obtained possession of the village during the reign of King John, after thrilling and romantic adventures. Fulk Fitz-Warrene owned Whitington Castle, in Shropshire, which his ancestors had won in a tournament. This property was seized by the Prince of Wales, and the King, out of hatred to Fulk—who had once beaten him in a game of chess—confirmed the Prince's possession. The Fitz-Warrenes demanded justice of the King and, failing to receive a favourable reply, renounced their allegiance to him, and, with the exception of Fulk, fled into Brittany. Then Fulk, to be revenged, turned highwayman, and with his followers came to Bradon Forest, near Cricklade, and lay in wait for the King's travelling subjects. One day a company of carriers, with a train of waggons full of valuable goods, came through the forest, and Fitz-Warrene and his men fell upon them and forced them to surrender. Then Fulk led them inside the forest and asked them who they were, and they told him they were the King's merchants and that the goods in their charge were destined for His Majesty. Thereupon Fitz-Warrene, in high glee, opened the bales of goods, unpacked rich stores of clothes and furs and divided them among his followers, telling the drivers of the waggons to return to London and salute the King in the name of Fulk Fitz-Warrene " who much thanked him for the fine wardrobe with which he had graciously provided them."

Then the King " went nigh mad with rage," and caused it to be cried throughout the kingdom that whosoever would bring Fulk, alive or dead, " to him would he give one thousand pounds of silver, and he would besides give to him all the lands in England which belonged to Fulk." Finding it difficult after this proclamation to remain in Bradon Forest, Fulk Fitz-Warrene fled into France. There he assumed the name of Sir Amice and distinguished himself in jousts and tournaments, and after various romantic experiences by land and sea, and having chivalrously rescued " certayne ladies owt of prison," he obtained the King's pardon. At the same time His Majesty allowed him the peaceable possession of Whitington Castle and furthermore granted him the Manor of Staunton in his native county of Wiltshire. It was Fulk Fitz-Warrene who, in the name of the Barons of England, bade one of the much hated Papal collectors get with haste out of these shores. "If you tarry three days longer you and your company shall be cut to pieces," cried he.

The village, according to local account, was not a parish of itself formerly, but was under Highworth. It obtained its independence very cheaply and with little trouble compared with what is necessary to obtain separation from another parish at this time. It seems to have been recognised, under the old order of things, that any village which could bring evidence to prove that it had relieved the wants of its own poor might claim to be a parish, independent of that to which it was officially joined. Accordingly, when a farm labourer, who was burdened with a numerous family, went to one of the churchwardens and asked for food for his children, he complied with the request and, in addition, gave him a shilling. Then the villagers published the fact far and wide and declared that Stanton Fitzwarren was a parish, which claim was duly admitted and confirmed by the authorities.

The church is dedicated to St. Leonard, who was known as the Forest Saint, either because of the fact that he built an oratory in a lonely place and dwelt there like a hermit, subsisting on wild herbs, fruits, and berries, or because the French King gave a part of the forest to the monastery to which he belonged. He is said to have been the son of a nobleman at the court of Clovis, King of the Franks, and his life's work was chiefly to ransom prisoners of war and to comfort and help those who were in prison by reason of their crimes, for which good offices the king would sometimes allow him to set prisoners at liberty. William of Malmesbury, with a zealousness characteristic of him, took advantage of this tradition to declare that "the Saint is said to be so especially powerful in loosing fetters that the captive may freely carry away his chains, even in sight of his enemies, who dare not mutter a syllable." St. Leonard was invoked by prisoners and slaves, and those who had been delivered hung up their fetters in churches dedicated to him, of which there are about one hundred and fifty in this country.

The burial ground without the church is very small; it is difficult to conceive how it should have contained the bones and dust of all who have died in the village, even within the last two hundred years. Possibly, however, it was once larger than it is now. In early ages not only the strict burial ground but all the lands contiguous to churches and, in some instances, all the domains of a church were comprehended under the name *cœmeterium*, cemetery.

The custom of burying the dead is supposed to have originated among the Egyptians, though the Rabbins claimed for it a greater antiquity, and affirmed that the idea was first taken from birds. Adam and Eve, said they, being at a loss what to do with the body of Abel after his murder by Cain, were relieved of their perplexity by observing a crow in the act of throwing earth and leaves over the body of one of its dead companions. Thereupon the patriarch, following its example, presently went and did the same to the corpse of his son. Both the ancient Greeks and the Romans disposed of their dead by earth burial; burning was first resorted to because of the savage treatment to which the bodies of the dead soldiers were subjected after battle by barbarian enemies, who dug up the corpses and mutilated them.

Sea burial was not recognised by the Greeks, and it was therefore customary for mariners and travellers by water to fasten to some part of their bodies a coin as a reward for whosoever might recover and bury them in case they should be drowned and washed ashore. Reference to this is made by Horace in the twenty-eighth Ode of the first Book—which is really a dialogue between the ghost of the Greek philosopher Archytas, a friend of Plato, drowned at sea, and a mariner in his ship. The spirit's solicitude for its unburied casket is poignant and tragical.

Omnes una manet nox,
Et calcanda semel via leti,

says the spirit, and afterwards :

Quamquam festinas, non est mora longa ; licebit
Injecto ter pulvere curras.

" One night awaits all, and the path of death must once be trod by everybody. . . . Though you are in a hurry you need not tarry long. You may sail as fast as you please when you have thrown three handfuls of dust upon my remains." The *injecto ter pulvere* was a part of the burial rite and corresponds to the modern formula : " Earth to earth, ashes to ashes, dust to dust." According to the poem it was not absolutely necessary for the body to be buried provided the funeral rite had been performed.

The Arwaces, a people of Guiana, pulverised the bones of their great men and drank them in their liquor ; and some natives of Brazil are said to have eaten their dead, not because of hunger, or any spirit of unfriendliness, but out of affection and reverence.

Burials by choice were usually on the south side of the church. A notion of evil was associated with the north, originating from the idea of Gog and Magog, or because suicides, criminals, and unbaptized persons were buried there. It is possible, too, that people preferred to be buried on the south because that is the sunny side, and the north is cold, dark, and comfortless.

The church feast, formerly held in honour of the good Saint Leonard, has now died out. The killing of a man at the backsword games was the prime cause of its abandonment. I have heard, when a boy, from my old grandmother—that, following a quarrel, a murder was committed near the village, and the culprit was tried, gibbeted, and buried on the roadside, and a sharp stake driven into the earth through his body. The news of the gibbeting travelled far and wide and attracted a big crowd. One venerable dame, whose boast it was that she had witnessed every public execution in the locality for three-quarters of a century, tramped a distance of twenty-four miles to see it, and made the forward and return journey each last two days, coming equipped with money and food to supply her on the way.

It was related to me by an aged person at Cricklade that when two young men, brothers, were hung from an oak tree outside the town, and the bodies were left suspended for the customary three days, the mother of the culprits took her sewing and sat beneath their bodies, apparently unconcerned.

A moderate-sized mansion and a farmhouse, several centuries old, occupy the site of the manor of Fulk Fitz-Warrene, the famous opponent of King John. A singular feature of the farmhouse is its fireplaces.

They are provided with a thin iron wheel, an inch and a half in diameter, fixed behind the chimney-piece; this was intended to revolve and so draw the smoke up the chimney. Another device adopted for the prevention of smoky chimneys was the hanging a brass globe, filled with water and provided with a small aperture, in the chimney at a height a little above the point reached by the greatest flame. As the water became hot it evaporated, and the steam was supposed to draw up the smoke that otherwise would loiter in the chimney.

In common with almost everything else the chimney was called upon to support a tax, the proceeds of which were called " chimney-money " and " hearth-money." By a statute of Charles II. it was decreed that the fire-hearth and stove of every dwelling or other house in England and Wales, except such as paid not to church and poor, should be chargeable with two shillings per annum payable at Michaelmas and Lady Day. The tax proved unpopular. The people declared it to be an oppression, and it was accordingly abolished, or, rather, exchanged for the impost on windows.

The lake below the House has been made for a hundred years, and is replenished by the clear spring that flows in at the upper end. The tall rushes and reeds, growing in the shallow parts, get stronger every year and push out, taking possession of new territory, to the satisfaction of the moorhens, coots, and dabchicks. In addition there are the thousands of white water-lilies that, with their large oval leaves, float on the surface in matchless beauty through the summer, and sink to the bottom, lashed and beaten by the vicious waves, when the stormy south-west winds blow. The water-lilies multiply with great

A DESTRUCTIVE SNAKE

rapidity. Fifty years ago the first two bulbs were planted in the lake, and they have now increased to such an extent as to cover over an acre of its bed. At the same time—the woodman, with mathematical nicety, informs you—there were but seven rushes growing on the banks; now they might be gathered by the waggon-load.

Numerous pike inhabit the lake and grow to an enormous size among the reeds and lily leaves. As the water is private they are not molested, and there are shoals of small roach for them to feed upon, with many a sleek fat rat and frog, young water-fowl, or snake, that finds its way into the jaws of the monster as it swims across from yonder bank.

Snakes eat minnows and small roach, which accounts for their frequent presence in water. In the aviary at Stanton House there was kept a choice collection of canaries that one by one mysteriously disappeared. At last the owner one morning discovered the cause. Inside the lattice a snake was imprisoned by reason of its having swallowed a large bird. Being late, and not having time to digest the meal, it could not squeeze through the meshes to freedom.

How quickly the kingfisher darts to and fro, and with what precision it enters the smallest aperture within which it has chosen to construct its nest! For several weeks I watched a pair flying in and out of a small drainpipe where the nest and young were situated. With the directness and velocity of an arrow they went whizzing into the hole; a little misjudgment would have caused them to be dashed to death against the rim of the pipe.

What possessed the old heron to play such curious pranks with the little fishes of the lake last year?

Thrice during the season there was discovered on the banks a perfect circle of small roach that he had made, presumably for amusement, since all the fish were intact.

The osprey has once or twice been seen here, and a pair of grebes nested amid the rushes several years in succession.

In the woods around the lake the "yukel," "yaffel," "eke-aw," or "ya-ha" dwells with the doves, owls, magpies, and sparrow-hawks. The beautiful nightingale sings amid the thickets and glades in early summer, and the lordly cock pheasant struts and crows beneath the oaks, challenging his rival to enter the lists and try the power of his wings and spurs. On cutting down an old pollard ash-tree recently the woodman found fourteen "bit-bats" inside it, clinging with their claws to the soft trunk, while hard by, fast asleep in an ivy bush, sat a foolish great owl that should have gone higher to roost. This the woodman's mate took with a wire, slipping the noose over its head and pulling it roughly off the perch. Afterwards the men stopped up an owl's entrance to the barn and were rewarded with a plague of mice, but when they removed the obstacle and allowed the owl to get inside the cunning little nibblers soon disappeared.

Numbers of squirrels haunt the plantations, and a few badgers have their home about the banks and slopes. The marten, or martlet, survived in Stanton woods and park down to the early part of the eighteenth century, though it is now quite extinct in the region of the Upper Thames. The marten was of the size of a cat, though with longer body, shorter legs, and claws less sharp. It was of a deep golden colour, with white throat and bushy tail, and it had its haunt

THE GREEN WOODS

and gave birth to its young in the tops and hollows of trees. It is said to have played great havoc with poultry and game, and on this account it was hunted like the fox, though the hounds were not permitted to eat its flesh by reason of its unwholesomeness.

There was a reason for the many twistings and turnings made by the single railway line that climbs through the wood and runs down into the hollow above the ruins of the ancient village. If the line had been cut straight through the meadows the cost of land would have been much higher than it was. By winding round the bottom alongside the little brook and through the copses, however, and ofttimes using no more ground than was occupied by the double fence of hawthorn, a way was acquired more cheaply, and the extra short distance was immaterial to the working of the line.

Under the great oaks and along the banks of the tiny brook that tinkles in the shade of the tall ashpoles and soft young hazel boughs the wild flowers bloom, drawing out their generations from earliest spring to latest summer and lingering on into the autumn. Scarcely has the little celandine opened its golden eye before the primroses rush forth. The blue and white violets awake beautifully out of sleep, perfuming the air; anemone and hyacinth strive to see which shall have the mastery of the copse and cover the open spaces between the trees with their mantles of clear silvery white and rich deep purple. Soon the wild cherry-tree bursts into snowy bloom; the laburnum hangs thick with bright golden chains, and the red and white honeysuckle overhead breathes its delicious fragrance abroad, intent on overpowering the sweetness of the campions that lift their heads high above the spreading ferns and wild strawberries.

After the fierce midsummer sun has slain Spring's brilliant children and the tall grasses wither, droop, and die beneath the oaks and hazel stumps, still the willow-herb and meadow-sweet thrive alongside the half-dried brook. The rosebay succeeds in masses, lighting up the interior with a lurid glow that threatens every moment to kindle tree and underwood, and strew the slopes and winding dell with unsightly ruin. Finally, as though to recompense the early loss, late summer brings on the hemp agrimony, that sheds a soft radiance throughout the thickets and groves—the last gleam before autumn comes scattering fire on every hand and the foliage of the great beeches burns steadily away with the consuming flame.

In a corner of the wood opposite a large cherry-tree, the top of which was broken off by the tempest, simple daffodils grow, blooming around a shallow well approached by means of several stone steps overgrown with moss, ferns, and violet. Many years ago a stone cottage stood on the spot, out of sight amid the trees and boughs, far from the high road and the village. In the cottage dwelt an old woman named Mary Taws, who might easily have been termed of evil repute, of the class of Bet Hyde and Moll Wilkins, but nothing is related of her by the villagers except that she loved the little old cottage, the well of sparkling water, the beautiful cherry-trees and the pretty " daffy-down-dillies." These she planted around the well and out beyond the garden fence, and in time they spread to and fro and filled that part of the wood with a sweeter beauty, inducing the boys and girls to come and pluck them with the primroses, violets, and bluebells. Every vestige of the cottage is gone now except the stones of the well, though the old woman's memory survives in the name given to that part of the wood, which is known to the villagers as " Moll Taw's Corner."

Poaching in the woods was common, and several kinds of gins and traps were set in the thickets to ensnare the depredators. Most dreaded of all were the man-traps. They were great iron gins having strong jaws fitted with sharp steel teeth that flew up and clutched a man about the calves and from which he could not extricate himself without assistance. Somewhat similar to them were the leg-traps. They were of steel and were so contrived that when they closed up they gripped a man firmly by the leg and locked automatically, and none but the keepers had keys to undo them. Spring guns were set among the low bushes and briars, and were provided with lines stretched across the paths at the height of a foot. Immediately the poacher's leg struck the line the straining of that both pointed the gun and fired it at the trespasser.

Another plan was to fix dummy pheasants to the branches of trees, and then to lie in wait for the poachers. When they fired at the dummies their whereabouts were discovered, and the keeper and his men promptly ran out after them. One Bob Lewis, the village sweep and a notorious poacher, when chased to his cottage by the keepers contrived invariably to disappear. In the wall, half-way up the chimney, he had built a secret recess. When he was hard pressed of a night he ran indoors, leapt up the chimney and descended into this, completely baffling his pursuers.

The timber of Stanton Woods is of a first-rate

quality. This value results from the properties of the soil in the bed of the hollow, and from its swampy nature. The waters of the lake frequently overflow, making the floor of the wood " goggy " and " patey," as the villagers say. The trees thrive on the moisture and the timber becomes extraordinarily tough.

Every species of tree—according to the woodman—is divided into two classes, the " he " and the " she "; and there is a corresponding difference discernible in the timber, whether it be of oak, elm, ash, beech, poplar, maple, or even the old stumpy hawthorn that grows in mid-field or by the roadside. The timber of the " he " tree—to follow the woodcutter—is always harder and tougher than the other; that of the " she " is soft and mellow, as befits the feminine nature. The " sexes " of the trees may easily be ascertained in the spring-time when the buds are opening. The female tree, bush, or bough, always shoots first. Those loitering, as though unwilling to put forth their velvety leaves and drink in the fresh air and sunshine, are invariably the males.

Every spring some part of a wood is cut and the timber sold on the spot by auction. The heaviest ash poles, intended for the wheelwrights, are trimmed and placed in separate piles. The lighter poles for fencing are similarly set by themselves and the small wood for faggots and pea-sticks is arranged in drifts. The usual crowd invariably attends, this one to make purchases, that one to look on: there are those who have not missed the event for over half a century.

The wood sale possesses an irresistible attraction for the aged roadmender, who walks forth to meet old friends and make a few purchases of poles, peasticks, or faggots, and is hailed by acquaintances whom he has not seen for a year.

A TRADE IN TIMBER

"Hello! Jacky! Bistn't thee dead yet?"

"No. More bistn't thee. But tha's ought to be."

"Oh! 'Ow's that?"

"Never done no good to nobody."

"I'm goin' to live as long as I can purpose to eggrivate everybody."

Here now is the auctioneer.

"Hello! Bridges. You're got over here, then!"

"Yes, sir. I brought a gentleman to do a bit o' business wi' ya."

"All right, Bridges. You know your way about."

"I don't know so much about that."

Presently a move is made, and the crowd, headed by the auctioneer, comes and stands by a pile of timber.

"Now, Bridges! Come on! How much for this lot? A pound? Twenty-five shillings, or what?"

"I'll gie two shillin's."

"What! You're getting generous, aren't you, Bridges? Two shillings I'm offered. Who says a pound?"

"Five shillings."

"Eight."

"Ten."

"Fourteen."

"Go on! There's plenty of room yet."

"Now, sir, Jacky's goin' to gie ya one more shillin', and only one. Fifteen. Now go on."

"All done at fifteen? All done, I say? Mind you, they're worth double. Once more; have you all done? Right! There you are, Bridges! Take 'em along. That's the cheapest lot that's been sold in the wood. Two tons of good ash poles for fifteen shillings, you artful old cove!"

Yonder cottages huddled on the hillside have sheltered a hardy stock, though their former occupants are extinct. There you may learn half the history of the village; of good Aunt Betsy, mortally afraid of a concertina, but who lived to a great age and became so childish that she set the bed on fire and was nearly roasted alive; of old Moll Garrett, " Kit " Rimes, and Patty Jones, who reaped and sowed, milked, thatched, and quarried stones as well as any man in the village. And you will hear of Mildenhall, the miller, so hearty and strong that he could pick up two sacks of flour—one under each arm—and race about with them, and, with a half-hundred-weight hung on his thumb, reach up and write his name on the ceiling of the mill; of " Nobber " Kibblewhite, the thresher, who lay in the barn with the rats and owls and the mysterious White Lady; of " Stivvy " Legg, who sat on the great sarsen-stone all night waiting for it to turn round at cock-crow; and, not the least famous, Tom Fowler, the carter, noted for an extraordinary feat of strength which he often performed for the entertainment of the villagers. Of him it is related that he would lie on his back beneath a farm waggon, place his feet against the hind axle-tree, lift up the waggon with the strength of his legs and back, and turn the two wheels round simultaneously with his hands.

The following is a record of Father Fowler's mowing, preserved since the summer of 1836 :

Stanton Mead.	Brick Field.
Wyld's Ground.	Call's Piece.
Bean Lands.	Ram's Close.

Number of acres, 45 0 10 perch. Sum per acre, 3s. Amount to receive, £6, 15s. 4d.

GREASING THE SCYTHE 271

One day the young shepherd went out mowing with the old man, though he could make but little progress. "Tackle wants graacin'," said he, darkly.

"You! What did the owl' fella mean bi saayin' as my tackle wanted graacin' ?" inquired the shepherd of his mate at night.

"Thee take an' gie'n a good piece o' bacon an' 'e'll put the zithe right far tha. Tha essent a got un zet right, locks!" answered he.

Old Farmer Hunter knew everyone's footprints but his own, so, when the boy Fowler borrowed his master's boots to go plum-stealing he was at a loss to trace the thieves and put it down to strangers.

Magpies at 4d.
Tomtits at ½d.
Skylarks at ¼d.

Twenty birds required to make a value of 1s. 8d.

Answer :   Three Magpies.
Fifteen Tomtits.
Two Skylarks.

To blow two bricks, weighing 14 lbs. and laid flat, off the table with the breath and so equal the carter's feat, place them upon a thin paper bag and blow up that with the mouth, when the bricks will leap off the table on to the ground.

The making a pocket-knife drop from a joist of the ceiling upon a sixpenny bit on the floor is assured by the following method. First stick the point of the pocket-knife slightly into the joist; next hold a cupful of water beneath the handle and mark where the drop falls when you have removed the cup. On that spot place the sixpence, then rap the joist gently with your knuckles, and the knife, if it be stuck in the wood truly, will fall on the coin.

Then there are the scissors and button-hook trick, the knife and needle puzzle—a magnetic game—the hot air juggle, making a penny stand on the rim of a tumbler, and the finding of magical verses in the Bible, all which the ploughboys learned at home on winter evenings, while their father was gone to attend to his horses in the stable, and their mother sang to them the piteous fate of William and Dinah, the unhappy lovers who poisoned themselves and who " lay both in one grave," or told how

> " There came three gipsies to the gate,
>   They sang brisk and bonny O,
>   They sang so neat and so complete,
>   That downstairs came the lady O ;
>
>   She pulled off her silken gown,
>   And with a blanket round her shoulders thrown,
>   Said she'd leave her new-wedded lord
>   And follow the draggle-tailed gipsies O."

CHAPTER XVI

Bide Mill Brook and Wood — Wych-Elms — Hannington Village — Giles Draper and the Cobbler Clerk — Farmer Baden's Courtship — Whistling Joe, the Blacksmith — Lye-Droppers, Potato Starch, and Rush-Lights — "Bang-Belly" and "Frog Water" — Wooding Rhyme — A "Journeyman Farmer" — Riddles — Rustic Lore — "Oby" and "Scamp."

THE small stream that flows through Stanton Woods, giving fragrance to the violets and toughness to the oaks and beeches, and goes singing between primrose-studded banks, whispering strange secrets of buried skeletons and white grinning skulls, spring-guns, and man-traps to the golden iris and blue-eyed forget-me-nots, is without a name until it winds round the slope below Hannington Church and plunges past the old Bide Mill. From this point—for its services rendered to the miller in times past—it is known as Bide Mill Brook. Henceforth it is free to wander at will adown the sunny meadows and seek out the flowery Thames that winds round to Inglesham and Lechlade.

Running along at the foot of the slope above the mill-pond is a wood of half a dozen acres so thickly grown with oak, ash, and towering Scots firs as to be almost impenetrable, and showing dark and gloomy from the road that leads down beneath the avenue of venerable wych-elms. No primroses, anemones, or bluebells grow within the wood, for the ground is wet and boggy; they delight in a dry situation and cannot live without pure air and bright sunshine. But though Flora shuns the dark wood, every summer sweet Philomela wakes the echoes by the brook-side, while the doves and jays build their nests and rear their young in the crowns of the high oak-trees. Swarms of cunning greedy foxes lie in the thickets and breed among the long grasses and nettles, and in the hollow " stowls."

On the face of a stone in the chancel wall facing the wood is an impression made by the foot of a prehistoric animal, larger than that of a fox or an otter, and which was furnished with four toes and rather a large pad. Doubtless the stone was obtained in the locality of the Thames, and the imprint records the passage of the animal along the wet sand in search of its prey ages before the river had shrunk to its present proportion, and before the mighty forest grew that filled the valley and stretched away to the distant Cotswolds.

Grand, rich, and stately as is the common elm, it is inferior in grace and light beauty to the wych-elm or wych-hazel—the " wild elm " of Scotland and Ireland. This, while it does not usually tower as high, comes to equal the common elm in bulk and often to surpass it in the quantity of boughs and foliage that radiate from the fork above the trunk and spread out like a giant umbrella, sometimes covering a space four or five hundred feet in circumference. From its abundance in Wiltshire the common elm has been called the " Wiltshire Weed." So prolific is it that it has been claimed that if the scythe and cattle were kept out of the fields for twenty years the valley would be covered with a forest as dense as it was in prehistoric days.

The wych-elm is propagated by seed, and the

common elm by suckers, since the fruit of the last-named rarely ripens in Britain. In former times the young wood of the wych-elm was used for making bows and was considered not much inferior to yew. Many villagers, in cases of cold or sore throat, strip off the inner bark of the young wands and chew it raw, or boil it and drink the liquor. This, when cold, settles into a brown jelly that is not unpleasant to the taste. I have often taken it as a boy, preparing it according to the directions given me by my old grandmother, who was skilled in the use of herbs and in the making of ointments from " Jack-by-the-Hedge "—garlic mustard—young primrose leaves, and other plants and flowers.

The village of Hannington lies beyond the avenues. At one time it was larger than it is now. When the land was laid down for pasture fewer hands were required. Little by little the population decreased. The houses were demolished and no more were built to replace them. During the last fifty years many cottages have been destroyed and not above half a dozen new ones erected. The two old inns—the Cat and Mouse and the Dog—have also disappeared, though a small farmhouse in the hollow was converted into an hostelry, and the sign of the Jolly Tar was hoisted above the door. An incident that occurred during the building of the inn did not tend to make the house popular, and it may be that it reflected the feelings of the villagers at the time. It is said that the local carpenter, after hanging the new sign of the Jolly Tar, went home and hung himself.

The two inns, the Cat and the Dog, played an important part in the life of the village, and though some of the proceedings carried on within them might have shocked those imbued with modern ideas of civil refinement, they were a proof of the hardihood of the population. The sports of bull-baiting, cock-fighting, wrestling, and boxing were regularly indulged in, and were witnessed and countenanced by the local squire and the parson, who admired the Greek nature of the games, and saw no harm in them, even though they might be attended with a little rough play towards the close, as in the case of Harry Waterman, the gamester of Highworth. For several years in succession he had come down to the feast and had made himself objectionable to all and sundry. At length, the villagers, headed by one Giles Draper, set upon him furiously, tore the clothes from his back, and chased him home naked across the fields to Highworth, in spite of the efforts of the constable, who shouted loudly for help " in the Queen's name," and tried hard to arrest the ringleaders.

The constable was a big burly man and was noted for several feats of strength. It is said that he could lift a heavy farm waggon from the ground on his back, so it was comparatively an easy matter for him to carry off refractory villagers to the Blind House, or to set them in the stocks that stood opposite the old Cat and Mouse Inn. It chanced that the last man to be imprisoned in the stocks, by name Davy Garrett, had a wooden leg. His offence was that of being drunk and unable to walk. He pleaded hard with the constable and begged that only his wooden leg might be infixed in the instrument, but the man of the law was inexorable and compelled him to sit there from sunrise to sunset during the next day, which was the Sabbath.

Giles Draper, who led the villagers against Harry

Waterman, disturber of the feast, was an old soldier and a famous mower. He was able to cut two acres of grass in a day and to keep up the effort for a week at a stretch. Such extraordinary exertions naturally made him very hungry and thirsty, and it is not to be wondered at that he discovered an enormous appetite, though it is difficult to believe that he really ate a quartern loaf and two pounds of bacon and drank a gallon of fresh beer at a meal. As he advanced in age the hard toil of the fields told upon him. His joints became stiff and feeble, and he thought of his earlier years. "I shall hae to do all that mowin' over agyen," said he to Dick Willis, the ox-man, who was puzzled at the time to know what he meant, though he understood it afterwards.

There was a long list of Hannington worthies while the ancient village stood. First was Squire Montgomery, who lived at the Hall. Next was Humphrey Baden—as good a farmer as ever brewed ale; Mary Rowlands, Moll Higgins, Sarah George, and Martha Hedges—haymakers, reapers, cheese-makers, and dairy women; Jack Woolford, cow-man, Finch the woodman, Daniel Yeates, the ancient miller, Joe Jarvis, blacksmith, and Bob Hewitt, cobbler, bell-ringer, church clerk, and gravedigger. Old Hewitt had earned renown as a cobbler and gravedigger, though he was deficient in his duties as clerk, which was probably a result of his too frequent attendance at the Dog Inn, which was a favourite resort of his. Almost every Sunday, during service at the church, he fell asleep in his pew beneath the high gallery, and as soon as he awoke, without waiting to see at which point the parson had arrived, he loudly shouted out: "Aaff-menn." Fixed to a beam in the ceiling at the Dog was a stout iron hook. From this the shoemaker clerk, when he felt so inclined, would hang with his left hand and continue chatting with one and the other till he had drunk a gallon of strong beer.

"By gad, Finch, this will never do," cried the new squire to the old woodman, meeting him one night on the way home with a large faggot, provided with two forks and a "stand up" at his back. "You'll ruin me, man."

"Baggin' yer pardon, sir, 'tis nothin' onusual," answered he.

"Nothing unusual!" exclaimed the squire. "What do you want with those two forks besides the faggot, there?"

"Them's the bear-aways, sir," replied the woodman.

"The bear-aways, eh! And what's the one hanging down behind you?"

"That's the teal-away, sir."

"Oh! the teal-away, is it? Well! for the future you shall neither bear away nor teal away my wood in this fashion, but be satisfied with a small faggot and one fork, and see you bring that back with you every morning."

Humphrey Baden courted one of two sisters, both of whom "wanted" him for a husband. The young lady of his choice being poor, that circumstance gave the other—who had money—an opportunity of pressing her suit. She accordingly met Humphrey in the lane one night and boldly addressed him. "If I was in your place I should look after somebody different to my sister, for her got nothing," said she. Thereupon Humphrey took the hint and proposed to her on the spot, and they were soon afterwards married.

Humphrey's fame as a good farmer and cultivator and a kind master had spread around the Vale, and was only eclipsed by that of John Archer, of Lushill. When the steam-ploughs came on the scene and other farmers got rid of their oxen, he kept his and went on as before. " Ya owl' fool ! " said a neighbour to him at length, " Why dossent zill the beyast an' 'ae the steam uns ? "

" I can work oxen an' aaterwerds fat em an' zell em, locks ! but neether thee ner I, ner nobody else, can fat a ploughin' ingine," Humphrey replied.

Strong and hardy, blunt and outspoken, but honest and straightforward were the women who toiled in old Humphrey's fields haymaking and harvesting throughout the summer and autumn. Sarah George, the carter's wife, was the recognised leader of the feminine element, and Moll Higgins was respected as her lieutenant. Without doubt a little scandal was sometimes discussed among the haycocks and wheat sheaves, but Sarah spoke her mind with perfect candour and answered a squeamish remark with : " Aa, damn tha ! Some fawks channges mutton for mutton, dwun em ? "

" Sally ! What sart of a tree do you call this un ? " inquired Jack Woolford, the cowman, of Sarah one day, pointing to an exotic shrub opposite the Hall.

" Why ! a ooden un to be sure, ya fool ! " replied she, passing quickly on her way.

After Moll Higgins' husband Tom died and the men took to chaffing her about marrying again she declared that she " wouldn't hev the brightest man as ever wore a head," though she finally succumbed to the charms of Dick Willis, widower. Then one of the daymen said to her : " Mary, I thought you said you oodn't hev the brightest man as ever werred a head, an' now yer be you agwain to marry Richat Willis, as ardinary a man as ever lived in Anninton."

"Ya fool! I 'edn't 'ed the chance to 'ev t'other un, 'ed I," answered she.

The old blacksmith, "Whistling Joe," what time he was not engaged shaping horseshoes and forging new shares and coulters on the anvil, made nails of scrap iron and sold them at 4d. a pound. He served his apprenticeship at Buscot and had to attend the neighbouring village of Kelmscott every morning in order to do the shoeing. When the Thames was in flood, he crossed the river at Buscot Lock, took off his clothes, tied them in a bundle, placed them on his head with his nail-box, hammer, and pincers, and walked naked for a mile through the flooded meadows, often with the water to his breast.

"I walked by myself, I said to myself, self said unto me—
'Beware of thyself, take care of thyself, for nobody will take care of thee,'"

is a favourite rhyme of the smith's. This he learned of his old master, the Buscot blacksmith; he often quotes it at the age of fourscore and five.

Those were the days of tinder-boxes, lye-droppers, rush-lights, home-made candles, and potato starch. Tinder-boxes have long disappeared from the cottages, and the old-fashioned lye-dropper has also become a thing of the past. The lye-dropper was used for the softening of water for the wash-tub before soda became cheap and common about the countryside. It was in the form of a box, eighteen inches or two feet square at the top, a foot and a half in depth, and about twelve inches square at the bottom, the board of which was perforated with a nail-passer. A quantity of charcoal was placed in the lye-dropper.

That was then set over a pan or tub, and the hard water was poured upon the charcoal and allowed to filter through into the vessel beneath. The water, after passing through the charcoal, was called the " lyes "—lees—and so the vessel was called the " lye-dropper." The process of water-softening was a rather tedious one and it was usual for the housewife to be engaged for several days at the " lye-dropping."

Potato starch was made by grating the potatoes into a pot or pan and adding a sufficient quantity of boiling water. All night, before Highworth Fair, Fanny Beckett toiled hard to have her new dress ready for the occasion, and only realised at three o'clock in the morning that there was no starch in the house to finish it.

" Oh, mother! whatever shall I do ? I shan't be able to wear my new frock, for we got no starch," cried she.

" Run out in the garden an' uck up a few taters," her good mother answered. So she ran and got the potatoes and made the starch, and between them they finished the dress, and Fanny looked very pretty in it and danced merrily in the booth with the young carters and shepherds.

The majority of the cottagers made their own rush-lights and, at a later date, their candles, using for the purpose tallow, or mutton fat. Old Elijah, of Inglesham, was highly expert in the making of both rush-lights and candles. To make the first-named he obtained rushes from the lowlands by the Thames, removed the green skin—all but one strip—from the pith, and when that was dry dipped it in the hot fat and allowed it to set.

The common way of making candles at home was

to obtain a supply of dry teasel " gixes " from the hedgerows, cut them into convenient lengths, draw a small string or thread through the middle, and then to fill them with hot fat. When the fat had set the dry gix was cut away and the candle was ready for use.

The meal for making " barley-dodkins," " barley-scawters," " barley-bangers," or " pot-cakes " was usually shaken through a piece of coarse muslin. When Sarah George and Moll Higgins were preparing their weekly batch, however, they sifted the meal through their Sunday bonnets.

Old Betty Ockwell's favourite dish—and one she provided for her children—was nicknamed " bang-belly." This consisted of milk, well stiffened with wheaten flour.

Frog-water was drunk in the place of tea when that was too expensive for poor people to buy. First a frog was placed in the teapot and boiling water poured upon it. After standing for a few minutes—or it might be boiled—the liquor was fit for use. The " frog " was the thick crust cut from the bottom of a loaf and blackened in the oven or before the fire.

" Plaaze to gie ma a bit o' 'ood to do mi bakin'," said Davy Garrett to " Lord " Withers, of The Nell, meeting him one day down Golden Rose Lane.

" Man ! Man ! Man ! I got no 'ood. All's I got to bake mi own loaves wi' is a bit o' green eldern, an' missis slips it into the o-ven an' ther' 'tis a 'oppin' an' poppin', spettin' an' 'issin', jumpin' an' crackin', an' when the bread bin in a hour an' moore chent narn a damn bit the doneder," returned he.

The omnivorous gipsies that encamped in Hannington Lane would dig up a pig that had been buried for three or four days and devour it, turning it into a savoury meal. They considered that any kind of flesh was good for food provided it would "take salt."

Four local farmers courted a beautiful dark-eyed gipsy girl, the daughter of Mark the Gipsy, who, though he practised the trade of a tinker, had twelve good horses and was said to own land "from London to Bristol." He had three daughters, and he caused it to be known that he was prepared to give a dowry of £1000 with each of them.

Not only gipsies but others have made use of swine that had died and been buried. Jack Hughes and Tom Bailey, hearing that the roadmender's sow had died in farrowing, and coming to know where it was buried, went to the spot at night, dug it up, plunged it into a large tub of hot water, dressed it, and then carried it off and sold it as prime pork in the town.

Farmer Hunter, having forty sacks of potatoes for sale, and having received an offer from a dealer at Chippenham, put them on rail, but took the precaution of getting in the waggon under the sheet and travelling down with them and demanded cash at the other end.

"Thenk ee ver a veow zwedes, maester," said Geb Zillard to old Pete Smith.

"Wants thaay for my ship," said he, striding by.

"Aw right, maester," said Geb quietly.

Presently the farmer turned round and strode back.

"Aa, Geb, thee cast hae some swedes," said he. "Thee cast go an' pull one, two, dree, vower, vive, zix, zeven, aaight, nine, ten, 'leven, twelve, up to twenty, an' when thaay be gone tha cast hev another lot, if thas likes to."

The following rhyme illustrates the ancient custom of wooding in the copses before coal was available, and shows how the farmer used occasionally to hide behind the trees, waiting for the rustics in the moonlight.

The Rustic appears.
"By the blessing of the Lord I lay down my cord;
By the blessing of the Moon I'll be back home soon."

The Farmer, leaping from behind the tree.
"By the blessing of the Sun I'll make thee run."

Hannington Feast, Marston Feast, and Wroughton Feast all fell on the same day, which chanced to be about the middle of haymaking. Jack Kibblewhite, having a chum at Wroughton, and wanting to see the backswording for which that place was famed, going there on the Sunday was induced to stop the week and was brought before the magistrates for being absent from mowing.

"I only went to Wroughton Feast, sir," said he to the Chairman, in extenuation of his offence.

Then David Archer, brother of the Squire of Lushill, gravely returned: "Ah! young man, we're all well aware of that, for it is a sure thing that if you hadn't gone to Wroughton Feast, Wroughton Feast would never have come to you."

Previous to that three men—one a cousin to Jack—had been sheep-stealing, and would have got clear if one of them had not turned Queen's evidence. When the other two were brought up, to every question addressed to them they soberly answered: "I was there," and uttered not a word besides. They failed materially to impress the squire, however, who merely remarked: "I quite believe you," and committed them to prison for a certain term.

A STRANGE SECLUSION

One Jeremiah Ewer lived at Crouch at that time. He was noted for acrobatic feats and was clever at somersaults, and particularly at standing and "walking" on his head, though he was so idle that he would not even put the rudge chain over the horse's back for the carter. He placed the boy Jack in charge of the women in the fields and called him his "bailey," and asked his advice on all matters pertaining to the cattle and crops. Jack was so sluggish that he would lie down anywhere and sleep for hours, but Jeremiah only laughed at him and called him a "lazy scamp" and a "wosbird," and "a purty fine fella to be a bailey." As Jeremiah advanced in years he became reserved and eccentric. He clapped on his knee with his hand so frequently that he wore a new smock into a hole in a week. At length he retired into the attic and stayed there for sixteen years without once coming down, not even when his aged father and mother died in the same house and were carried off for burial.

What is a "Journeyman Farmer"? He is not really a farmer at all, but a labourer, a "Jack of all trades," that can turn his hand to ploughing, sowing, hoeing, reaping, mowing, threshing, shepherding, sheep-shearing, cartering, milking, hedge-cutting, ditching, draining, tree-felling, thatching, hurdle-making, faggoting, and anything else that may be needed of him, as well as being able to help the master with particular advice concerning the exact times for sowing and the quantities of seed required according to the soil and season, cutting and carrying crops, complaints in cattle, and being a reliable weather prophet into the bargain. Such were old Elijah Iles of Inglesham, "Wassail" Harvey of

Cricklade, Tom Hancock of Blunsdon Hill, and Gabriel Zillard of Hannington.

> "When the moon lays on his back,
> Then he holds wet in his lap."

and

> "If it rains on Easter Day,
> Plenty of grass but not much hay,"

say the villagers. If the ducks and geese quack and cackle clamorously and come running home from the pool, or the cocks and hens rub themselves in the dust, or the old sow runs squealing to and fro grubbing with her snout; or if the bees remain in the hives, or the spiders run up and down the walls at night, or the water boils away swiftly in the pot, or the mischievous moles cast up the earth with more than their usual energy, rain is sure soon to follow. But if the cows lie down, or the bull follows the herd to pasture, or the swallows mount high, or the pretty pimpernel, wood-sorrel, and dandelion open their petals in the early morning, that is a sure sign of fine weather.

There are many other sayings and rhymes touching the weather which are not so well remembered by those of the present generation, though some of the old folks occasionally make use of them, usually more by accident than intention. Such are the following:

> "March winds will search you, April will try,
> May will tell you whether you will live or die."

> "A cold April with no leaves
> Will fill the barn chock-full of sheaves."

> "When the cuckoo comes to the bare thorn,
> Sell your cow and buy your corn,
> But when he comes to the full bit,
> Sell your corn and buy your sheep."

"If a cock moults before the hen,
 We shall have weather both thick and thin.
 But if the hen moults before the cock,
 We shall have weather as hard as a block."

"A rainbow at eve, it will rain and leave.
 A rainbow at morrow, it will neither lend nor borrow."

"A Thursday's moon and a Friday's full,
 Allus was a flood and allus 'ull."

"Sow your barley, be it dry or wet,
 When the old sloe tree's white as a sheet."

"No weather is ill
 If the wind be still,
 But rough wind and storm
 Works plenty of harm."

"A Tuesday's moon always comes too soon
 If it only comes once in seven years."

When Betty Kinch, the cowman's wife, wished to know whether it rained or not—unless there was a heavy downpour—she gave one of the children a good cuff and sent it running down to view the surface of the big pond that stood in the meadow at some distance from the house, and would not otherwise be satisfied.

Come riddle me, riddle me, riddle me, ree,
None are so blind as those that won't see.

"It walked upon earth,
 It talked upon earth,
 It never committed a sin,
 It will neither go to heaven nor hell,
 And never will enter therein."

("Why hast thou smitten me these three times?")

"In a garden there stayed
 A beautiful maid,
As gay as the flowers of the morn;
 The first hour of her life
 She became a wife,
And died before she was born."

Answer: EVE.

Riddle, heard at Coleshill Feast, in the year 1830:

" When first the marriage knot was tied between my wife and me
My age exceeded hers as much as three times three does three,
But when ten years and half ten years we man and wife had been
Her age approached as near to mine as eight is to sixteen."

Answer: At the time of their marriage the age of the bridegroom was forty-five and that of the bride fifteen. After fifteen years the husband was aged sixty and the wife thirty.

"There was a man and he had no eyes,
And he went out to view the skies;
He saw a tree with apples on,
He took none off and left none on."

It appears that the man had one eye, and the tree two apples. Of the apples he took one and left one.

" Shrove Tuesday, Ash Wednesday poor Jack went to plough,
His mother made pancakes, she didn't know how,
She tossed them and rolled them and made them so black,
She put too much pepper and poisoned poor Jack."

When the ancient Saxons tilled the land around Highworth, they fastened their horses to the plough by their tails in order to draw them along. They never sheared their sheep, as we do, but plucked the wool from the backs of the living animals every spring-time. The month of May they called "Trimilki," because they then began to milk their kine three times daily.

" There was a man indeed,
He sowed his garden full of seed.
When the seed began to grow
'Twas like a garden full of snow.
When the snow began to fall
'Twas like a bird upon the wall.

> When the bird began to fly
> 'Twas like an eagle in the sky.
> When the eagle began to roar
> 'Twas like a bulldog at the door.
> When the door began to crack
> 'Twas like a stick about my back.
> When my back began to smart
> 'Twas like a penknife in my heart.
> When my heart began to bleed
> 'Twas like the kernel of the seed."

If you are a true rustic, you will take particular care
> never to view yourself in a glass when you are ill;
> never to let a young baby see a looking-glass;
> never to lock the door upon a dead person, and always to have a candle burning beside it;
> never to give away a knife, which would certainly cut off love;
> never to cross two knives on a plate at table, which signifies strife;
> never to pass anyone on the stairs, or have snowdrops or hawthorn blossom indoors, or allow a woman to be the first to enter your house on New Year's Day; and be sure never to look upon a new moon for the first time through a closed window.

It is also considered of evil omen to dream of eggs, snakes, money, or water, or to walk beneath a ladder leaned against a wall or haystack; but it is lucky to dream of lice, to "fall upstairs," to put on clothes the wrong way, or to do anything backwards, to pick up coal, a nail, or a horseshoe, and especially to have a mole on the right side of your body.

> "A mole on the neck
> Brings money by the peck,"

and

> "Two moles within a span
> Marry a man with house and land,"

they say, but

> "A blue vein across your nose
> You'll never wear wedding clothes."

"Dream of the dead and you'll hear of the living;
Dream of a wedding and you'll hear of a funeral;
but
"Dream of flowers out of season
You'll have troubles without reason."

Most cottagers' wives occasionally have the "newsbells" in their ears. If, at such times, they are careful to hold their tongues they will be sure to hear interesting revelations, but if they go on chattering like magpies Rumour will not come their way. If the ear burns and tingles someone is talking of you—the right ear for spite and the left for love.

To produce warts—according to an ancient belief—wash the hands with water in which an egg has been boiled. To cure them take an elder twig, strip it of leaves and knots, and drive it into the earth out of sight, taking care not to visit the spot for seventeen days afterwards.

The old-fashioned sort of farmer is careful to eat only those parts of the beast upon which the sun shines.

"Wher' be I to go wi' tha looadd, maester?" inquired "Scamp" of old "Oby" the farmer, wanting to shift a cartload of manure from the stable yard.

"Damn tha! take it up to the farks o' that tree an' shoot it out ther'," replied he angrily.

When "Scamp" was told off to help Jimmy in the garden the roguish under-carter whispered a secret in his ear, as to the best way of handling the old fellow. Arrived at the potato patch, everything went smoothly for a time. Then "Scamp," who was setting the potatoes, suddenly blurted out—"Kip the line tight, Jimmy!" whereupon Jimmy pitched the fork at him, and chased him through the muddy brook and back into the brewhouse, where he took refuge up the chimney till "Oby" came on the scene with his gun and scared him out of it, as black as a sweep.

Wine made of peggles and ipsons—that is, of the berries of the hawthorn and wild rose—has a delicate flavour and was popular with the old folks, though it has gone out of fashion of late years, chiefly by reason of the abundance of superior fruits.

CHAPTER XVII

A Retrospect—The Thames in Flood—Gramp's Cottage—
" Farmer Bernard and Yellow-breeches the Lawyer "—
Healths and Toasts—" Parson Jingle-Jaw's Adventure "
—" Sweet Peggy O "—Skit on the Fast ordered by
Parliament at the Time of the Cotton Famine—The
Mumming Play of *Robin Hood and Little John.*

IT was haytime when we met in the meadows at Lushill, before setting out to explore the country and villages. On every side the busy toilers were at work, some slaughtering the ripe, heavy crops full of orchis and the rich, crimson-seeded sorrel; others raking up the hay ready for the pitchers and loaders. In the deep ditch and alongside the river bloomed the beautiful loose-strife, valerian, and iris; the hedges were laden with wild roses and blackberry blossom. Overhead the sun shone warm and bright. The birds—except the cuckoo—sat mute in the boughs. The fields, trees, and atmosphere quivered with the heat; it was perfect summertime.

A great change has taken place. Summer has flown. Autumn has come and gone, and grizzly Winter bestrides the vale. The flowers have withered, and the fields are brown and sere. The rugged, massive elms are naked and desolate, and the beeches in the wood stand bare and beautiful, drooping their smooth branches down to the ground. The day is short and usually dull; the whole valley and the

Cotswolds beyond look intensely blue beneath the cold wintry sky.

Several times of late the Thames has been in flood. The south-west wind—that lay low throughout the autumn—awoke from sleep mightily about the beginning of December, and, racing up the wide Atlantic, lifting and driving the heavy waves before him, panting and puffing, burst furiously upon the land, bringing torrential rains. All day and night the tempest raged and the drenching torrents fell. The old elm-trees swayed to and fro noisily and beat their boughs together, and the poplars bent their tops over crescent-wise, while the dripping oaks stood immovable. The hills and downs were hidden with masses of grey rolling clouds, and everything in the valley was blotted out. Adown the hills a hundred torrents ran splashing, shouting, and leaping in headlong haste, as though eager to see which should come first to the lowlands. As the hatches were not yet removed, the streams overflowed their banks and covered the meadows in the upper parts of the valley.

It took twenty-four hours' incessant rain to cause the flood, with ten hours added in which to allow the water to be carried down by the brooks and streamlets. Then thousands of acres on both sides of the river were covered a yard deep or more; the hedgerows were submerged, and only the tops of the hawthorn clumps and withies were visible. The merry Cole leapt over the top of the hatches and roared and foamed below like a mad bull; but the Thames was silent, and rolled his torrent along steadily, though with tremendous power. In less than three days the flood subsided. Then crowds of wild-fowl sailed over the meadows, searching for small fish, and the great chubs that came out of the river went wriggling home again with their backs and tails half out of water. A week afterwards the storm repeated and the river rose again, and so on several times until the wind finally sank and the pale moon shone in a calm, cloudless sky.

The continual rains, winds, and floods greatly perturbed grandfather Elijah of Inglesham. It was not that he was afraid of the water. His cottage is too elevated for that to reach, even at the highest floods. He is, moreover, used to the inundations, for he has known them these ninety years, and he understands the old Thames perfectly. While others view the sea of waters with real alarm and wonder how much higher it is going to rise, he surveys the scene calmly from the window and sits down again in his arm-chair beside the fire. "Tha bin dippin' an't up out o' the Channel an' chockin' an't over thaay owl' 'ills agyen. A good job when 'tis gone to make room for zum more," he complacently remarks.

Why, then, is he anxious now? Or what makes him impatient? It is simply this. He has been promised a special visit, one that should last a whole night without interruption, and he is eagerly looking forward to having the engagement fulfilled. The fact is, grandfather Elijah has several old songs he wants to sing, and one or two quaint rhymes to repeat, and he is furthermore very anxious to recite to us the play of *Robin Hood and Little John*, as acted by the Mummers when he was a boy. With so much wind and wet prevalent and the floods out in so many places this had to be again and again postponed. At last, since the time of year was drawing on, it was considered advisable to wait till Christmas.

"P'raps the owl' dooman ull be out for fine then, an' the wind ull a zunk a bit," said Gramp.

A spell of fine weather followed the wind and floods. By day the sun shone softly from a silver sky, and at night the stars came out and peeped through long lines of transparent clouds, and the season was mild. The water in the river fell to its normal winter level and the pools in the meadows gradually disappeared. Vast flocks of rooks and starlings settled in the fields where the floods had been, and even ran about in the shallow waters, splashing and spluttering in their eagerness to outdo each other in snatching up the unhappy worms and insects. Every night, in the starry silence, you could hear the Cole leaping into the broad pool where the great trout lie beneath the naked willow boughs. Across the meadows, the steady Coln thundered over the great hatch-doors at Whelford Mill. With a sweet, low sound the Thames glided over the weir at St. John's Bridge; the *chow, chow* of the iron wheel at Buscot could be heard a mile distant.

The few remaining days before Christmas passed by quickly. For a week the children had gone round to the farms every night, singing and begging. They carried lanterns made of swedes hollowed out, with a piece of candle fitted inside, and held them by the stump, warding off the draught with their hands. Then came "Gooding Day," or "Begging Day"— which is always eagerly looked forward to by the village children—and, finally, the day before Christmas itself and the date of the proposed meeting at old Elijah's house.

A little before four o'clock the sun set, dropping down behind Lushill, and soon afterwards the station lamps at Highworth were lit, showing afar off like the lights of a ship at sea. The interior of Gramp's cottage was warm and bright. A fire of logs blazed up the chimney-back and a large lamp stood in the centre of the table beneath a rather low ceiling. Numerous pictures and photographs hung on the walls around. Above them were set sprigs of holly and mistletoe, or little boughs of ivy. On each side of the chimney was a recess fitted with cupboards and shelves containing dishes and chinaware, mugs, and tumblers, gleaming in the merry firelight. The small clock on the mantelpiece was twenty minutes ahead of time. This is not an uncommon thing to find in the cottages, for the villagers love to be deceived in the matter of moments, and to feel that the hour is not really as far advanced as is indicated by the hands of the instrument. Inside the door was a thin partition to protect the fireplace from draught. Behind this old Elijah always sat, and never thought of shifting his position out of consideration for any.

Each of the visitors to the cottage had brought Gramp a small present. Clothes he needed not, nor yet a new pair of boots, for he seldom wore anything but slippers, either indoors or out. Books and newspapers were useless to him, for he could not see to read, and he had a sufficient stock of knowledge crammed into his old head to last him for the rest of his days. This his children and grandchildren knew, and so did not trouble to buy him anything that would be of no use. Instead they brought him a few good things to eat—cakes and oranges, a piece of beef for Christmas dinner, several ounces of tobacco, and a little flask of whisky. With all these Gramp was greatly pleased, though it was easy to see that he most preferred the tobacco and the small flask of barley juice, which, after all, was quite natural for one of his years. His delight in the tobacco was unbounded. " Ho ! ho ! ho ! H'm ! h'm ! h'm ! " chuckled he, taking up the packages and holding them in his mouth one after another, and tossing his head the while, before he stowed them away on the shelf beside his pipe and spills, and sat down in the arm-chair with a triumphant expression upon his countenance.

Gramp was the hero of the hour. This he knew, though he tried to be natural and to conceal his joy at having the company present. His daughter called him " a regular owl' toff " and teased him about wanting a " hair-cut." The grandchildren laughed and chattered like magpies, but old Elijah smiled the smile of one who is master of the situation and sat quietly and comfortably in his chair, smoking, and awaiting a convenient time for beginning the entertainment. He was dressed in corduroy trousers, with woollen waistcoat and cardigan jacket, and he had on a new felt hat such as is worn in the fields at haymaking. His wooden pipe was laid aside for a new clay with a long stem. His long snow-white hair fell gracefully over his shoulders and gave dignity to his form ; he was really a grand old man, whose worth could not be over-estimated.

When the table had been cleared of the tea-things there came a lull in the conversation. Then Mrs. Lawrence, Gramp's daughter, gave the fire a vigorous rout, brought more coals and set on the kettle again. Suddenly, without warning, Gramp burst into song with a clear, ringing voice, and we knew the time for festivity had arrived. He only sang one verse of the ditty. This was concerning two farmers who took refuge in the church porch during a heavy thunder-shower.

"Says Mark O to Peter O—'This is very funny weather.
This will make the little seeds to grow and all things spring up together.'

"Says Peter O to Mark O—'I'll trudge along, in spite of the weather,
For three wives buried have I got snug in this churchyard together.'"

Then he went on: "I was jest a thenkin' now 'e be got yer 'e med as well do zummat, 'cos Time's on the wing an' waits for no man, an' 'tis a very good thing to do the same as Farmer Bernard when he went to zee owl' Yalla-britches, the laayer, an' never put off till to-morra what you can do to-day. What be us to hae fust? A bit of a zong or a tale, or what? We'd better lave owl' *Robin 'Ood* till last, 'cos ther's a longish piece o' 'e. 'Tool take two or dree hours to spake 'e off, all an in."

"Wha's that about owl' Yalla-britches?" inquired Mrs. Lawrence.

"'Bout owl' Yalla-britches? Why, Farmer Bernard an' 'e."

"Well, what is it?"

"Farmer Bernard was at a loss what to do wi' 'isself, an' bolts off to market. Ther' a met wi' other farmers. Walks an' strakes about the market. Couldn't zee nothin' to 'tract 'is attention. Goes by owl' Yalla-britches' office.

"'Le's go in an' zee owl' Yalla-britches, an' yer what 'e got to talk about.'"

"Knocks at the door. Out comes Yalla-britches.

"'Oh, good morning.'

"'Good morning.'

"'What's the business?'

"'I come for a little o' your advice to know 'ow to get on in the world.'

"Yalla-britches stood an' considered a bit. Goes to 'is desk, lays olt of a bit o' paper, pen an' ink—all at 'and. Writes on paper—'Never put off till tomorrow what ought to be done to-day.'

"Wraps it up, gies it to Bernard. Bernard takes it.

"'What's the fee?'

"'Zix an' aaight pence.'

"Farmer Bernard thought he was foolish to gie zix and aaight pence for what he know'd afore. Anyhow, he got 'is owl' nag in the trap an' went off early, an' 'is missis congratulated un for bein' home early. 'Ad 'is tea an' telled the missis about owl' Yalla-britches. Rap comes at the door.

"'Maaster come home?'

"'Yes.'

"'Wants to zi'n.'

"Bernard goes to the door.

"'What's the matter, carter?'

"'Nothing the matter, maaster, but ther's that bit o' whate. We be anxious to get it in. If you be agreeable we'll ac't in 'fore us gies out.'

"Well! tha went on an' got it done. All comes in to zupper. Off home to bed. Latish. In the night a thunder-storm comes on. Farmer Bernard opens window.

"'It rains cats an' dogs, missis. A double zix an' aaight-pence the fust night.' Jumps into bed. Everybody else's whate washed away but his'n."

"Oh, bad luck it can't be prevented,
Fortune she smiles and frowns,
That man's best off that's contented,
And mixes the ups wi' the downs."

Several suggestions were made as to songs. One asked to hear "The Jolly Tinker, or Preaching for Bacon," others preferred "Lord Bateman," "On the Banks of Sweet Dundee," "Butter and Cheese and All," "The Carrion Crow and the Tailor," or "The Oyster Girl," all which Gramp knew. Finally the matter was left for himself to decide.

Then Gramp said: "Zeein' as we got a goodish company I thenks we ought to hae healths fust an' drenk to one another."

A jug of ale was accordingly brought and the tumblers were reached down from the shelf. A little weak whisky and water, with sugar, was made for old Elijah. Then the glasses were clinked, and the young people stood up to drink.

"Now, then! What is it to be?" inquired Gramp of the first.

Then the granddaughter replied:

"Here's a health to the world, as round as a wheel,
Death is a thing we all shall feel;
If life were a thing that money could buy
The rich would live, and the poor would die."

"Aa! Tha's a very good un. Go on wi' t'other," said Elijah.

Here the grandson spoke:

"Here's success to the plough, the fleece, and the flail,
May the landlord ever flourish and the tenant never fail."

"Aa! Tha's a owld un, that is. I've yerd my grandfather saay 'e many a time when I was a bwoy. Wha's the next un?"

Elijah's son spoke next:

"Here's a health to that as 'll do that good when the body and soul is taken from it!"

"H'm, h'm, h'm. Tha's a teert un. Don' know the meanin' o' 'e—No."

"Yes you do know, too. What is it as does a ooman good when 'er baby's born? You knows as my mother allus used to gie a cup o' hot beer to the ooman as soon as the child was born when 'er went a nursin'."

"Ah! ah! ah! To be sure. I forgot that. Tha's as much as to say: 'Yer's a health to the cup o' beer as doos the ooman good when 'er baby 's barn.' Go on wi't."

"Here's to the man with a ragged coat,
And with no means to mend it,
And here's to the man with plenty of cash,
And who doesn't know how to spend it."

"H'm! h'm! 'E dwun' live at our 'ouse, nat the last un, awhever. Ther's one more to come."

"Happy have we met,
Merry have we been,
Happy may we part,
And merry meet again."

"Ah! ah! An' there's one very similar—what I med zaay—agrees wi' that un very well.

"Let them be merry merry there,
And we'll be merry merry here,
But—who can tell wher' we shall be
To be *merry another year?*"

'Ev 'e all done? Spose 'tis my time now then?" said grandfather, rising from the chair and taking up his glass from the table, while all eyed him eagerly. Holding the glass on high and inclining his head a little to one side, old Elijah delivered his toast:

"Here's to the inside of a loaf and the outside of a gaol,
A good beefsteak and a quart of good ale,"

cried he, and drank off the contents of the glass amid much laughter.

"But you got neether beefsteak nor yet ale, for you drunk whisky an' water," cried Mrs. Lawrence.

There was no holding Gramp after that. His old face wore an ineffable expression, and he shook with frequent laughter. First he sang "Paddle your own Canoe, my Boys," then ran into "The Four and Nine," and ended with "Blow the Candle out." Afterwards followed a short bit of patter, then came "Parson Jingle-Jaw's Adventure" and the song of "Sweet Peggy O," newly remembered after sixty years.

"All you that have ears to hear, eyes to see, tongues to taste, and throats to swallow, draw near, draw near and pick up the crumbs I'm going to scatter about amongst you, the crumbs of comfort wherewith you must be crammed till you become chickens of grace and cooped up in the coop of righteousness, there to make bubble for somebody's dinner. And if your hearts are as hard as a Cheshire cheese or a Norfolk dumpling my discourse will make them as tender as it were on a cobbler's lapstone, till they become as soft as custard meat and to melt in your bellies like a marrow pudding."

PARSON JINGLE-JAW'S ADVENTURE

Parson Jingle-Jaw was out on his rounds visiting his flock, and came to the house of Mrs. Wallops.

"Good morning to you, Mrs. Wallops! How are you this morning?"

"Oh, better in health than I be in temper."

"Better in health than you are in temper! What's the meaning of that, then?"

"Ye see, I bin mendin' my owl' man's milkin' slop, an' I an't a done 't right. I must pull 't off an' do 't afresh."

"It's like this, Mrs. Wallops! Of them that sow the same shall they rip, and you've got to rip that. I can see I'm not wanted here. I must go on to the next cottage."

Jingle-Jaw accordingly passed on his way and came to a second cottage. There he met with four elderly women and a younger person, who were sitting around a three-legged table busily sewing.

"Well! I'm glad I'm come, for this is quite a place of industry," said Jingle-Jaw. "You've all been stitching away, I can see, and have done your work exceedingly well. They tell me this young woman has made a remarkable book-mark."

Here the young woman runs and gets the book-mark and shows it to Jingle-Jaw, who reads the text worked upon it: "Fade me lambs."

"Fade—me—lambs! How could the lambs feed you? It's 'Feed *my* lambs.'"

"You've got no lambs to feed," cried the young woman.

At that moment one looked out of the window and saw Mrs. Wallops coming.

"Here's old Moll Wallops a-comin'. Let's put the pig in the cradle," cried she.

The pig was accordingly put in the cradle.

"Excuse me, Mrs. White," began Jingle-Jaw, "you've got your patch on bottom-upwards, inside outwards."

"Can't help that," said she.

"But it looks as if 'twas shot on with a blunderbuss," remarked Jingle-Jaw.

Just then Moll Wallops entered,

"I'm come to see your baby, Mrs. White."

Goes to the cradle and removes the coverlet.

"Massy ow! Jest like 'is faather!" exclaimed she.

How could that be; the pig like his father, thought the women, at the same time showing signs of great displeasure at the remark.

"The pig may be like his father, but neither Mrs. Wallops nor I have ever seen the pig's father," suggested Jingle-Jaw.

Hereupon a general quarrel ensued, and Jingle-Jaw, to pacify the women, remarked: "The pig is probably like his father and the child is like his father, but I can see that Mrs. Wallops knows no more about the child's father nor yet the pig's father than a bull knows about his own father."

This brought the parson into hot water, and he deemed it wise to beat a hasty retreat.

"I must be going," said he. "My children will want their dinner, and I have the key of the cupboard. So good morning, and do the best you can."

SWEET PEGGY O

"There was once a Captain in Derby O,
And he was come recruiting O,
But a pretty chambermaid
His heart she betrayed,
And she was called 'Sweet Peggy O.'

The Captain went to the foot of the stair—
'O, come down with your golden hair,
Come down,' cried the Captain O,
'For I to Killarney must now haste away,
Then bid me farewell, pretty Peggy O.'

And at Killarney he became so helpless,
For his troubles he never would confess;
Love alone filled his breast,
And he never could rest,
So he died for the pretty girl at Derby O."

"And that put an end to 'is growin'," added Gramp.

"But that's not in the song," cried one of the young people.

"I didn't zaay as 'twas," returned he, "but ther's a bit of a toast as goes wi'n, jest to finish un off."

TOAST TO PEGGY

"The god of love his wanton power displays,
And oft torments us in a thousand ways;
And yet on Peggy none can lay the blame
For not complying with the Captain's flame."

Just then a galloping of horses, accompanied by a loud, rumbling sound, was heard outside.

". There goes the mailman from Lechlade! 'E's late to-night, cried the hostess, looking up at the clock on the mantelpiece.

"Aa, 'e got a smartish load. 'E'll 'ev a job to get up Hywuth 'ill to-night. But dur-saay a got double 'osses," returned Gramp. "I was thenkin' about a bit o' zummat us used to zeng at the time o' the fast as tha 'ed by Act o' Parliament a good many years ago.

"There was such a jolly game, you know, on Wednesday last,
Some did swear and some did dance, but very few did fast,
For Lord John Russell ate a pig, likewise a large cow-heel,
And old Duke Nosey swallowed a gun and a bushel of barley meal.

Little Billy ate his trap, and poor old Joey Hume
Had three cartloads of cabbage plants put into his bedroom,
And invited Tommy Duncombe to dine on Wednesday last,
And when they'd bolted all the greens Tom Wheatley holloed 'Fast!'

Lords Palmerston and Derby cried—'We very hungry be,'
And Radnor eat a sausage as big as a chestnut tree,
He was so hungry in the night he started up from bed
And swallowed the pantry furniture and fourteen loaves of bread.

Lord Morpeth he had such a gorge of salmon, sprats, and eggs,
And finished off the dainty dish with nineteen wooden legs ;
Then in steps young Disraeli, with a belly like a whale,
And drank six quarts of shandygaff and a dozen of bottled ale.

The Bishop of St. Asaph's unto the Lords did prate,
And told them what a sin it was to touch a bit of meat,
Then Lord George Bentinck he jumped up, with a bun as big as a mask,
And drank eleven pots of beer, and that's the way they fast."

"And how about 'The Bonny Bunch o' Roses O'?" inquired one of the young people.

"What! Afore owl' *Robin 'Ood* ?"

"Yes. We can have that afterwards."

"H'm! h'm! I was gwain to zeng 'Barbara Allen.'"

"Never mind about 'Barbara Allen' now."

"Then you don't want to yer 'e. 'Ow about 'Woodman Spare that Tree?' I gied my dinner for 'e when I was drivin' plough a'top o' Badbury 'ill yander."

"No. Let's have the other."

"'E got some heavyish lines. 'Tis a long, rollin' zong. I caan't bust un out like I could use to."

"You'd better begin *Robin Hood* else you won't get through 'n to-night," cried the hostess.

"Aa! Better 'ae owl' *Robin' Ood*, cos Time's on the wing, an' if 'e dwun 'ae'n to-night 'e mightn't 'ae the chance aaterwerds. You'll be zumwher' else to-morra," Gramp replied.

Thereupon Mrs. Lawrence made Gramp a small tumblerful of weak whisky and water, while he filled his pipe, lit it with a spill taken from the shelf beside the mantelpiece, and sat down in his arm-chair again. When he had half finished the tobacco he extinguished it with the top of his thumb, replaced the pipe on the shelf, emptied his glass—wishing good luck to everybody—gripped a stout stick standing in the corner holding it between his legs with both hands, and sat rigid in the chair with his felt hat pulled down tight on his head, and his bushy eyebrows lowered. Then, after a few words as to the number of players, the manner in which they were dressed, and so on, he proceeded with the piece.

ROBIN HOOD AND LITTLE JOHN

Enter a TANNER.

TANNER :
    Give room, give room, you gallants all,
    And give me room to rhyme,
    I'll show you an activity
    This merry Christmas-time,
    An activity of youth,
    An activity of age,
    And such an activity you never saw before
    Nor acted on a stage.
    I am a Tanner from Nottingham,
    My name is Arthur O'Bran,
    There's not a squire in Hampshire
    That dares bid me to stand.
    With my long pikestaff on my shoulder so high
    As I go I clear the way,
    By one, two, and three
    I make them to flee,
    And give them no leave to stay.

As I walked forth one summer's morning
To see the forest of merry Sherwood,
To view the red deer
That run here and there,
It was there I espied Robin Hood.
As soon as bold Robin gave me the spy
He thought fine sport to make,
He pulled out a wand
And bid me to stand,
And thus unto me he did speak.

Enter ROBIN HOOD.

ROBIN HOOD :
Hold! Who art thou, bold fellow,
That reigns so boldly here ?
I swear by my brief
Thou look'st like a thief
That art come to steal our king's deer.
I am the keeper of this forest,
The king he has put me in trust,
To look to the deer
That run here and there,
And stop thee, bold fellow, I must.

TANNER :
Speak clear, my good fellow,
And give better terms to me,
For thee I correct,
And thy neglect
Will make thee more manly.
And if thou art the keeper of this forest
And hast such a great command,
Thou must have more
For taking of store
Before thou can'st make *me* stand.

ROBIN HOOD :
I have no more
For taking of store,
Nor any have I need,
For here is my staff
From another oaken graff,
And I'm sure he'll do his deed.

A HARMLESS DUEL

They fight: the TANNER *yields.*

TANNER :
> Hold your hand! Hold your hand!
> And let our quarrel fall,
> Or we may get our bones to smash
> And get no coin at all.
> What little proud fellow is this coming down the hill?

ROBIN HOOD :
> That's Little John, my man, who shall fight with thee thy fill.

Enter LITTLE JOHN, *who goes to* ROBIN HOOD.

LITTLE JOHN :
> What's the matter then, master?
> I pray unto me tell.
> To see you stand
> Your staff in hand,
> I fear all is not well.

ROBIN HOOD :
> This is a Tanner that stands by my side,
> He is a bonny blade,
> Even now he swore he'd tan my hide
> Like a master of his trade.

LITTLE JOHN :
> He is to be commended
> If he the deed can do,
> And if he is so stout
> He and I will have a bout,
> And then he can tan my hide, too.

They fight for some time. Each alternately cries "Bout" (rest) and then pause for breath. At last LITTLE JOHN *strikes the* TANNER'S *knee. The* TANNER *falls on one knee.* LITTLE JOHN *cries out*:

> Doctor! Doctor! Where bist thee?
> The Tanner's wounded in his knee.
> Doctor! Doctor! Play thy part,
> The Tanner's wounded in the heart.
> Four guineas or five pound
> If this noble doctor can be found!

Enter DOCTOR *with a tin box containing marbles.*

DOCTOR :
    See ! Sir, comes this noble doctor.
    I travel much at home,
    I carry good pills
    To cure all ills,
    Past remedy and time to come.
    I am this noble doctor,
    With my courageous hand
    I can quickly purge the blood.

I can cure this man or any other man if he's not quite dead. If you were to bring me an old woman seven years dead, seven years laid in her grave, if she can rise up and crack one of these golden pills

    In the bond I'll be bound
    Of fifty pound
    Her life to quickly save.

You must not think I go about as rag-shag quack-doctors do, rather to cure than to kill. I go about for the good of my country, rather to kill than to cure.

    I can cure the itch, the pitch, the molly-grubs and the
        pimple-pomples,
    All pains within and without ;
    Mend a bee's broken sting,
    Or a gnatfly's wing,
    And charm away shingles and gout.
    Break your neck and I'll set it again,
    I charge you nothing for the pain.
    Horses I cure, bulls, poultry, or pigs,
    They give me the name of Mr. Cleverlegs.
    I've travelled through Ireland, Scotland, and France.
    Rise up, bold Tanner, and let's have a dance !

Here they dance a three-handed jig.

They tell me there's the grandest man goes tramping about, by name Jack Vinney.

Enter JACK VINNEY, *Clown.*

JACK VINNEY : My name's not Jack Vinney. My name's Mr. Vinney, a man of great respect and property ; could do more than you or any other man.

SONG OF THE MILKMAID

Doctor: I wonder what you can do, then?

Jack Vinney: I can cure a magpie of the toothache.

Doctor: Very clever bit, John, but I never knew a magpie with the toothache yet.

Jack Vinney: First I wrist off his head and throw his body in the ditch; he never has the toothache again. As I was walking down street this morning I hitched my toe in a whimble-straw, fell over a barn, and saw a pig-sty thatched with candlesticks. I knocked at the maid and the door came out, and she asked me if I could drink a crust of bread and cheese and eat a cup of ale, and I said, "No thank you, if you please, miss." After that I fell in love with her and I said:

" Suppose that I should marry you, my pretty, fair maid,
  With your red rosy cheeks and your coal-black hair?"
" Please yourself, and that you may, kind sir," she quickly said,
" It's rolling in the dew makes the milkmaid so fair."

" What should you do for wedding clothes, my pretty, fair maid,
  With your red rosy cheeks and your coal-black hair?"
" I'll cut my holland milking-smock, and that will make a pretty frock—
  It's rolling in the dew makes the milkmaid so fair."

" Suppose that I should run away, my pretty, fair maid,
  With your red rosy cheeks and your coal-black hair?"
" Of curds and cream I should not lack, my sand-red cow would call you back—
  It's rolling in the dew makes the milkmaid so fair."

" Suppose I *shouldn't* marry you, my pretty, fair maid,
  With your red rosy cheeks and your coal-black hair?"
" You can wait until you're asked, kind sir," this maiden said—
" It's rolling in the dew makes the milkmaid so fair."

After finishing the song old Elijah sat back in the chair, replaced the stick in the corner, and took up his pipe, by which we knew the play of *Robin Hood* was ended. Then one of the young people exclaimed disappointedly:

"Is that all?"

"Whatty?" returned Gramp.

"Is that the lot of *Robin Hood*?"

"Aw, eece! Tha's all o' *Robin 'Ood*."

"But you said 't 'ood take two or three hours!"

"Ah! so 't 'ood, probably, if you was playin an't, cos you could make it last as long as you liked, but we spoke un off quick. 'Tis a purtyish zong at the ind an in, but owl' Jack Vinney got took in one. What! be 'e off a'ready, then? Thought 'e was gwain to stop a bit," continued Elijah, as one of the company prepared to leave.

"Another half an hour and it will be Christmas morning," replied he.

"Well! good-bye to 'e, if 'e *must* go. Look out for the owl' black dog o' Engleshum," said Gramp, and the visitor, after wishing every one "Goodnight," and "A Merry Christmas," opened the door and left the cottage.

The night was calm and clear. Above Coleshill Wood the yellow half-moon was rising, topsy-turvy; the stars glittered brightly overhead in the frosty sky. Down below the sound of the Cole leaping through the hatches could faintly be heard, otherwise there was perfect silence. The street lights were out in the town on the hill, but the old church tower stood black against the sky and was visible several miles off. As I passed beneath the dark trees a black dog came running by, and I thought of Gramp's parting words at the cottage, in which he referred to the Inglesham Ghost, though that was probably one let loose from the neighbouring farmyard.

Old Elijah became so merry after my departure that he stayed up till after two o'clock, and it was feared that he would not be got to bed at all. Even after he was put there he kept singing, and only fell asleep an hour before daybreak, to wake again with a song when the postman's rat-tat came at the door signifying the arrival of the Christmas letters and parcels.

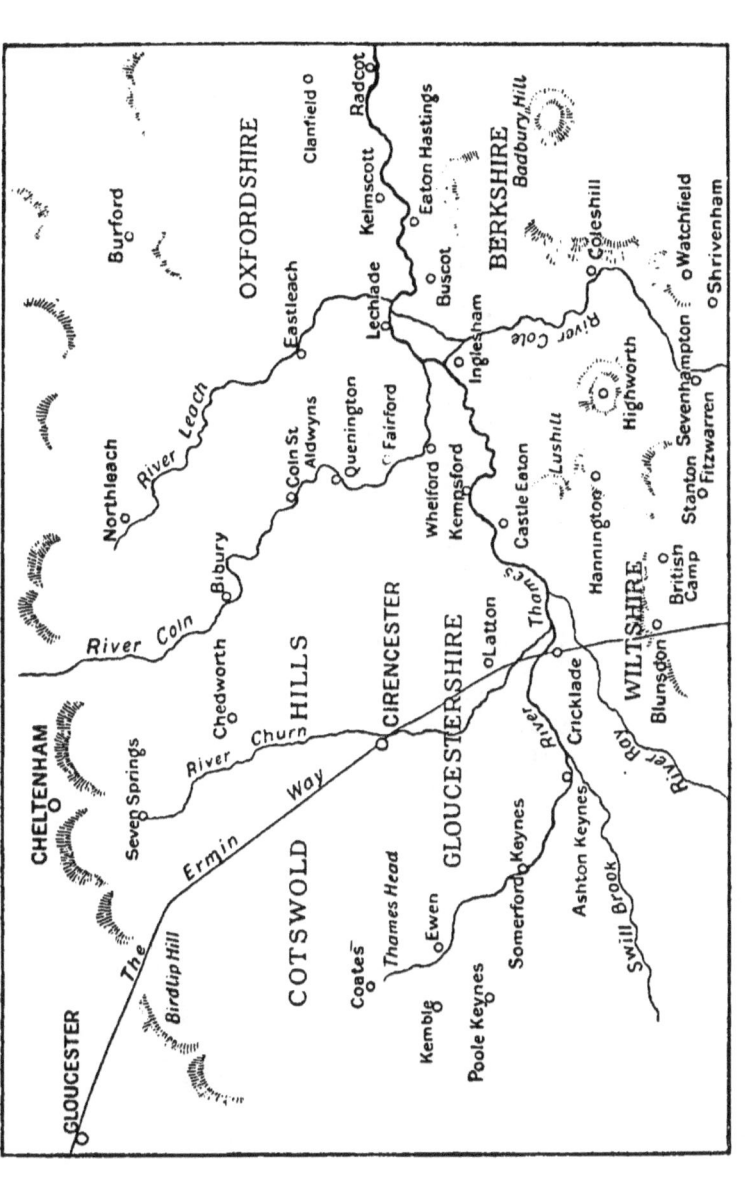

INDEX

Aaps, Flemish artist, 136.
Abingdon, 119.
Ablington, 132.
Achilles, H.M.S., 48.
Acorn pie, 27.
Aldsworth, 151.
Ale-taster, 38.
Alfred, King, 22, 120.
Archbishop Parker, 205.
Archytas, philosopher, 260.
Arwaces, the, 260.
Ashton Keynes, 223.
Auriole, golden, 175.

Back-swording, 72.
"Bang-belly," 282.
Bark-harvest, 232.
Barley-dodkin, 282.
Baronial wars, 186.
Barrington, Lord Samuel, 48, 50.
"Bastard House," 250.
Belgæ, the, 27.
Bibury, 132, 133.
"Bit-bats," 264.
Blackbirds, 64.
Black Death, the, 119.
"Blind House," 53, 276.
Blunsdon Hill, 235.
Borough of St. John, 34.
Bradon Forest, 257.
Bristol Avon, 219.
Bull-baiting, 52.
Bulrushes, uses of, 89.
Burne-Jones, artist, 98.
Bury Town, 254.
Buscot village, 97.

Canute, King, 219.
Carps, 103.
Cassivellaunus, 237.
Castle Eaton, 206.

Charlbury Tump, 48.
Charlton Abbots, 132.
"Chasing the Cock," 108.
Cheap Jacks, 123.
Chedworth, 132.
Cheltenham, 32.
"Chimney-money," 262.
Chubs, 115.
Coates, 219.
Cold Harbour, 249.
Coleshill House, 70.
Coln, river, 23.
Coln Rogers, 132.
Coln St. Aldwyns, 133.
Coln St. Denis, 132.
Cologne Cathedral, 120.
Corinium, 220, 223.
"Cotswold Shepherd's Scolding," 145.
Cotton Famine Fast, 305.
Court Leet, 53, 230.
Cricklade, 226.
Culkerton, 219.

"Dandy horse," 249.
Disraeli, 50.
Down Ampney, 204.
Duke of Lancaster, 180.
Dürer, Albert, artist, 136.

Earl of Cornwall, 120.
Eaton Weir, 108.
Edward IV., 121.
Edward Mortimer, 121.
Ermin Street, 218.
Ethelmund, King, 185.
Ethelwold at Cricklade, 224.
Ewen, 222.

Fairford windows, 136.
Faringdon Folly, 22.
"Flea Fair," 116.

318 INDEX

"Flower of Berks," 69.
Fulk FitzWarrene, 256.
"Funnel trick," 227.

"Gallibird," 56.
Gilbert White, naturalist, 55.
Gipsy funeral, 141.
Glove-making, 224.
"Gooding Day," 295.
Gospel Oak, the, 226.
"Gridiron Saint," the, 122.

Hannington Wick, 183.
Ha'penny Bridge, 95.
Harvest-home healths, 142.
Hatherop Castle, 133.
Herons, 104.
Highworth, 32.
Hinksey, 21.
Horace, Latin poet, 260.
Horse-threshers, 137.
Hugh de Spencer, 121.

Ichthyosaurus, 236.
Inglesham Church, 86.

"Joe the Marine," 248.
John Tame, 135.
"Journeyman Farmer," 285.
Judge Hughes, 49.

Kelmscott, 109.
Kempsford, 188.
Kingfishers, 113, 263.
King John, 86.

"Lady of the Mist," 186.
Lanier, Sidney, 131.
Liddington Hill, 94.
London Bridge, 114.
Longworth Lodge, 77.
Lord Craven, 59.
Lord Radnor, 72, 75.
"Lye-dropper," 280.

Mabuse, artist, 98.
Malmsbury, 220.
Mandrakes, 63.
Manor of Eiton, 206.
"Man-traps," 267.
Mark the Gipsy, 283.
Marten, the, 204.
"Moll Taw's Corner," 267.
Monks of Beaulieu, 86.

Moreau, French poet, 134.
Morris, William, 98, 133.

Naseby, battle of, 34.
New Inn, Lechlade, 124.
"News-bells," 290.
North-leach, 129.

Oliver Cromwell, 28, 34.
"One o'clock bush," 48.
Otter, the, 83, 113.
Otter-hounds, 174.

Papal collectors, 258.
"Parish Kettle," 72.
Parson Jingle-Jaw, 303.
Peasant's Revolt, 119.
"Peggy-wiggy" Pie, 139.
Penda, King of Mercia, 225.
Ploughing-match, 148.
Poole Keynes, 222.
Potato starch, 281.
Prince Erik, 156.
Purton Stoke, 231.

Quenington, 133.

"Rat-catcher Joe," 242.
Reeve Leet, 230.
Riddles, 287, 288.
Riot, Fairford, 143.
Robin Hood, play of, 307–310.
Roman Empire, 255.
Round House, 87.
Rushlights, 281.
Russley Down, 48.

Saxons, 223.
Sea-swallow, 106.
"Seed-cake," 141.
Sevenhampton, 22.
Shearing Feast, 141.
Shelley, 123.
Shorncote, 223.
Shorthorn, rhyme of, 196.
"Skim Dick," 212.
Slan Feast, 241.
Somerford Keynes, 223.
Squire Archer, 200–205.
Squire Campbell, 97, 200.
Steam-ploughs, 92.
St. Augustine, 225.
St. Florentine, the, 49.
St. John's Bridge, 114.

INDEX

St. Leonard, 258.
St. Lucia, battle of, 48.
"Sweet Peggy O," song, 304.

Tewkesbury, 121.
Thames and Severn Canal, 87.
Thames Head, 189.
Theocritus, 99.
"Tib Day," 38.
Tinder-box, 280.
Toasts, 300, 301.
Trafalgar, battle of, 90.
"Trimilki," 288.
Trout Inn, 115.
"Twig Budget," 84.

Uffington, 21.

Vale of White Horse, 21.
Van Dyck, 137.

Warneford Place, 66.
"Wassail song," 221.
Watchfield, 62.
Water Eaton, 233.
Water-gardens, 102.
Waterloo, battle of, 90.
Water-turbine, 179.
Water-wheel, 99.
Wayland Smith's Cave, 48.
Wetherell, Sir Charles, 66.
Whelford, 175.
White Horse Revels, 49.
Whitington Castle, 256.
William of Malmesbury, 259.
Winson, 132.
Witches, 125, 126, 249, 253.
Witney, 32.
Woodford, Dr., 185, 203.
Wooding rhyme, 284.
Wych elms, 274.

"Yukel," the, 264.

www.ingramcontent.com/pod-product-compliance
Lightning Source LLC
Chambersburg PA
CBHW030102170426
43198CB00009B/458